Sister Sharon J Smith

6493353

647-3474

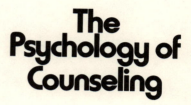

The Psychology of Counseling

BOOKS BY DR. NARRAMORE . . .

How to Tell Your Children About Sex

Life and Love

The Psychology of Counseling

Young Only Once

Encyclopedia of Psychological Problems

Counseling Youth

The Psychology of Counseling

Professional Techniques for Pastors, Teachers, Youth Leaders, and All Who Are Engaged in the Incomparable Art of Counseling

by

CLYDE M. NARRAMORE, Ed. D.

Zondervan Publishing House
Grand Rapids, Michigan

THE PSYCHOLOGY OF COUNSELING
Copyright 1960 by Clyde M. Narramore
Pasadena, California

Zondervan Publishing House,
1415 Lake Drive, S.E.,
Grand Rapids, Michigan 49506

Library of Congress Catalog Card No. 60-10242
ISBN 0-310-29930-6

Printed in the United States of America

88   89   90 / 39

A PERSONAL WORD . . .

This book is written to meet the needs of ministers and other Christian counselors. During the preparation of the manuscript I received a letter which aptly expressed the need for such a publication:

Dear Dr. Narramore:

The longer I am in Christian work, the more I realize the need to counsel effectively with men and women and young people. I would like to be able to recognize symptoms, then know how to deal with them. My weapons are, of course, the Word, prayer and the Holy Spirit as I point people to Christ as the answer to their problems.

Yet, some who come to me need psychological help either before or after conversion. In many instances I feel that I am failing to help them and I am frustrated as to what to do next.

Undoubtedly my ministry would be much more effective if I had additional insight and training. I shall be grateful for your suggestions.

Sincerely,

Counseling is indeed complex, embracing many concepts and techniques. May I suggest you consider each chapter of this book as only one aspect of counseling, integrating the other chapters with it to make it meaningful. In this way you will gain a comprehensive picture of counseling rather than a one-sided, limited view.

May God bless you mightily as you engage in the incomparable art of counseling.

In His Matchless Service,

CLYDE M. NARRAMORE

ACKNOWLEDGMENTS

When asked, "How long does it take to write a book?" an author replied, "A lifetime."

There is much truth in such an answer. One writes things he heard or read when just a small child. And through the years a person gathers valuable information which finds its way into a writer's manuscript.

The author is deeply grateful to the many people who have touched his life and who have had a part in this book. He especially wishes to recognize the following ministers, psychologists, educators, marriage counselors, editors and secretaries for their important contributions: Jeanette Acrea, Lloyd Ahlem, Margaret Atwood, Alice Elliott, Geraldine Folk, Marion Ferguson, Forrest Forbes, William Georgiades, Sylvia Locke, Ernest Schellenberg, John Tuel and Benjamin Weiss.

Loving appreciation is also expressed to the author's wife, Ruth, for her months of planning, writing, and editing. Without her help this book would not have been attempted.

CONTENTS

A Personal Word

Part I — Basic Concepts and Techniques of Counseling

1. The Importance of Counseling 11
2. To Whom Do They Turn? 14
3. The Counselor 18
4. Professional Ethics 24
5. Counseling Arrangements 30
6. The Counseling Process 37
7. Your Best Attention 40
8. The Value of Discussion 43
9. Accepting the Counselee 46
10. Waiting for the Real Problem 50
11. Recognizing the Therapeutic Process 54
12. The Significance of Pauses 58
13. Problems and Their Setting 61
14. Tracing the Origins 66
15. Physical Causes 72
16. Multiple Perspective 78
17. Motives for Discussion 81
18. Focusing on the Client's Problem 84
19. Encouraging Self-Reliance 89
20. Handling Direct Questions 93
21. Involvement 96
22. Responsibility for Referrals 100
23. Extending Your Counseling Ministry 105
24. The Great Physician 112
25. Success in Counseling 118
26. Growing Professionally 122

Part II — Special Areas of Counseling

27. Counseling with Teen-agers 133
28. The Mentally and Emotionally Ill 160
29. Basic Guides in Marriage Counseling 184
30. Problems of Sex 206

Part III — The Use of Scripture in Counseling; Appendix

31. The Use of Scripture in Counseling 237
32. Terms 274
33. Books and Recordings 298

part one

BASIC CONCEPTS AND TECHNIQUES
OF COUNSELING

1 | THE IMPORTANCE OF COUNSELING

A minister phoned a psychologist friend one morning and asked for a referral suggestion. "This case really shocked me," the pastor said. "He is a member of our church, apparently a fine spiritual man. But yesterday the police picked him up on a serious charge."

After discussing the problem for several minutes the psychologist asked, "What does this experience indicate to you?"

"Several things," replied the pastor, "but especially this: there is a great need for counseling. If I had allowed time for individual counseling, he might not have committed this crime at all."

Most pastors realize the importance of the pulpit ministry but some have not fully considered the significance of the counseling ministry. It has been said that a minister who does not place a strong emphasis on counseling is only "half a minister."

There are some basic reasons why counseling is so important. One is that it focuses on the needs of *individuals*.

Pulpit preaching is a blessing, but it may not always meet one's *specific* needs. Gloria, for example, is very concerned about a matter that stands in the way of marriage. But she does not get the particular help she needs from a sermon.

Don, on the other hand, has a very different problem: homosexuality. He knows that unless his situation improves he is likely to have serious trouble. Does he get anything from the speaker at the youth meeting? Yes, but not the individual help he needs for his own peculiar problem.

Mrs. Smith's daughter has gone away to college. During the year she has written her mother saying that she will not return home next summer. She thinks she will spend the time in a nearby city. Mrs. Smith realizes that her daughter is slipping away from the Lord. Naturally, Mrs. Smith is concerned. She needs counsel — individual guidance. On Sunday she does not receive much benefit from the message because her mind is preoccupied thinking about her daughter.

So it is, every person has his own interesting world. And we do not enter people's worlds by taking a "pot-shot" at them. Someone has said that people are not born in bunches and we usually do not solve their problems in bunches. We help people most when we talk with them *individually*.

Another reason why counseling is important is because it enables one to work on highly *personal* problems. Wonderful teaching and inspiration can be found in books and lectures. But some topics do not lend themselves to public or mass discussion. When we counsel with people individually, however, we reach their personal and innermost problems.

Counseling is important because it is *two-way* communication. The counselee as well as the counselor talks. And we do not grow or change much unless we are given the opportunity to discuss our problems thoroughly. A message or a lecture is *one-way* communication. We talk *at* people. We consider them targets which we hope to "hit." But when we counsel individually, the counselee also has something to say. He thinks and talks with the counselor. This is two-way communication — and it brings results.

Counseling is also important because it has a *depth aspect*. We can only go part way with such media as books, lectures and television. Sometimes our efforts are, at best, only superficial. But work with individuals is more thorough. The client gains a much greater depth of understanding. This brings about sounder and more permanent solutions.

Every Christian worker should consider the emphasis he places on counseling. He should keep in mind that God is intensely interested in the *individual*. In Jesus' ministry here on earth, He manifested His interest in individuals. True, He was pressed by the throngs and He fed the multitude. But He called

His disciples one by one. He met Nicodemus alone to talk over the things of God. Another time He sat by a well and explained to a woman of Samaria how she could have satisfying, living water. And in a jostling street procession Jesus looked up and spotted a man sitting in the branches of a tree. He ordered the man to come down. Then Jesus left the throng and went with Zacchaeus to his home so that He could *personally* discuss this man's needs. Still again Christ heard the pleading cry of poor, blind Bartimaeus and stopped on His way to minister to him and to give him sight. And even in the midst of the crowds who pressed closely about Him, Jesus felt the touch of *one* woman in need and said, "Thy faith hath made thee whole." Yes, Jesus gave His life for *each* individual and salvation is an *individual* matter.

The good Shepherd left the ninety and nine to help *one*, poor wandering sheep. Can we do less than give people our personal attention? It is God's way — and it is the effective way to help people with their individual needs.

2 | TO WHOM DO THEY TURN?

One of the signs of a healthy personality is the desire to reach out beyond one's self and become a blessing to others. This quality is especially apparent in Christians. When a person trusts in Christ as his Saviour and begins to grow into a mature Christian, he looks beyond himself for opportunities to serve. He sees people, perhaps in far away lands, perhaps in his own community, who need help. This same urge to serve mankind makes men want to counsel and help others.

However, some Christian leaders find it difficult to reach people. They have a desire to help, but it seems that problem-laden people do not gravitate in their direction. A question which seminary students and young ministers often ask is, "How do we get people to come to us with their problems?" This question is also raised by mature, experienced men and women. "We are sure we could help people," they say, "but very few confide in us."

There are some people who seem to attract others almost immediately. A study of the men and women to whom people readily turn indicates that these people usually possess certain essential qualities — characteristics which draw others to them. What are these traits? The following suggestions will help any Christian leader improve his "counselor personality."

① *People usually turn to someone they know.* It is only natural that people take their problems to a person with whom they feel comfortable — someone they know personally or to whom they have at least spoken. The more any Christian leader mixes with people and increases his personal contacts, the more likely people are to seek his help. Meetings, picnics, class parties, and scores of other occasions give any man or woman an opportunity to associate with others and acquaint himself with them. It is easy to understand why people do not usually seek strangers for help. The man (or woman) they *know* and in whom they have confidence, is the one to whom people are likely to turn in time of stress.

② *People take their problems to someone they like.* It is usually not enough to know a person. Most people want to take their problems to someone whom they feel is a friend. This close identification grows out of friendliness and genuine warmth. When a person is friendly, one who can laugh, or sympathize, and one who seems to understand others, he is usually well accepted. True, it is easier for some people to show friendliness than it is for others. Yet, any Christian leader can become a warmer, friendlier person by consistently noticing others and talking with them.

③ *People take their problems to someone they respect.* The person who lives an exemplary life, who is wise and discreet in his behavior, is the one who is respected and held in high esteem. This is the kind of person to whom others feel secure in taking their burdens.

Concerning respect, it is important to remember that since man looks on the "outward appearance," it is essential to dress neatly and appropriately and to conduct one's self in a manner becoming a Christian leader. When a person's walk before God and men is such that others admire his behavior and decorum, people immediately respect him. They see that God is controlling his life and that he is a man of honor. This kind of respect opens the door for counseling.

④ *People are most likely to seek help from Christian leaders who indicate their interest in counseling.* It is often said that people are constantly sending out signals. Their actions, either obviously or subtly, tell people about such things as their interests and abilities. Pastors and other Christian leaders are no exceptions. Through the many little things they do and say, people can soon tell whether they are genuinely interested in counseling.

If a pastor, for example, preaches practical sermons that apply to everyday problems, the congregation knows that he is interested in people's needs. They feel that he is a person with whom they can talk. Sermons on such topics as "The Christian Home," "Consecration," or "Youth's Greatest Decisions" indicate to the congregation that the minister is interested in counseling about such matters. In the same way a youth leader or a Sunday school teacher can let people know that he is interested in their problems by using appropriate illustrations in devotionals and talks.

Another subtle but very effective way of telling people that you are interested in them is to place the right books in your library. For example, if a person walks into the study or the home of a pastor or Christian leader and notices books about teen-age problems, marriage, sex, mental health, and such topics, he realizes that the pastor is interested in these problems. But if people never see books of this type in the pastor's library, they may feel that he does not have much concern about people's everyday, personal needs.

One of the best ways for a pastor to get close to his people and to show his willingness to help them with their problems is to conduct a series of study groups throughout the church. For example, in one church the pastor and the youth director conducted three Friday night meetings for the young people on the subject, "Courtship and Marriage." The meetings were enthusiastically attended. It wasn't long after this series that several of the young people began coming to the pastor and youth director for counsel about some of their personal problems.

Another pastor had a similar experience. He conducted two Friday night meetings for the parents of teen-agers in his church. The topic was, "What Makes a Good Christian Home?" The pastor noticed that after these meetings, the parents felt more free to come to his study and discuss their problems. Indeed, one of the best ways to encourage people to consider their problems individually is to conduct study groups, seminars and similar meetings in the church. Through these sessions people are impressed with the importance and the serious consequences of unsolved problems. And through this means they gain confidence in their leader.

People turn for counseling to someone whom they feel is competent. Although other attributes are important in counseling, they do not take the place of competence. Today's counselor must

16

have more to offer than mere "talk." He must be well informed and skilled.

If a person is competent, people soon realize that he is prepared to help them. Since counseling is vitally important, it deserves all the preparation one can afford. Reading books, taking courses, and getting as much information as possible about counseling helps a person to be prepared.* And if he is competent, people will certainly make a path to his door.

People take their problems to someone who observes professional ethics.† People want to be especially sure that a counselor is strictly confidential. They want to be certain that he will not divulge personal information to anyone else.

It is well said that a man's reputation "goes before him." If he is not confidential, the word soon travels around and in a short time people avoid talking with him about personal matters. Unfortunately, it only takes a few "slips" to crystallize an undesirable reputation.

One of the best ways to establish yourself as a dependable counselor is to make sure that what is said in your office never goes any further. Even the most gifted, brilliantly trained counselor will not be sought after if he fails to be confidential. "Confidence in an unfaithful man in time of trouble is like a broken tooth, and a foot out of joint" (Proverbs 25:19). People refuse to take chances on what they consider "private affairs." So, if you would have people turn to you, be sure you guard their confidences.

Finally, people turn to the counselor who knows God. In time of turbulence and trouble people want *Divine* help. They have tasted the mouldy wisdom of man. They have drunk from civilization's broken cisterns. Now they want the pure, omnipotent help of God. They want counsel from one who is redeemed and full of the wisdom of the Scriptures.‡ They want to take their troubles to a person who is in touch with God — someone who can pray and trust and believe. Surely, in time of need, people turn to one who walks closely with the Lord. They look for "a man (or woman) of God."

---

*See Chapter 26, *Growing Professionally*.
†For a discussion of professional ethics see Chapter 4.
‡See Chapter 31, *The Use of Scripture in Counseling*.

3 | THE COUNSELOR

People sometimes ask, "What is the most important thing in counseling?"

The answer is, "The counselor."

Naturally, the counselor's techniques are very important. He should also have an understanding of human behavior and knowledge of bibliography as well as sources of referral at his command. But the most important element in counseling is the counselor himself.

Counseling is, in a sense, a projection of the counselor.

You have heard the comment, "We rub off on people." This is especially true in counseling. The counselee subtly learns to consider problems in the same way as does the counselor. As time is spent together, the counselee is greatly influenced.

A counselor is more than an arsenal of techniques and a bag of ideas. He needs to be a firm believer in Christian principle. He needs to be energized by the power of God. He should not be like the exorcists in the book of Acts who thought they could ride along without any personal convictions, casting out evil spirits in the name of Jesus "whom Paul preacheth." The demons were much better informed than were the exorcists concerning the ground rules. We read:

"But (one) evil spirit retorted, Jesus I know, and Paul I know about, but who are you? Then the man in whom the evil spirit dwelt, leaped upon them, mastering two of them, and was so violent against them that they dashed out of the house (in fear), stripped naked and wounded" (Acts 19:15, 16 ANT).

Actually, no one should be better qualified to counsel than the true man of God.* He has accurate insight into human nature. True wisdom and understanding emanate from God. Through His Word, the believer finds the answers to life's problems. Not only that, he has the powerful resources of prayer. As he grows in grace and in the knowledge of his Lord and Saviour, Jesus Christ, he develops an attractive personality that radiates Christ. All of this by-passes the unsaved man. *The Amplified New Testament* (ANT) reads: "But the fruit of the (Holy) Spirit, (the work which His presence within accomplishes)—is love, joy (gladness), peace, patience (an even temper, forbearance), kindness, goodness (benevolence), faithfulness; (meekness, humility) gentleness, self-control (self-restraint, continence). Against such things there is no law (that can bring a charge)" (Galatians 5:22, 23). These qualities are ones that attract counselees. They are the qualities that make us *approachable* and qualify us to help others. God says that these are the products of the Holy Spirit dwelling within us.

To be good counselors we must first be the right kind of people ourselves. We must let the Lord take charge of our lives. When we do, we will have the "wisdom that is from above." And this is the wisdom the Apostle James speaks about, the kind we must have if we are to be effective.

"But the wisdom that is from above is first pure, then peaceable, gentle, and easy to be intreated, full of mercy and good fruits, without partiality, and without hypocrisy" (James 3:17).

This wisdom is first PURE. It is not tainted by worldliness or selfish gain. It is not contaminated by our own faulty ideas. It is *sound* and *right* and *righteous!* It comes from God. Everyone gives advice; but much of it is far from right and pure. A Christian girl once went to an unsaved psychiatrist for help with an emotional problem. The psychiatrist, among other things, suggested that she "throw off all crippling restraints and live it up." Such nonsense! This advice is satanic.

The Bible teaches that those who help others should be spirit-

---

*See Chapter 24, *The Great Physician,* and Chapter 31, *The Use of Scripture in Counseling.*

ual: "Brethren, if any person is overtaken in misconduct or sin of any sort, you who are spiritual — who are responsive to and controlled by the Spirit — should set him right and restore and reinstate him, without any sense of superiority and with all gentleness, keeping an attentive eye on yourself, lest you should be tempted also" (Galatians 6:1 ANT).

When Mrs. Harvey, a Christian woman, had serious marital difficulties, she sought help from a man in her community. But she went to the wrong person. She by-passed the godly people and went to a backslidden Christian. Naturally she did not receive *pure* counsel.

Truly, it behooves every Christian counselor to live righteously so that he will have *pure* wisdom.

His wisdom is also PEACEABLE. Some people have the right answers but the wrong attitude. We do not help people by arguing with them. We only set up walls of resentment.

An effective counselor is peaceable. His life is marked by a peaceful nature. Peace is a rare quality. You look in vain to find it among nations and you rarely see it in individuals. You *do* find it in some Christians; but regrettably, too few. God's Word teaches us to "rest in the Lord." Many of us trust Him as our Saviour, but we don't *rest* in Him. There is much peace available for the receiving. He says, "*Peace* I leave with you, *my peace* I give unto you: not as the world giveth, give I unto you. Let not your heart be troubled, neither let it be afraid" (John 14:27).

Peace is the presence of Christ; and peace is the result of confessed and forgiven sin. Sometimes it seems easier to hide or excuse sin than to ask God's forgiveness. Someone has said that peace is just as close as the nearest prayer closet. But it is closer than that. It is as near as any fervent, sincere prayer. We are prone to "figure" things out ourselves. But that is unnecessary. God merely wants us to come to Him in prayer, confess our sins and ask Him to forgive us. Then He will give peace. He does not always change conditions — they may even remain the same. But in the midst of those conditions He gives wonderful peace.

"I remember so clearly one time," said a man, "when I was troubled about a certain situation. For several days I thought about it, trying my best to find a solution. My heart and mind were in turmoil. Then finally, after much fretting, I got alone on my knees

and talked to the Lord. I committed my burden to Him. He took
the burden and replaced it with peace. Then I thought to myself,
'I should have done this several days ago.' My mind turned to the
words of an old hymn:

> O what peace we often forfeit,
> O what needless pain we bear
> All because we do not carry
> Everything to God in prayer."

This serene, wonderful peace of God is what every counselor
needs. People have confidence in one whom they sense is at peace
inwardly as well as outwardly.

Godly wisdom is also GENTLE — and easy to be entreated.
How important it is to be the kind of person who is "easy to be
entreated" — approachable, understanding, warm, friendly, sincere.
Life for many is hard and cold. Their world is cruel and un-
sympathetic. Little wonder, then, that people respond to gentleness.

One of the marks of a truly born-again Christian is *gentleness*.
Gentleness means carefulness in our approach to others. By nature
we are children of wrath, but when God lays His hands upon us,
He tames us, takes away our harshness and gives us gentle natures.

This characteristic is required in dealing with others. Have
you known Christians, or even Christian leaders and ministers,
who were not approachable? Their trouble may have been that
they were not gentle. They were not fully under the control of the
Holy Spirit. God's Word says, "And the servant of the Lord must
not strive but be *gentle* unto all men . . . ." (II Timothy 2:24).

Is your personality characterized by gentleness? If not, you
can well understand why you are not used more of God. "But the
wisdom that is from above is . . . gentle, and easy to be entreated."

Godly wisdom is FULL OF MERCY — not critical or overbear-
ing, but forgiving. When we think of our own shortcomings and
weaknesses, it should cause us to be tolerant of others. When we
think of God's mercy toward sinners, we should become more
compassionate ourselves.

Sometimes counselors are prone to judge and blame. But this
is not God's way. And naturally, it is not psychologically sound.
True, we must help people learn to balance on their own two feet,
but in all our dealings we should be filled with mercy.

21

Without any sympathy for sin, there must still be real compassion and love for the sinner. When this is lacking, little help can be given. Even among Christian leaders (who are Satan's target), there are victims who need loving help rather than cold indifference or scorn. When the enemy has been able to hook a Christian with some idolatrous bait, he lashes him into an agony of suffering that no one can know unless he has also experienced it. Satan knows no mercy; he is a foul and sly operator. Even the Saracen Saladin called a gallant truce when Richard the Lionhearted fell ill of malaria. He sent him lime water for his affliction. Not so Satan. He knows nothing of truce or fair fighting. The enemy of our souls does not strike where men and women are strong and noble. He knows where they are weak and mean and vulnerable. He strikes there.

Happily, the Christian counselor can have the armor of defense and offense that has long proved adequate against all the enemy's stock pile of weapons. This marvelous equipment of the Christian is fully described in Ephesians 6:11-17.

Godly wisdom is full of GOOD FRUITS. It is easy to "tell" people what to do but it is a different thing to actually help them do it. Advice is not enough. There must also be works. Goodness is an old-fashioned quality, but it is still priceless and effective in our modern society. As twentieth century people, we are taught to be sophisticated, suave, sly, smart, and clever. But unfortunately not much emphasis is placed on goodness — being filled with good fruits.

"When I think of good people," a man said, "I think of my own mother. She was a good woman and thoughtful of others. Mother often invited people to our home, even though many times it was not convenient for her. When worn out by the day's work of caring for seven children, she stayed up at night and sewed for someone who was in need. Her goodness shone through her everyday deeds and her actions revealed that she was truly a handmaiden of the Lord."

People often do not understand religion but they do understand goodness. In God's Word we are taught: "As we have therefore opportunity, let us do *good* unto all men . . ." (Galatians 6:10).

When "good fruits" become a part of a counselor's daily living, he will emerge as the kind of person in whom others will have confidence. And his counseling will prove effective.

When our wisdom is from above it will be WITHOUT PARTIALITY.

To be impartial is a difficult assignment. Our own feelings enter in so easily. But spiritual wisdom does not take sides — except against evil.

Impartiality is one of the basics of counseling. A counselor must guard against taking sides. Partiality thwarts good judgment.

For example, Mrs. Cane went to see a counselor about a marriage problem. She had serious conflicts with her husband. After the second session, she had told "her side" of the story so convincingly that the counselor "judged" the case and advised her accordingly. One error: he gave the wrong advice.

When we daily read God's Word, talk with Him in prayer and obey His commandments, He floods our lives with wisdom that is without partiality — a *must* in counseling.

Wisdom must be WITHOUT HYPOCRISY. You can be sure the principle of "do as I say but not as I do" does not spring from God. Wisdom that is from above is without hypocrisy. As translated in *The Amplified New Testament,* it is "free from doubts, wavering and insincerity."

You have heard the time-worn saying about all the world being a stage, and all the people actors on it. This is amazingly true. The world is filled with actors — people taking a part which is inconsistent with their true feelings. Unnatural players. Saying one thing and doing another. Advising others to do what they are unable to do themselves.

When a man turns his life over to God and sincerely serves Him, God makes him *genuine.* A Christ-honoring man no longer needs to live a double life — one that he aspires to and another which he accomplishes. A saved, consecrated man is reliable. He is forthright and honest. This is the kind of man (or woman) who makes a good counselor, one who is not a hypocrite.

As we are called upon to counsel, may those with whom we counsel see godly wisdom in us. "Wisdom that is from above — first PURE, then PEACEABLE, GENTLE, and EASY TO BE ENTREATED, full of MERCY and GOOD FRUITS, WITHOUT PARTIALITY, and WITHOUT HYPOCRISY."

4 | PROFESSIONAL ETHICS

"I'm certainly glad that you will be assisting me," Pastor White told the new associate pastor. "We have a wonderful church family. The people here are gracious, cooperative and for the most part, godly Christians. But, as in any church, there are also many problems — family difficulties, marriage upheavals, youth problems, and many other serious situations. I have found that a great deal of my time is taken with counseling. I surely welcome your help in this needy area."

As these two servants of God discussed their responsibilities in counseling, they spoke about the importance of observing professional ethics. "All one's 'know how' and techniques amount to very little if he is not careful about his counseling ethics," Pastor White pointed out.

Indeed, ethical standards are essential to all counseling. Every counselor must consider them. They are too important to overlook or ignore.

Perhaps the first and most important element in professional ethics is the *confidential treatment of all personal information*. After you have seen a number of people with the same kind of problem, it is easy to feel that such difficulties are routine. But to the counselee, his problem is one-of-a-kind. No other situation is quite the same. He has come to you because he trusts you. He wants understanding, sympathy and respect for the seriousness of his situation. As he begins to reveal his problem he will expect you to guard the information with care.

Another important reason for keeping case material confidential is the effect it may have on others. Many personal disclosures may not seem shocking to you. But to the counselee's family, friends and associates, it could be devastating. For years he may have hidden the fact that he harbored strong feelings of hostility toward a loved one. No one may know of his sexual misbehavior, dishonesty, guilt or anxiety. Now that he has revealed this, you are the only person who holds this information. Naturally, if you violate his trust, either intentionally or through carelessness, severe repercussions may result. This will only worsen his condition and weaken whatever assets he still has. Personal information falling into the wrong hands can cause much trouble for the counselee. He may lose friends, be ostracized, lose his job, be sued or suffer estrangement from his family.

A doctor, lawyer or minister is protected by law from being forced to reveal confidential information given him by a client. This is a matter of tradition. Surely the Christian counselor has no less responsibility. Personal information must be guarded as a sacred trust.

Many counselors intend to be confidential but often information leaks out through carelessness. Just because a person is a wife, husband, relative or personal friend does not mean that we should share strict confidences with them. Undoubtedly many a minister has dwarfed or destroyed his counseling ministry because he has shared personal confidences with his spouse.

Another caution concerns *the handling of written information.* If possible, case material should be filed securely in a locked place. It is not that we expect someone to steal anything. But church workers and even officials have been known to succumb to a little "harmless" curiosity about Mrs. "X" who looks so worried and has been seeing the pastor for the past three weeks.

"But," you may ask, "doesn't it help to give *some* information to a deacon or spiritual leader who is competent to help or pray for the person?"

At times this may be wise. But if so, it is better to explain the situation verbally. One suggestion is to observe the policy the government follows about defense secrets: let only the person know *who needs* to know and then only *as much* as he needs to know to do his job.

It is not advisable for the counselee to see your notes on his case. They will seem cold, abstract and critical and may reveal facts about himself that he is not ready to accept.

Another professional pitfall is the temptation for ministers and other public speakers to *use case material for illustrations.* This practice presents serious drawbacks. Naturally names are changed and other identifying information is altered, but still there is a risk. If the person who supplied the material hears it, or even hears about the illustration, he will feel sure he has been betrayed. No one in the audience may have the slightest suspicion as to whom the speaker referred. But the person involved will think everyone knows. People with problems feel that they are transparent. Obviously, if an individual believes he has been betrayed, a counselor's ability to further help him will be lost. Even when the one you are discussing is not in the vicinity, another with a similar problem, and whom you have counseled, may think you are speaking about him.

When we use case material for illustrations too frequently, other people with problems are hesitant to come to us. They are afraid of also becoming *illustrations.*

Should a counselor, then, never use cases for illustrations in messages or talks? Not necessarily. But when he does, the following precautions should be followed:

(1) Do not use material from cases you are *presently* carrying.
(2) Do not use material *similar* to that of any current case.
(3) Do not always reveal that the source of your illustration stems from counseling.
(4) In any event, *change identifying information.*

Confidence is a precious commodity. It should be safeguarded at all times.

But protecting confidential information is not the only aspect of professional ethics. There are several others to consider.

First: *Do not talk about other counselors.* It is quite possible that a person may have seen another counselor before he came to you. This counselor's technique and philosophy (especially if he is *not* a Christian) may differ considerably from yours. You may also find yourself *competing* with him to give this person *more* help than he did. You may be tempted to criticize him to the counselee. Criticizing another counselor is like "knocking a competitor's product." It destroys confidence in the one who is making the criticism. A counselor is wise to concentrate on helping the person concerned rather than minimizing the other counselor.

Of course, *a counselor does not discuss others with whom he is now counseling or has counseled.* One can never be sure that others are unknown to those with whom he is currently working. Also, a person may get the impression that he also will be discussed. This will increase defensiveness and destroy rapport.

Counselors should not touch a counselee unnecessarily, especially of the opposite sex. Although it is important to be cordial, we must also be discreet. A counselor must be especially careful when working with those who are upset or disturbed. Such people may have strong, unnatural cravings for affection. They are more apt to misinterpret a mere friendly gesture. Those who have sex problems may project their feelings toward the counselor, considering his kindnesses as personal advances.

Slanderous stories have started this way. But counselors sometimes bring criticism on themselves. Even if the disturbed person does *not* project his feelings, much harm can be caused by unwise physical contact and other stimulating, affectionate gestures. As for therapy, it tends to make the counselee more dependent upon the counselor. He is likely to become affectionately and personally attached to you. Since counselors are human and have affectional needs, this may seem pleasant at first. But the counselee may begin to develop intense feelings. Rapport will be destroyed and he will be left in worse condition than before.

But what does one do if, in spite of all precautions, a person still makes advances?

Sometimes this happens — and through no fault of your own. If it does, remain firm but kind. Explain the counselee's own feelings to him. If he persists in making advances, you should drop his case and ask him not to see you again. Unfortunately, some counselors have yielded to emotionally disturbed counselees and have become involved in homosexual practices, love affairs and other shameful activities.

Naturally it is much easier to *prevent* personal advances than to cope with them after they arise. Desirable ways to prevent them are these:

(1) Avoid physical contacts other than shaking hands.

(2) Avoid satisfying your own desires intellectually by probing for unnecessary intimate details. It is well to keep in mind that when your own personal desires are unsatisfied, it is easy to be unconsciously seductive toward another person. After marriage a man may find himself even more vulnerable at times, especially if he and his wife are separated for an extended period. This fact is so important that Paul discusses it thoroughly in I Corinthians 7.

(3) Keep the counselee from becoming emotionally involved too fast. This can usually be done by limiting the length of your interview to an hour or less. The therapeutic (getting well) process is not limited *only* to the time spent in an actual counseling session. If it is really effective, the process will continue its effectiveness *between* interviews. As the counselee gains insights he will become less and less dependent on you. This *should* be your goal. But you need to make certain that some hidden need of your own does not interfere with the therapeutic process.

Also, *be sure you counsel in an appropriate place.* Counseling is something like surgery. The place where the operation is performed *is* important. In surgery a sterile operating room is used to prevent infection. For maximum effectiveness in counseling, an appropriate place is also advisable.

The place where counseling is done brings with it many subtle influences. Such things as distractions, unhealthy associations with the place of counseling, lack of privacy, immature behavior on the part of the counselor can hinder the therapeutic process.

A wise counselor avoids counseling in inappropriate places like a secluded corner or a parked car. Not only are such locations unprofessional but there are also many distractions. To counsel in such places is indiscreet. Even the most Freudian analyst sees little psychological similarity between foam rubber car seats and the analytical couch!

28

3. Closed doors and secret sessions can lead to suspicion and criticism. This is why some pastors take steps to guard against unfavorable gossip. A nearby secretary, a door left ajar or a convenient but not distracting window may assure needed privacy without suspicious seclusiveness.

But what about a private *home*? This still has some disadvantages. Here, too, there may be distractions. The counselee may remain defensive due to lack of privacy — the danger of being overheard by other family members. Also, the counseling session may be confused with a *social* situation.

Some locations lend themselves to counseling much better than others. Experience shows that most counselors find the ideal place to be their own offices. Here distractions are at a minimum. Too, the counselee comes to feel that this is a special place where help can be received. Familiar surroundings also aid the counselor in handling a person's problems with ease and confidence. If a Scripture verse is needed, his Bible is near. If a call for further referral is warranted, his address book is on his desk. When he wishes to recommend a certain book, his library is at hand. The counselee learns to appreciate the efficiency of the counselor in helping him with his problems.

A fixed place and time greatly help to structure a counseling situation. The desk and surroundings become a symbol of the counselor's competence. The counseling relationship can be clearly defined. This gives a counselee the assurance he needs.

Another aspect of professional ethics concerns attitude toward referrals. *A counselor should recognize his limitations*. When a case is not within his training and ability he should refer the counselee to another specialist such as a medical doctor, a Christian counselor, a psychologist or a lawyer. No one counselor is competent to handle all cases. It is a sign of maturity when a counselor knows that he is not capable of making all of the necessary diagnoses and is willing to refer a counselee to one who may be better able to meet his particular needs. This attitude will add stature to the counselor and people will respect him for it.

Professional ethics, essential to everyone who counsels, may mean the difference between failure and success.

5 | COUNSELING ARRANGEMENTS

The old saying, "For want of a nail . . . a kingdom was lost," points up the significance of details in life. In counseling, too, details are very important. In fact, some of the "little things" carry so much weight that they often make or break all counseling efforts.

Effective counselors are conscious of details. Thus, they give careful thought to such arrangements as:

- Setting the Appointment
- Preparing for the Interview
- Beginning the Interview
- Determining the Length of the Interview
- Closing the Interview
- Recording the Interview
- Handling Persistent Cases

1. *Setting the Appointment*

A counseling session is worthy of a definite appointment.* Even though a fee may not be involved, the help received is valuable and the time spent should be established in a professional manner.

Making a definite appointment tends to increase your counselee's respect for you. He knows that you are efficient and orderly, that you are taking his case seriously. In addition, a regularly scheduled appointment indicates a wise stewardship of time.

---

*See Chapter 7, *Your Best Attention.*

2. *Preparing for the Interview*

A person coming for counseling should be received with at least as much courtesy as an invited guest. He may already feel guilty for "taking your time." Thus, he may react adversely to any sign that he has interrupted your plans or is in any way imposing upon you. This is the reason it is important to spend a few moments *preparing* for your interviews with him.

A room (and desk) in readiness makes it clear that you were *expecting* your counselee. Stacks of papers or other work on the desk may impress a person as to your busy schedule, but it can also provide food for his guilt feelings. He may marvel at how kind you are to lay aside this work in order to see him. But he will also consider how selfish he is for taking your time. This can prove embarrassing and make him ill at ease. But a counselor and a room (or office) in readiness indicates to the counselee that he is expected — and wanted.

For maximum comfort and rapport, the counselee should not have to face bright light. He should also have a choice of seating. Thus he need not sit across the desk from the counselor unless he prefers to do so.

The counselor also makes sure that counseling takes place where there will be no interruptions. Time reserved for the counselee should be safeguarded as carefully as possible. Interruptions have a way of breaking in at the wrong moment — just when a person is discussing something important or perhaps just as the counselor is offering a suggestion. Arrangements should be made to have someone take all phone calls and inform the caller as to when the counselor will be available. He may find it advisable to phone his family before beginning an interview to let them know that he will be busy.

If a counselor's office or study is situated so that people often knock on the door or walk in, a sign reading "PLEASE DO NOT DISTURB, IN CONSULTATION UNTIL . . ." may prevent interruptions.

If a counselee has had previous sessions, it is advisable for the counselor to check his confidential file and review pertinent data. Keeping good records and reviewing them just before an interview, may prevent embarrassment and needless error. Naturally, your counselee wants to feel that *his* case stands uppermost in your mind. And a brief review of his record will help him to feel that you are sincerely interested.

The most important preparation for an interview is prayer. Ask God to make you sensitive to the real needs and problems of your counselee. Read an appropriate passage from the Bible, not forgetting the unique power of God's Word in "discerning the thoughts and motives of the heart" (Hebrews 4:12). Commit the interview to Him and rest assured that He will guide you and bless you in your efforts.

3. *Beginning the Interview*

Beginning the interview may pose an awkward problem, especially for the inexperienced counselor.

"What should I say? What should I do?"

After a cordial exchange of greetings, a direct approach is usually the most appropriate. The counselee has not come to talk about the weather. So he will appreciate your direct approach to the conversation. Further structuring may be indicated later in the interview but your directness at the beginning will help keep the counselee from floundering.

4. *Determining the Length of the Interview*

Time limits for counseling interviews serve several purposes. For example, they tend to give the counselee a sense of *security*. He knows where he stands. He does not need to feel that he may be overstaying his welcome or, on the other hand, leaving too soon. Also, the counselee is less likely to interpret the termination of the interview as a sign of rejection.

With counselees who are especially dependent, the counselor may find it advisable to arbitrarily set the time limit. However, in most cases it is wise to discuss the counseling time together and thereby reach a mutual understanding.

When setting time limits, several factors are usually taken into account:

(a) *Your time:* You should avoid undue demands upon your time which would impose upon your schedule or which might make you unconsciously resent the counselee. Also, your family has a right to some of your time. Care must be taken that every spare moment is not occupied with counseling. Problems are very demanding.

(b) *The counselee's time:* The counselor should be sensitive to the strain he might place on the counselee's relationships to other people, for example, his employer or his family.

(c) *The nature of the problem:* Each case is different. Some problems may require only informational discussion and nothing particularly emotional. Since these discussions will often be concluded in a single interview, it is sometimes best to extend the time beyond the customary hour limit. For example, Wally, a bright and likeable young high school senior had recently dedicated his life to full time Christian service. He was happy in his decision but he did not know into which field the Lord might be leading him. So he went to his pastor for certain information. The pastor spent considerable time one afternoon discussing the matter.

Another kind of problem may call for a "standard" counseling interview. Such problems are not particularly involved. Structured time limits of 45 to 60 minutes for these sessions are usually optimum.

Another kind of problem may be more serious. In cases where highly emotional, unconscious material is likely to present itself or where strong dependency motives exist, it is usually best to limit the time of each interview. Perhaps 30 to 45 minutes may be desirable. A shorter period of time tends to limit excessive leaning on the counselor. It also helps prevent the too rapid escape of repressed material. A disturbed individual who is allowed to continue too long during one interview may become frightened and balk at further therapy.

(d) *The degree of progress:* Other things being equal, it is wise to have frequent short interviews (30 - 45 minutes, twice a week) during the initial catharsis period. When a person enters the stage of insight and positive planning, longer and less frequent interviews (45 - 60 minutes, once a week) may be advisable. During the follow-up period you may wish to see him for a brief session at monthly intervals. In general, the frequency of interviews should be inversely proportional to their *length.*

5. *Closing the Interview*

At first the counselor will want to take the responsibility for bringing the session to a close. Naturally, the interview is not terminated suddenly as the second hand sweeps past its zenith. The counselee should be prepared. Perhaps at the beginning of the interview the counselor may casually say, "If it is all right with you, we'll spend 30 minutes to an hour discussing your problem." Then, as the session progresses, he may suggest, "For the next few minutes let's discuss . . ." At the end the counselor might comment, "Our time has gone by so fast. We'll have to close now. Shall we continue our discussion next week?"

What is the purpose of preparing the counselee? It gives him security. He knows where he stands and how much time he has. He need not be caught short. This tends to limit "beating around the bush" — which saves your time and his. Because the time limit has been agreed upon from the start, he need not feel that something he said may have been offensive to you and prompted you to close the interview.

As you near the end of the interview you will find it advantageous to tie the session together by summarizing the main thoughts discussed. This will not only serve as a recapitulation; it will bring the session to a natural, desirable close.

6. *Keeping a Record of the Interview*

Each counselor develops his own method of keeping case notes. But every counselor who works with more than a few people a year *should* keep records of some kind, even though they may be brief. No matter how phenomenal a memory a person may possess, he is likely to confuse the details of different cases, unless, after the session, he makes a few notes. One also tends to overlook the subtle nuances of each individual case and generalizes among similar ones — unless he keeps a written summary.

Besides the value good notes afford in helping to understand the counselee and sense his progress, the counselor's notes on various cases can provide an index to his own professional growth.

It is usually best not to take notes in the presence of the counselee inasmuch as the counselor is prevented from giving his full attention to the discussion. Furthermore, the client may not feel free to divulge certain information if he sees the counselor taking copious notes. There are times, however, when the counselor may ask permission to jot down a point or two. Occasionally a written note during the counseling session enables the counselor to remember some pertinent fact. Also, a thought may come to the counselor which he wishes to introduce later. Simply noting it will help him remember it at an appropriate time.

Methods for keeping records vary considerably. Some counselors keep essential information on convenient 5 x 7 cards. Others write more extensive notes and keep them in file folders. One can suit himself. But enough detailed information should be kept to recall the case should there be a need to refer to it in the future.

One caution: it is essential that confidential information be kept securely out of reach of prying eyes. Just as the counselor does not want his innermost thoughts to become topics of general discussion, neither does the counselee.

7. *Handling Persistent Cases*

Unfortunately, not every case can be brought to a successful conclusion in a few interviews. Worse still, some cannot be completed in *any* number of interviews. These are the perennial, persistent cases.

Some individuals have extremely dependent personality structures. These are often the most difficult to handle. Such people come back again and again. Unless you take firm steps to set the limits, they may push you to the point where you actually reject them. Their extreme dependency has characteristically been met with rejection by other people and, if you show them much attention or sympathy, they will attach themselves to you tenaciously. Such was the case of Elmer. He was in his twenties, unemployed, unmarried and generally "unwanted." When he found that the pastor was kind to him, Elmer beat a path to the church office. He came and came again. Finally it became a menace to the pastor's time. The pastor did not want to hurt Elmer's feelings and yet he realized he could not help him. "He has some kind of mental problem," the pastor often thought.

There is no magic solution to the problem of "clinging" clients. It is very hard *not* to hurt them. But, of course, if possible you want to avoid rejecting them. It is best to offer sincere help, yet set definite limits as to the time you will spend with them, then refer them to specialists if the case so demands.

Details, from setting appointments to keeping records, are essential in any counseling situation. Because these arrangements appear to be peripheral to the psychotherapy itself, some counselors underestimate their importance. Yet, failure to properly take care of these details can handicap your very best efforts. All are essential to your success in counseling.

6 | THE COUNSELING PROCESS

Counseling is a process, not a lecture. Too often after a counselor has talked with a person for a few minutes, or even an hour, he may think that he has "solved" the problem. But effective counseling is seldom done quickly. Since counseling is a *process*, it requires time.

Has anyone ever phoned you saying, "I need to talk with you for a few minutes"?

True, he may need to talk with you, but surely for more than a *few minutes*. Undoubtedly he needs to discuss his need with someone for *several hours*. When people have rather serious problems, you may be certain that it has taken years for them to develop. Naturally, it takes a number of counseling sessions to do much about these maladjustments. Serious difficulties are not solved with the exchange of a few words. Undoubtedly, one of the biggest mistakes that ministers, youth directors, and other Christian leaders make in counseling is to consider counseling as a lecture rather than a process.

"But," you say, "I'm a minister and I am very busy. I marry people, bury people, settle quarrels, prepare messages, and I must spend some time with my family."

This is true. And you may not have as much time to counsel as you would like.* However, as a person comes to know the importance of counseling and as he learns additional professional skills, he usually gives it a more prominent place.

---

*See Chapter 23, *Extending Your Counseling Ministry.*

Why does counseling require so much time? A number of reasons. When you counsel you are actually expecting several things to take place. One of these, of course, is that both you and the counselee develop a thorough understanding of the problem itself. Precisely, what is the problem? What are the ramifications? Who are the people involved?

Also, you are seeking the true *causes* of the problem. When you "lecture" to a person — talk with him for a few minutes, you do not give yourself or your counselee time to consider the real problem. But when you meet with a person for several sessions, you can lead him to uncover the roots of his difficulty.

Even if you should see the sources of a problem immediately, the counselee may not. And it may require several sessions before he is able to grasp the actual difficulty. He will know the symptoms — but he may not be able to delineate the problem. One reason is that causes are often hidden — subtly concealed underneath strong feelings and varying circumstances. The counselee may require several sessions before he understands and *accepts* the real problem. When a person is preoccupied with symptoms, it is often difficult for him to see through to the true causes. Furthermore, he may be so upset with his immediate troubles that he has only one goal in mind — to get out of his present "hot water."

There is no substitute for time. An old Latin proverb states, "Time discovers the truth." (*Veritatum dies aperit.*) In counseling, we can attest this fact. Time, indeed, is a truth finder.

When several sessions are arranged, the counselor also has an opportunity to think the problem through. Perhaps you have had the experience of giving advice, then later thinking of much better solutions. You have said to yourself, "I wish I had thought of that before. That would have been a much better suggestion than the one I made."

People need time to change. A counselee, for example, might like to feel differently, but changes in attitudes do not come automatically. Several sessions may be required. It was Plutarch, a first century Greek philosopher, who said, "Trust to time; it is the wisest of all counselors." This, in a sense, is true.

When counseling is a process rather than a lecture, it affords more opportunity to pray about the matter — both on your part and on the part of the counselee. We often see the motto, "Prayer Changes Things." If this is true (and it is), then the more we pray, the more things will change. God is in the "changing business." He gives us new outlooks and new attitudes. Setting up counseling on the basis of several sessions permits more time for prayer for all concerned.

You cannot blame people for expecting you to solve their problems in two minutes or two hours. They come to you because their burdens are pressing. They need and want help. And they want it as soon as possible. But permanent help is not usually supplied in a "rush order." It is up to you to guide the counselee into a process of several sessions.

One night at the close of a youth rally a number of young people came to the front of the auditorium to meet the speaker. One of the boys shook the speaker's hand and said, "My name is Bill. Could I speak to you about a problem, please."

"Certainly," he replied, "but I am wondering, Bill, if you can wait for a few minutes until I have a little more time."

Bill agreed that he could "hang around" for a while. The speaker greeted the others who were waiting. Then he talked with Bill alone. Immediately he sensed that the boy's problem was a serious one. So the speaker made arrangements to see Bill several times during the next few weeks. Soon Bill was making real progress. How much wiser this was than handing out a "pat solution" while shaking the boy's hand at the close of the meeting.

People's problems are serious and they should be dealt with seriously. Most difficulties have been a long time in making — and it will take time to resolve them. A counselor is never at his best until he recognizes the fact that counseling is a process — not a lecture.

7 | YOUR BEST ATTENTION

There are many embarrassing moments in life. But one of the most humiliating comes to the counselor when he is caught short because he has failed to give the counselee his undivided attention. His mind wanders a little and a few minutes later he is left guessing what the counselee has or has not said! It has happened to everyone, even to experienced counselors.

A pastor was counseling with a woman about her problem. After she had talked continuously for nearly ten minutes, scarcely taking a breath, he became disinterested. A few minutes later his mind had strayed miles away. Suddenly the pastor realized that he had not been listening. Almost immediately the embarrassing fact stared him squarely in the face: he needed some vital information about the woman's family, but alas, he was afraid that she might have already given it.

A person readily senses whether a counselor is wholeheartedly listening to what he is saying. Each individual problem is vitally important to the one concerned, and a troubled person cannot fathom a counselor not remembering the things just said.

One of the basic principles of counseling is to give the counselee complete attention. But unfortunately this aspect of counseling is often ignored. Take, for example, the minister who, as he shakes hands with the members of his congregation, throws in a little counseling on the side. This, of course, hardly deserves to be called counseling. It is impossible under these circumstances to give people the undivided attention they need.

Many a speaker makes the mistake of counseling with people as they come to him after a meeting. Suddenly the speaker finds himself surrounded by about twenty-five or thirty "clients" — all wanting to greet him. Most of them seize this opportunity to mention some problem. This, they feel, is their chance to get some advice.

When a speaker is surrounded by numerous well-wishers and hand shakers at the close of an address, he should, if possible, arrange some other time when he may meet any with serious problems and consider each case individually.

Take, also, the case of the youth leader who is conducting a question and answer period. If he is not careful, he will publicly counsel a few people whom he should see privately.

There are Christian leaders who sometimes try to counsel as they walk from one building to another, out in hallways, or various other places. Under these conditions they cannot possibly devote their best attention to either the counselee or the problem.

What can be done when people seek personal attention at inconvenient times and places? Every counselor should consider all of these gestures as *contacts* for counseling; not counseling sessions in themselves. In other words, if at the close of a Sunday morning church service a lady corners a minister about a problem, he should suggest that she phone to make an appointment to see him later. Every minister knows that delivering a sermon is giving of himself. He may be so exhausted that he will not even retain details of problems disclosed during split second greetings at the door.

It is a disadvantage to attempt counseling with a person when you are not quietly seated. Being relaxed is an initial step in therapy. Furthermore, it is an injustice to the counselee to allow him to believe that you are helping him if you are unable to give him your undivided attention.

A counselor cannot possibly understand all the ramifications of a person's problem unless he concentrates on it. And when a counselee says something, he should not be asked to repeat it. The counselor should be so intent on what is being said that he not only perceives the main thoughts but also picks up accompanying nuances and overtones.

41

When you arrange to see a person in an appropriate, quiet setting, it is easier to think things through and analyze the problem. It is only as you grasp the details that you can understand a person's actual involvement. For example, a counselor talked with a lady about a certain situation that existed in her home. If he had not listened intently he might not have realized that it was primarily not her problem; rather, it was actually her sister's problem. Her interest was indirect. So it is that when a counselor gives a person his utmost attention, he can learn the extent of the counselee's involvement.

When we listen carefully we are apt to pick up vital bits of information. This was true of a psychologist who talked with a man about his son. In a passing remark the father mentioned that the boy once had a little seizure. Because he was alert, the psychologist pursued the statement and found that it was a clue to the entire problem. During the following sessions it was revealed that the boy had experienced a number of convulsions. In fact, his persistent facial tics and bodily twitching were actually being caused by an epileptic condition. If the counselor had not been attentive he might not have caught this. As a result, the boy might not have received the help he so desperately needed.

People are continually sending out signals to one another. They unwittingly tell much about themselves in all that they do and say. By their appearance, dress, walk, talk, preoccupations and in many subtle ways they indicate the kind of persons they are. Psychologists and psychiatrists take professional courses to learn these signs and their interpretations. They also give tests which render valuable information. But the average counselor can also pick up many signals by being observant and alert. These signals will undoubtedly fall into such categories as general health, physical ability, emotional health, social poise, knowledge, intelligence, preoccupations, spirituality, adaptability and other personality characteristics.

When the counselor quietly observes and carefully listens, many hidden aspects come to light. A new world of information and understanding is open to the counselor who gives a counselee his best attention!

8 | THE VALUE OF DISCUSSION

When God created Adam and Eve He gave them the power of speech, and ever since, people have spent much of their time talking. The air waves are flooded with words — words from a baby's prattle, a lecturer's podium, words in every language and in every circumstance. It makes little difference whether the words are said in a shop or in an office, over a telephone or across a back fence, at clubs, at parties, at church or at home in an easy chair, people will talk. They *must* talk. Language is an outlet for human expression.

There is an old saying that "talk is cheap." But this is not always true. Talking may have real value. Although some talk seems to have little or no significance, it is usually more than just a succession of words. It is therapy.

① Talking is thinking. A good way to consider a thing is to put it into words. Some authorities claim that there can be no thought without words. And, of course, expressing a thought out loud helps to clarify it.

Yes, talking is thinking — but it involves more than that. *② Talking is sifting.* Discussion helps us to sift our good ideas from the poor ones.

Have you ever had a "tremendous" idea, one that you thought was "great" — great, that is, until you told it to someone else? Then, somehow, it just seemed to fall flat! It did not *sound* so good out loud. Perhaps one or two points were worth salvaging. But for

43

the most part, the idea just could not stand up under the audio test.

Why do spoken ideas usually seem different from ones that have never been verbally expressed? Because speech is an effective filtering agent. Many things flood our minds, but talking sifts our ideas to separate the chaff from the wheat.

People need to sift their thoughts. And this is where the counselor is so valuable. When you counsel, you are helping people sort their ideas. Many people make wrong decisions simply because there is no one to go through this "sifting" process with them, no one with whom they can discuss their thoughts.

Talking is clarifying — bringing into sharper focus. It helps us to define just what we really *do* think. It shows up the true issues and points out possible danger or good.

Betty, for example, was a high school girl who wanted to quit school. She disliked the teachers and had few friends. Everything was wrong. Finally Betty saw the youth director at church. He encouraged her to talk. As she did, she began to clarify her thinking. "All" school wasn't bad, and "all" teachers were not stupid. In fact, it wasn't "school" that she really wanted to run away from. Through much discussion she came to see that most of her difficulty stemmed from the fact that she was poor in Geometry. Also, she faced up to the fact that her study habits were poor. So instead of running away from school, she and the youth director discussed some basic guides to improve her study habits. She also asked her math teacher for extra help. In a short time Betty's entire attitude toward school improved. What happened? She had talked the situation through sufficiently to clarify her specific problems. Through discussion she gained new insights. Now she knew which direction to pursue. But it was not until she had discussed these things thoroughly that Betty received the help she needed.

Talking is release. Through discussion we rid ourselves of poisonous feelings and pent up emotions. After we have aired our thoughts we see things differently. Even the world about us seems to take on a more pleasant atmosphere.

44

Janet, for example, was a young married woman who lived with her in-laws. She was most unhappy but she had no one with whom to talk over her problem. Finally she decided to tell her pastor about it. She really had not expected to say much, but after she began, she could not stop. At the end of a long counseling session she took a deep breath and said, "Pastor, you don't know how much this has helped me. Having someone to talk to — just getting it off my chest — gives me relief. Now everything seems better."

And our emotions are that way. When feelings are continually suppressed, we are likely to become nervous or ill. Our tensions may manifest themselves in a variety of symptoms. But talking brings relief. When we see things more clearly, we feel differently and we are better able to cope with difficulties.

6 *Talking is therapy*. It has been said that people who have serious problems seldom make good adjustments until they talk. Sadly enough, however, many people have no one with whom to talk. Can a person share his problem with the neighbors? No, neighbors usually want to do the talking and advising themselves. Yet, that is *not* what a person needs. *He* needs to do the talking. What about talking the problem over with a husband or wife or other relative? There are times when this is possible; but in many instances, family members are part of the problem. When this is the case, they merely become a stone wall to discussion.

To whom, then, shall they turn? This is where *you* play an important role. People come to you because you are a counselor with professional skill. You can draw them out, help them discuss their problems, find release, think things through, sift their ideas, clarify their thinking, gain new insights, rid themselves of impulses, trust in the Lord and become well adjusted. THIS IS COUNSELING!

9 | ACCEPTING THE COUNSELEE

One hurdle which every counselor faces is his own attitude toward the person he is counseling. Counselors are often prone to judge others rather than patiently gain an understanding of the forces working in their lives. Until a counselor eliminates condemnatory attitudes, he cannot possibly offer his best. Blaming a person is no solution.

What are some of the attitudes that one must erase before he can counsel effectively? They are many, but here are the typical ones. Careful examination will help a counselor evaluate his own attitudes.

1) He Should Have Known Better.

Undoubtedly all of us have, at some time, allowed this attitude to throw up a barrier between us and the counselee. But this point of view also suggests, "I did know better. I am much wiser than he." Naturally, this attitude of superiority does not aid us in establishing rapport with a person.

2) If He Had Stayed Away from the Wrong Crowd, He Would Not Be in Trouble.

Here we show our resentment, not only of the counselee, but of his friends. Yet, there evidently is something in his associations that meets his basic needs. A person is usually drawn into certain friendships because they seem to offer him something that he lacks. The fact that a person associates with the wrong people should be a clue to the counselor.

46

③ *A Little Plain, Common Sense Would Have Prevented This Trouble.*

Common sense is important. But most people do not function or make decisions on the basis of what they know. They act on how they feel. Certain experiences may have warped their outlook. Part of the counselor's responsibility is to help them gain different attitudes. When they feel differently, they will act differently.

④ *The Right Kind of Discipline Would Have Straightened Him Out.*

Discipline plays an important role. But self discipline is even more desirable.

It is true that some parents contribute to delinquency. But many have sincerely done the best they have known. It does little good to blame parents. Even if parents are at fault, we cannot undo the past. Our challenge is to work with the problem as we find it.

Concerning punishment, people in trouble usually suffer for their own deeds — many times over. And when they come to a counselor they respond to acceptance rather than further rejection. They deserve to be understood and helped.

⑤ *He Is Just a Trouble Maker.*

When we do not understand the causes of behavior or know how to help a person, it is easy to chalk up all trouble to a "mean streak," or a "bad disposition." But this suggests no remedy. We still do not know *why* he is a trouble maker or what makes him act the way he does. Problems are usually deeper than a person's actions.

⑥ *He Got What He Deserved.*

True, "Our sins will find us out" and "the way of the transgressor is hard." But counselors are not to mete out punishment. "Vengeance is mine, saith the Lord." The counselor's role is to help uncover the causes of behavior, then aid the counselee in gaining new direction in life.

⑦ *He Was Just Weak and Easily Led.*

God's Word tells us, "The heart is deceitful above all things and desperately wicked. Who can know it?" (Jeremiah 17:9).

47

This applies to the total human race; not just one individual. We all have weak natures.

In addition, some people have had unfortunate experiences. If a person has been led into trouble, our concern is to learn why, then help plan a program of rehabilitation. Side-stepping an issue by calling a person "weak" offers no solution, nor does it cast any new light on human nature.

8 He Is Only Trying to Get Sympathy.

This is often true. The human heart reaches out desperately for friendship and understanding. In fact, one of the basic psychological needs of man is love and affection. But some people have been denied this essential at every turn in life. As Christian counselors we can lead a person to Christ who alone fully meets the need of love and affection.*

9 There Is Something Physically or Mentally Wrong with Him.

Since there are many related causes of behavior, this is quite possible. Studies show that many behavior, emotional, and mental problems have their origins in physiological disorders. In a recent study of delinquent boys, for example, more than twenty-five percent were found to have neurological impairments (brain injuries). But such causes do not excuse us from counseling effectively. Our responsibility may lie in referring clients to a specialist.

10 He's Just Low Class. That Kind of Person Will Always Be That Way.

Some people do come from families classified as "lower class." In such cases, their experiences and values may differ greatly from ours. But this information should only help us to understand them better. Knowledge of a person's background should give us more insight and patience.

11 Why Doesn't He Snap Out of It?

Undoubtedly he would if he could. But this is precisely the reason he is talking to you — he *can't*. Most people in trouble are trapped; they are emotionally and mentally immobilized. They

---

*For a full discussion of man's basic psychological needs see the annotation of *This Way to Happiness*, in Chapter 33.

must be *helped* out of their situation. And this is the great privilege of counselors.

12) He Must Be Lacking in Good Spiritual Training.

Some people have had excellent spiritual training. But like others (even David), they have been "drawn away of their own lust and enticed" (James 1:14). If a person is a Christian, he needs restoration — renewed fellowship with Christ. If he is unsaved, he needs to be born again. We have a spiritual obligation to everyone with whom we counsel.

13) A Good Lecture Should Straighten Him Out.

Although instruction is always a valuable part of adjustment, people rarely respond favorably to lectures. They already feel condemned. They need a *process* involving a number of counseling sessions. They must gain new attitudes and new skills. They stand in need of a new nature through Christ. And these are not obtained through lectures.

14) Why Didn't Someone Help Him Long Ago?

Undoubtedly someone should have. On the other hand he may not have *wanted* help earlier. Now he is ready and is seeking help. Perhaps God has brought you into his life to assist him. You may become a great blessing, both to the counselee and those who are close to him. Through this experience you may also become a stronger, more mature person yourself.

Although a counselor may not condone, it is not his place to condemn. God hates sin, but He loves the sinner. Jesus set an example of acceptance when He did not condemn the woman taken in adultery. Even in a clear-cut case of immorality Jesus said, "Neither do I condemn thee: go, and sin no more." Likewise, the counselor may reject the unfavorable conditions that brought about the problem, but he accepts the counselee. He can never expect to help unless he meets his counselee where he is. *When the counselor's attitudes are constructive, they are likely to be greeted with success!*

10 | WAITING FOR THE REAL PROBLEM

People often hesitate to divulge their basic problems when they first talk to a counselor. They may begin with one thing, when actually they came to talk about something quite different. The wise counselor is conscious of this tendency and is willing to wait for the *real* problem to rise to the surface.

It is unwise for any counselor to "jump at conclusions." For example, a husband and wife went to see a marriage counselor. During the initial visit the couple discussed many things including several mutual grievances. The counselor quickly "sized up" the situation. He discussed it with them, then made several definite suggestions. At the close of the session the counselor suggested that they would not need to return.

"But," said the wife to a friend several weeks later, "we never even discussed our *problem!* I suppose we hated to reveal it, especially to a stranger, so we never got around to it. And the counselor, to this day, doesn't know what our real difficulty is."

This hesitancy to reveal true problems is also noticed by physicians, psychiatrists, attorneys and other professional people who counsel.

Why do people often start with a question or with "talk" which is not actually their real problem? Why do they seemingly dodge the issue when they have come to the counselor for help? There are many reasons. One is that they may feel ill at ease: *they may not know just how to begin.* To them, one way to get the conversation started is to talk about something else, something that they can discuss easily. Then a little later they will feel more secure about moving into their true problem.

Some people do not begin talking about their real concern until they have worked through one or two counseling sessions. This may be due to the fact that *they do not know what their problem actually is*. People with severe difficulties are often confused. They have little objective insight and they may be quite bewildered. This is part of being heavily problem laden. If a person were not confused and bewildered, if he *did* have insight into his own difficulty, he probably would not be entangled in it. He *does* know the symptoms: headaches, indigestion, resentment toward the spouse or other complaints, but he may not know the deeper problem.

A counselor was talking with Miss Deck who was disturbed about not being able to get a credential to teach in the public schools. During the first session she talked constantly about the fact that she had worked hard to get her college education and now that she had it, the State Department of Education refused to grant her a credential. As the counselor listened, he sensed that this was not her primary conflict. He realized that undoubtedly there was an underlying cause of which she was unaware. During the second session, however, she began to gain insight into the fact that her problem was deeper than not being able to obtain a license to teach. Her greatest difficulty was a serious personality problem. This was the thing that stood in the way of her credential.

Like Miss Deck, many counselees cannot put their finger on the real problem. It may require several visits before they can completely grasp and pinpoint it. This requires skill on the counselor's part. Realizing that the counselee may be confused and upset, the counselor should create an environment in which the real problem and its causes can be uncovered.

Another reason why people may not hand their problems to you when they first begin counseling sessions is that they *may be unsure whether you are competent to handle their particular difficulty*. People sometimes think that their troubles are so great and over-powering that only someone who has had years of psychiatric or psychological training can possibly help them. When such a person talks with a minister or some other Christian leader, he may circumvent his real concern until the second or third session. It may take time for him to recognize the counselor's ability.

Another reason why people do not talk about their basic problem the first time they come to you is because *they may find it too painful to discuss.* A serious difficulty is usually several years in the making. It has become deeply imbedded in one's pattern of life. To get to that problem immediately and start probing around it, may be extremely unpleasant. So when mistakes, sin and shame are discussed, a person wants to feel at least a measure of ease and security in doing so. This means that you may have to wait until near the end of the first session or even the second or third before the counselee is willing to go into the embarrassing or shameful aspects of his problem. People do not like to incriminate themselves. Realizing this, a wise counselor will refrain from "pumping." The counselee will start talking about these things when he feels comfortable enough to do so.

At a Bible conference one summer a tall young man named Tom walked up to the senior counselor and asked if he might talk with him privately. They arranged a time to meet together. As they sat down to talk, Tom said, "You know, my problem is about my mother and dad. They don't get along well together. While I am away at college, I keep worrying about the folks fighting at home."

He continued at length talking about his parents. But the seasoned counselor had talked with other young men like Tom and he began to wonder if this was the boy's problem at all. Tom did not seem deeply concerned. In fact, he talked quite glibly about the conflicts at home. It seemed to the counselor that Tom was not deeply involved in his parents' difficulty. But he listened patiently and encouraged him to talk. After about forty minutes, Tom said, "I also have another problem."

"Another problem?" the counselor asked.

"Yes."

"Would you like to discuss it?"

"It's about my girl friend." Tom's face turned red; he struggled in speech. Then he said, "We were at Central Park the other night. Oh, it was a terrible thing." Then putting his face in his hands he continued, "I never thought I would do it—but now my life is ruined . . ."

The counselor thought, "This is the problem." And, of course, within a few minutes he knew it was. This was Tom's *real* concern. But at first it was too distressing to talk about.

Some people conceal their real problem the first few sessions because *they want to be certain that the counselor is confidential*. Take, for example, the experience of Pastor Norton. A young lady in his church was having serious marital problems. Eventually she sought out her pastor. During the initial counseling session, she kept repeating nervously, "Of course, this is highly confidential."

What did this indicate? It signaled the fact that she did not yet rely on her pastor as a confidential counselor. And this was natural. However, as the session went along, Pastor Norton noticed that she made the statement less and less. He was careful not to probe too deeply and was cautious about mentioning other people. He wanted her to feel that he could be trusted with personal information. During succeeding visits the young lady was assured that her pastor would keep her confidences as a sacred trust. When she was convinced that he would not divulge personal information, she discontinued saying, "Of course, this is confidential."

When counseling, do not be offended if a client questions your ability to safeguard confidences. Merely work with the person until he arrives at his own conclusion that you are a person of integrity — one who is highly confidential and can be trusted with any kind of information.

Another reason why people may not present their major problems at first is because *they may not be sure of your attitude*. Sometimes a counselee circumvents the real issue with inconsequential chatter until he learns the counselor's general attitude and point of view. A person will not confide in another if he feels that he will be condemned. He is seeking guidance, not disapproval. When he finds that you accept him, he will reveal his true difficulty.

An effective counselor is always sensitive to the significance of an individual problem. He is aware that people may start with *anything*. He knows that he must not judge, but listen patiently. He continually asks himself, "Is this really the major problem?" Then he does not rush the issue or take an early detour. This is basic to sound, professional counseling.

11 | RECOGNIZING THE THERAPEUTIC PROCESS

For months Mrs. Dunn had wanted to talk with her pastor about a personal problem. Finally she summoned up enough courage to call him and make an appointment. It was three o'clock one afternoon when she walked into his office.

"Good afternoon, Mrs. Dunn," the pastor said. "I'm so glad you have come. Won't you please be seated?"

Mrs. Dunn had many things on her mind, including the fear of revealing some facts that she had quietly hidden for years. The pastor had several things on his mind, too. But uppermost was the thought that he needed to leave the city by four o'clock. He knew that if Mrs. Dunn did not "move pretty fast," he could not possibly make it.

During the interview he kept thinking, "Why doesn't she come to the point? If she has something to say, why doesn't she say it?" So as they talked, the pastor kept pushing. And before the hour ended he had "yanked" considerable information out of Mrs. Dunn.

Why do some counselors "yank" information out of counselees? There are several reasons. Sometimes, like Mrs. Dunn's pastor, they are under the pressure of time. On the other hand, some are unwholesomely interested in other people's private lives. Still others unwittingly press for information without realizing that they are endangering their client-counselor relationship. And there are some counselors who feel that a quick and complete emptying of sinful facts helps the counselee to get them out in the open where he can ask forgiveness.

But "yanking" is usually dangerous and unwise. If a counselor is to be his best he must let information and thoughts *emerge*.

Extracting information hurts. It not only hurts the one with whom you are counseling; it also damages your relationship to him. Have you ever had a tooth pulled before the anesthetic took effect? Then you know that just as a tooth must be prepared before an extraction, so a person must be emotionally ready before he yields certain information. An effective counselor is always sensitive to readiness.

There is a comfortable sequence in counseling that differs with each individual. Hurrying information out of people destroys the therapeutic process which is so vital in helping them gain insights.

After the counselee has taken the first step in seeking help with a problem, the next step is to feel comfortable about discussing it. But in this desirable therapeutic process he does not talk about just any part of the problem. He selects, session by session, those segments which are easiest for him to think about and discuss. He may not realize it, but he does not want the counselor to disrupt the succession which he chooses for revealing information. In fact, he may not know what he is going to reveal, but during the session various aspects of his problem emerge naturally. Each aspect comes at the right time for him. The counselor realizes that by remaining a catalytic or a "furtherance" agent, he allows this process to evidence itself. At this point the counselor may actually do harm by pulling out or insisting upon certain information and insights which are not timed to the counselee's own readiness. The counselor does not know what the order of the process should be. Neither *can* he know beforehand because it differs from person to person. However, he should be sensitive to the process which is taking place and not disorder it by pulling certain information or forcing insights ahead of their natural emergence. If he does disorder the arrangement, the counselee will, possibly unconsciously, resent it and feel frustrated.

This natural "coming out" or presentation of the problem relieves the counselee from the tension of self consciousness. It also enables him to feel at ease about hearing himself say what he does. He is not fearful of what he has said; neither does he regret having verbalized it, because it came without force or coercion.

The next logical step in the therapeutic process is the counselee's desire to carefully think and talk through each part of the material he has presented. He senses that merely "saying" it, is not enough. It must be handled and examined if it is to result in clearer understanding and eventual effectiveness. The impulses which bind him must be loosened a strand at a time, and each one requires its own scrutiny and disposal. So he discusses each point in detail.

As the counselee comes face to face with each force that has combined to make him feel and act as he does, he begins to entertain, at least verbally, new ways of reacting to old problems. He thinks of ways to overcome his problems. He rationalizes new steps to take. But his willingness to do this depends largely upon the counselor's skill in aiding, rather than disrupting the natural therapeutic process. If things have been upset and tangled, the counselee will find it difficult to think of or earnestly follow a reasonable program of rehabilitation.

Many people coming to a counselor are readily advised what to do in order to improve. But the counselee finds it difficult to follow something for which he is not prepared. If, on the other hand, the counselor carefully leads the counselee to the place where, in his own readiness, he can see likely solutions, he will be more apt to accept and begin following them.

For example, Les, a married man, took his in-law problem to a Christian leader. The leader soon saw the picture, and he could have advised Les what to do but he knew that the man would not, at present be able to follow his advice. So he waited. In the sessions that followed, Les gained many insights. Through detailed discussion he eventually uncovered the sources of his problem. Without any pressure from the counselor, he slowly traced each cause to its present result. In time he began to see some possible alternatives for improving his in-law situation. This was followed by thoroughly discussing the advantages and disadvantages of each alternative. Finally he reached the point where he felt justified in taking a course of action. And he did so, successfully.

Les's counselor was indeed wise not to jump ahead in the counseling sessions and destroy the natural sequence of events. Skillfully he had let the process take its own natural course.

It is not difficult to get a person to open the flood gates of emotion and tell all. But unless such catharsis is desired by the counselee, he may later resent it and wish that he had not told so much. In other words, you can "win" the counseling session while you are with the counselee, yet lose it as he leaves your office and thinks about it on his way home.

A counselor may help a counselee discover and follow his own unique pattern by observing the following:

- Provide a place and atmosphere conducive to uninterrupted discussion.
- Encourage the counselee to talk and express himself freely.
- Reflect and restate what the counselee says, thereby encouraging him to clarify his own thoughts and to say more.
- Do not register surprise at any information which the counselee reveals.
- Refrain from censoring or judging what the counselee says.
- Encourage the counselee to suggest and discuss his own possible solutions.
- Maintain a confidential attitude toward all discussion.

So whether you are sitting in the chair of a professional counselor or discussing a problem with a buddy at the office, or just talking over a cup of coffee with your best friend, keep asking yourself, "Am I 'yanking' information out of this person?" This caution pays off in big dividends. It is a vital concept that Christian counselors cannot afford to overlook.

12 | THE SIGNIFICANCE OF PAUSES

Through the centuries wise men have been telling us the value of silence. An old German proverb says, "The art of silence is as great as that of speech." It was Thomas Carlyle who said, "Silence is more eloquent than words." Another ancient proverb states that "speech is silver; silence is golden."

These are especially true in counseling. A vital part of counseling is the pauses — the quiet moments when both the counselor and the counselee remain silent. These silences are not only golden, they are moments that pay off in excellent results. Unfortunately some people seem to think of counseling as a talking contest. They feel that every moment must be packed with words. They measure their effectiveness by the amount of talk. But this is the badge of an amateur or a poor counselor.

A guidance professor, holding a professional seminar in counseling, kept emphasizing the value of pauses. "When your client comes to a pause," the teacher asserted, "don't begin talking yourself. Just quietly let him think. Thirty seconds is not too long to wait."

This point hit home to one young counselor in the group. *I will try out the professor's idea and see how it works,* he thought. So the next time the young man was in a counseling situation he watched for a pause. And it didn't take long to find one. He was counseling with a fellow named Jim who had been talking considerably. Then Jim stopped. He just sat there, staring across the room. The counselor thought to himself, *Here is my chance to test the professor's "thirty second" theory.*

Finally he looked at his watch again. *Twenty* seconds had slowly ticked by — but *it had seemed like an eternity*. The counselor felt as though he would explode if someone didn't say something soon. But he was determined to sit it out for thirty seconds. And he did. Finally Jim looked up and said, "Do you know what?"

"Yes?" asked the relieved counselor.

"I was just thinking," said Jim. "I was just thinking about something that happened when I was a kid. I guess I wasn't more than about five years old. I think I was in kindergarten."

For some time Jim talked about the experience. Then he brought up the fact that he had faced several similar experiences both at home and at school. He continued to look back into his childhood, picking up hidden threads from the time he was a toddler to an adult.

The counselor quietly let him talk — and think.

What had taken place? This: Jim had begun to unearth some of the persisting experiences of his life, then link them to the way in which he felt and acted today.

As Jim left the office, he turned to the counselor and said, "Thanks so much for the wonderful session. You know, I think you have helped me more this time than all of the other sessions combined."

The counselor smiled to himself and thought, "And I said *less* than ever!" Actually it was the series of long pauses that helped Jim so much. These quiet times had given him the opportunity to delve into his problems and come up with important insights.

Most skilled counselors do their finest work when they lead the counselee to a point where he can start thinking and talking; where he can see the relationship between his past experiences and his present feelings. The insights gained in this setting usually have lasting value since they have been uncovered by the counselee himself. Because he has thought of them, he is more willing to accept them.

The counseling session is a good place to produce thought. In fact, some people have little opportunity to think. Not at home, in the office, on the job, nor at school. The world is a place of constant hustle and bustle. When people are not frantically rushing from one activity to another, the television is glaring, the radio blaring, or the phone may be ringing. Time for quiet thought and meditation is pushed aside. But *things* crowding in are not the only deterrent to sound, logical thought. The people about us are often the greatest hindrance. Our friends, our family, our neighbors are eager to tell us what *they* think we should do. Talk is fluid and advice is free. Other people do the talking — and prevent us from thinking.

Thinking helps a person climb to a new perspective. It clears the air. It helps him see the causes of his problem and what he can do to change the situation. In fact, unless a counselor fully understands the value of pauses, he will never be at his best. Sir Isaac Newton, the great English mathematician and scientist, said, "What I have done is due to patient thought."

Indeed, pauses, quiet times of patient thought and reflection, are not mere empty, vacant spaces, awkward and hard to endure. Rather, they are the golden moments when a counselee gains insights and when a counselor is working at his professional best!

13 | PROBLEMS AND THEIR SETTING

A problem seldom stands alone. It is surrounded by a setting. It may include people, financial concerns, strong feelings, and other contributing factors. These tie-ins are like tributaries that feed into a river.

Unfortunately, the tributaries in a problem are not always obvious. That is why the counselor encourages the counselee to explore the context of his situation. Eliminating its tributaries may reduce a great river to a mere trickle. So it is in counseling. By properly dealing with the setting, one may erase the problem itself. Like explorers, the counselor and counselee search together for the sources of confusion and distress.

As they move forward, they will come to tributaries emptying into the main stream. The counselee should explore each one. The wise counselor encourages him in this because this process leads to insights and eventually to new attitudes. Unfortunately, a counselee is often hurried on to what the counselor thinks is the cause. In so doing they may both by-pass the real source.

When we look closely at the setting of a problem, there are usually several people involved. Take the case of Fred and Sandra, a young married couple. For them life was a series of arguments. It had reached the point where Fred had begun to stay late at the office and go other places to avoid coming home. Sandra was considering separation. Finally Fred went to his pastor who realized it would take time to resolve Fred's difficulty. During the first few sessions Fred told about his many arguments with Sandra: money, sex, and disciplining the children. But it was not until the third interview that Fred first mentioned his mother-in-law.

"Your mother-in-law lives with you, doesn't she?" the pastor asked.

"Yes," Fred replied, "she's been with us for several years."

Fred began to discuss his mother-in-law's role in their home. As he did, he could see that her subtle influence was a primary factor in their marriage difficulty. As Fred talked the problem through, he saw that she was "sweetly and inoffensively" controlling their home. Sandra was so accustomed to being quietly dominated by her mother that she gave more heed to her than to Fred. Not fully realizing the dynamics of the situation, and not being able to put his finger on anything his mother-in-law had actually said or done, Fred had turned his hostility toward Sandra. She was more outspoken, usually echoing her mother's ideas. Sandra unconsciously resented the fact that Fred did not take a stand against her mother and become the head of the house. But Fred, himself accustomed in childhood to mother domination, seemed unable to assume the role Sandra desired for him.

The insight he gained from the counseling sessions with his pastor enabled Fred to have several frank talks with Sandra about her mother. Not long after, the couple had several sessions together with the pastor. In time they made real progress toward the solution of their problem.

Sometimes the focal person in a family problem is a child. Dick and Helen, for example, could not agree on the discipline of their son, Ricky.

"All you do is baby him," Dick accused.

"No, I don't," Helen retorted. "You just don't understand him."

On and on they went, arguing with each other until the situation was almost unbearable. Both agreed that the boy certainly had a severe behavior problem — but they blamed each other for it.

Finally the couple sought the help of a Christian psychologist. Dick complained that Helen was hard to get along with. She claimed that all he did was argue. However, the psychologist was not misled by these superficial complaints. As he worked with them individually he encouraged each to explore the context of his problem. Then Ricky was brought into the picture.

As the sessions progressed the counselor arranged to see the boy alone. During the second interview with him the psychologist administered an individual intelligence test. The results confirmed the psychologist's suspicions. They showed that Ricky had below average intelligence. Although he was a good-looking child and clever in some ways, he could not understand and grasp ideas as rapidly as others his age. The psychologist spent two sessions with the parents tactfully explaining the boy's problem. The parents were encouraged to cooperate with the maturity found in their child. Gradually they came to accept his retardation and made every effort to bring about a good adjustment. As they began to understand their son's situation, they ceased blaming each other. Naturally, this paid off in better home relationships.

This good adjustment came about as the result of wise counseling. The psychologist realized that problems do not exist outside of a context — that they are nearly always influenced by other things or people. He searched for the setting, and in so doing, he uncovered the real problem.

Another tributary to the main stream of a problem is a person's *environmental limitations*. Such was Dave's case. He had been suffering from nervous tension and had seen his family physician several times for minor physical complaints. The doctor suspected that these were of psychological origin, so he referred Dave to a Christian psychiatrist.

After several interviews the psychiatrist saw this picture: Dave had exceptional intelligence and high aspirations. But each day found him drudgingly selling bolts, nuts and screws in a hardware store. Dave had married at nineteen and had taken this job to support his wife. In time two children were born. Even though Dave was dissatisfied with his work, he dared not take the risk of changing jobs because of his family responsibilities. College and graduate study? They were out of the question. But the unresolved conflict hammered relentlessly. This intense frustration was the main cause of his nervous tension.

Gradually, Dave began to see the relationship between his "nerves" and the fact that he was a vocational misfit. He saw that he would have to set new goals in the light of reality. The counselor helped him to understand the important and unique contribution he could make to his wife and two wonderful children. He was also encouraged to serve the Lord by teaching a Sunday school class. In addition he arranged to take an evening course to qualify him for a job which would offer more challenge.

Through counseling sessions and wise planning Dave's health improved. In time his nervous tension and physical complaints disappeared.

Another factor that contributes to people's problems concerns their personal limitations. Marjorie, for example, was a college sophomore and had studied piano for years. Her dream was to be a concert pianist like her Aunt Celia. She drove herself harder and harder until she neared the breaking point.

One day Mrs. Wilson, the church organist, casually asked Marjorie about her music study. After talking awhile, Marjorie burst into tears. Mrs. Wilson then encouraged the girl to tell what was troubling her. Marjorie talked about her disappointment in music. During the past two years she seemed to have been standing still, although she had faithfully practiced several hours a day. She had forced herself to practice longer, but to no avail. "Why can't I do better?" she asked. "I hate myself for being so stupid."

Mrs. Wilson had several talks with Marjorie. Soon the girl began to see that it was not her aunt who had really encouraged her to be a concert pianist. Rather, it was her mother. Gradually, the picture came into sharper focus. Marjorie's mother had always envied her own talented younger sister, Celia. Therefore, her mother determined that Marjorie should excel in music. Unconsciously she thought, "Marjorie will fulfill my dreams."

As Marjorie talked and reasoned, one question began to demand an honest answer: "Am I trying to be an outstanding pianist when I actually have only average ability?" This was the fear that had been pounding at the door of her mind. Now, with the help of Mrs. Wilson, she had the courage to open the door and face this possibility. This was the key to her problem. In a later talk with Mrs. Wilson, Marjorie decided to continue her musical training only as an avocation. She joined the church choir and began playing for the primary department in Sunday school. For the first time she discovered the joy of using the talent she had to serve the Lord. Now music became *fun*.

As in the case of Marjorie, or Dave, or Fred and Sandra, each counselor should ask himself:

What is the *context* of this problem?

Who are the *persons* involved?

Which *environmental factors* are contributing to the difficulty?

What *other conditions* are impinging upon the situation?

Every problem has its setting. Often this setting is the key that opens the door to effective solutions.

14 | TRACING THE ORIGINS

Mrs. Chambers, Christian Education Director, was just opening her office Monday morning when the phone began to ring. She lifted the receiver and found that it was one of the ladies of the church.

"Mrs. Chambers," she said, "I wonder if I could come over and talk with you about a problem. I hate to take your time, but it's got me worried. It's — well, it's very serious."

"I'd be very happy to talk with you, Mrs. Aldrich. When would it be convenient for you to come?"

"Any time before three-thirty. That's when the children get home from school."

"How would one o'clock be?"

"That would be just fine. I'll be over at one; and thank you *so* much. You don't know how much I appreciate this."

That afternoon Mrs. Aldrich revealed her problem — a marriage difficulty which she felt started "several months ago."

Mrs. Chambers thought to herself, "Several months ago? No, it probably started several years ago."

Being an experienced counselor, Mrs. Chambers knew that serious problems, like mature trees, have *long, persistent roots*. In fact, the root systems may be much larger than the branches above ground. The extensive roots of problems often wind their ways back into early childhood. In Mrs. Aldrich's case, the problem which she thought started "several months ago" was actually the result of misinterpretations and fears of years past. Now they were rearing their ugly heads and interfering with her marriage. With weeks of careful counseling, however, she gained understanding and reached solutions to her problem.

Pulling up a weed without removing its taproot gives no guarantee that you have eliminated it. Just so, erasing the symptoms of a problem without dealing with its *source* may not prevent its reappearance in another guise.

Take the case of "Ole" (as his friends called him). He had been with the firm fourteen years. He was a quiet, likeable man and nobody wanted to see him get into trouble. So his fellow workers covered up the fact that he had recently been coming to work drunk. But one morning as he was getting on the elevator, Ole staggered right into Mr. Hendricks, the personnel manager. Fortunately, the personnel manager was a well trained industrial psychologist. He suggested that Ole come to his office the following day after lunch.

Mr. Hendricks knew that alcoholism did not develop over night; that it was usually a symptom of an emotional, physical, mental or spiritual problem whose roots may reach far into the past. So as he interviewed Ole he was on the lookout for three main types of information: (1) other *symptoms* (in addition to excessive drinking), (2) the *setting* of the problem (the precipitating factors), and (3) the *source* of the problem (the predisposing factors).

As they talked, Mr. Hendricks observed that Ole had symptoms of mild depression, anxiety and guilt. Only recently Ole's mother had died. This was a part of the *setting* of the problem — a precipitating triggering factor. Mr. Hendricks knew that he must look further if he was to find the source of Ole's problem. So he arranged a series of appointments with a psychiatrist. During these appointments Ole was encouraged to talk about his childhood. Predisposing factors of his problem began to appear. He was the youngest of five children, and seven years younger than the nearest sibling. He was the only boy. His father was killed in an accident when Ole was only five. His mother was a nervous person who focused her "smother" love on him, particularly after his father's death. When he was a teen-ager, his mother opposed his dating, often embarrassing him in front of his friends. "Your first responsibility is to your mother," she continually reminded him. Finally he quit dating altogether. His sisters left home and married early, apparently to escape from their mother's domination. When Ole finished high school, he was offered a scholarship at a college in another state. This meant leaving home, and, of course, his mother opposed it. But he determined to go anyway. Two days before he was to leave, his mother had a heart attack. Ole cancelled his plans and went to work with a local firm to support himself and his mother. Her physician later diagnosed that her symptoms were caused by "nerves." The symptoms persisted so Ole made a home for his mother and himself. For the past 14 years his only "freedom" took the form of having a few Saturday night drinks at the corner bar.

It was now clear that a basic source of Ole's drinking problem was a passive-dependency reaction. Ole had never been allowed to grow up and face life on his own. He was still tied to his mother's apron strings. She controlled him through her symptoms and her insistence that his responsibility was to her. With every attempt for independence he was made to feel that he was deserting his "poor, old, sick mother." Unconsciously, he built up an intense hostility toward her—a bitterness for which he felt considerable guilt. Then, at her death, the full weight of this guilt dropped upon him. He was left alone, anxious and dependent, faced with living without her.

In this dilemma he turned to the one other thing which through the years he had depended upon — the bottle. He was accustomed to venting his emotions this way. Intoxication enabled him to forget his fears and to be temporarily confident again. In addition, the intense guilt he felt over his hostility toward his dead mother seemed to demand punishment. Here again, alcohol seemed to fulfill this requirement in the discomfort of the hangover and the threat to his most important remaining asset — his job. At the bar he found sympathy among others who had similar problems and it gave him release to talk about his troubles.

As the psychiatrist worked through the case Ole began to gain insights into his own inadequacy. As new understandings unfolded, he began to seek his own independence and personal development. But the greatest help of all came from an understanding Christian businessman who told Ole about the One who alone can satisfy the natural dependency needs of man. In time Ole gave his heart to Christ. With the understanding he had gained about himself and with the new life he had found in Christ, he did not need the bottle any longer. Instead, as a "newborn babe" in Christ, he began feeding on "the sincere milk of the Word." He became active in the Lord's work and gained many new friends. For the first time in his life he became an adequate, independent man.

The case of Ole illustrates how important it is for a counselor to take time to unravel a problem. The counselor must help his client look for clues. He must encourage him in the process of examining the past so that he might trace the origins of his trouble. It is obvious that Ole would have received no permanent help if Mr. Hendricks and the other counselors had been in a hurry. If they had jumped to conclusions about the reason for Ole's alcoholism, more than likely his basic dependency would have been overlooked.

But dependency is not the only problem with long roots. Many *fears* (in both children and adults) have sources that stem back to an early age. Children are often afraid of the dark, of storms, animals, water, and high places. They may fear the "bogey man," competition or certain people. All too often these fears persist into adulthood. In serious cases they may severely circumscribe the life of their victim. But the trained counselor knows that fear is the *symptom,* not the problem. The situations that arouse or trigger it may be considered its setting and are often clues to its source.

Fears that grip parents may be either consciously or unconsciously passed on to their children. When parents unwisely and continually threaten small children with such disciplinary measures as, "If you're not good the bogey man will get you," an ugly imprint is left that may be hard to erase. Traumatic experiences like falling into water and nearly drowning may leave an indelible mark. In addition there are conditioned fears which may be learned by the association of some harmless object with a frightening experience in which it played a role.

Take the case of Kathy, a second grader, who was brought to the school principal after she had begun screaming uncontrollably. That morning her class had taken a field trip to a farm and Kathy had apparently been terribly frightened by a white rabbit. The principal talked with Kathy, gained her confidence and helped to calm her. Then the principal called Kathy's mother and requested that they discuss the situation with the school psychologist. Her mother arranged to stop by when she brought Kathy to school the next morning.

As Kathy's mother and the psychologist discussed the girl's uncontrollable fear, she remembered one incident that might have had some bearing on the case. She explained that she hesitated to mention it because it had happened when Kathy was only a baby.

"When Kathy was about 13 months old," the mother related, "we were visiting relatives in the country. They had a frisky white puppy who had taken quite a liking to Kathy. So much so, in fact, that he kept jumping up on her. One afternoon when Kathy was sleeping, the puppy jumped up by her and knocked the lamp over. It fell with a terrible crash. Kathy woke up screaming and it took me two whole hours to get her calmed down.

"What I don't understand," continued the mother, "is why she was always afraid of the *puppy* after that. The puppy had jumped up on her several times before but it had never scared her — she liked it."

"Had Kathy been frightened by loud noises before?"

"Oh yes — in fact she was quite sensitive to noise. I'm sure it was the crash of the lamp that scared her so badly . . . But she may have thought it had something to do with the puppy."

"Yes, undoubtedly she transferred the fear of the noise to the puppy. Children often do that — even adults. We call it *association* or *learning by conditioning*."

"I can see why it might have made her afraid of dogs," said the mother, "but why should she be afraid of rabbits or other animals?"

"This is very interesting. We have found that, especially with children an idea often spreads out to take in similar things. This process is called *generalization*. The idea of the original object of fear, the white puppy, probably extended to take in all white puppies and eventually all small white furry animals."

"Well, I can see that. But can anything be done to get rid of this fear?"

"Yes, these fears can usually be eliminated. In fact, they are often outgrown. In Kathy's case, as she has pleasant experiences with white furry animals, these times will outweigh and overcome the unhappy ones. In addition, quietly talking with her about her fear will help her see that there is no reason to be afraid. Then, in time, her feelings will change."

As the school psychologist and Kathy's mother worked on the basis of this understanding, they were able to help Kathy overcome this phobia.

As in the case of Kathy, a counselor must encourage people to reach back into the past, to re-examine almost forgotten experiences, to dig out the tap-root of the problem. This was true in "Ole's" case, in "Kathy's" case, and in most of the cases counselors encounter.

But such treatment takes patience and time. Yet, when we deal with human personalities, can we begrudge the time and effort it takes to see a person become well adjusted? Helping a person recover psychologically is, in many ways, more rewarding than seeing him recover physically. Think of it this way: a psychologically sound person can face physical illness, but a psychologically disturbed person often cannot even face good health!

15 | PHYSICAL CAUSES

Today, men with professional training in medicine, psychology, religion and related fields are recognizing the value of the team approach. They know that their combined efforts bring about the best results. This team effort is based upon the fact that causes are multiple. There are usually a number of factors that create a problem. Any one, or any combination of these causes may bring about illness, maladjustments and various serious problems.

When people bring their troubles to a counselor, they are often unaware that these difficulties may stem from physical causes. Thus, it is the responsibility of the counselor to consider the possibility of medical or physical origins. Until recently certain physical causes have remained virtually hidden. But research has uncovered some of these. Now we know that a physical problem may be disguised in mental, emotional or even spiritual attire.

The case of Mark, a ten-year-old boy, bears this out. He came from a fine home where love and Christian graces shone through everyday living. His father was the Sunday school superintendent in a fine gospel church.

Yet, with all of this in Mark's favor, he never seemed to do as well as he should. His eight-year-old brother was a well adjusted child — a joy to be around. But not so Mark. In both public school and Sunday school he left turmoil in his wake.

Mark claimed to have accepted the Lord as his personal Saviour. His parents had talked with him about full surrender. They pointed out that his actions were displeasing to God. Mark usually repented — and then went right back to his same pattern.

One day when Mark's parents were talking to the pastor about their concern, the pastor suggested they take the boy to a psychologist. Since there was none in their town, the parents wrote a letter to a Christian psychologist in another city describing the boy's problem and asking for an appointment. The letter contained this description:

> His reading is very poor. It is only first grade level even though he is nearly ten years of age and in the fourth grade. His teachers say that he is smart enough, but they have had to keep him back one year already because he does such poor school work.
>
> He has a terrible temper and always blames others for his own faults. He cries easily. Yet in some ways he is a very sweet boy.
>
> He seems nervous, always on the move, and he doesn't stick to things long at a time. He is also easily upset. He is getting better at sports but still he is not up to the others his age. He doesn't have many friends because he doesn't know how to treat them. He often fights and quarrels. He has been taken to doctors but they can't find anything wrong with him. He seems confused much of the time.

Reading the letter carefully, the psychologist noted a number of descriptions which, when combined, offered significant evidence.

- Poor reader
- Apparently intelligent
- Low achievement
- Bad temper
- Blames others
- Cries often
- Gains sympathy
- Nervous
- Short attention span
- Easily upset
- Poor coordination
- Few friends
- In constant conflict
- Confused
- No help found

Appointments followed. As they discussed the boy's problem the psychologist began to suspect that Mark's difficulty might stem from an organic cause. During the next few visits the psychologist gave tests. The results pointed to a neurological impairment.

"Has the boy ever suffered a severe fall, or perhaps had a continued high fever when he was a young child?" asked the psychologist.

"No," the parents replied, "but he did have a very difficult time at birth. In fact, we almost lost him then."

The psychologist then referred the boy to a neurologist who ordered an electroencephalogram (brain wave test) at a local hospital. The test revealed diffused disrythmia with localized disrythmia in the left occipital lobe.

"This condition," explained the doctor, "undoubtedly accounts for much of Mark's behavior. The apparent damage to the left occipital lobe results in a perceptual distortion which has affected his reading. Even though his eyes appear to be normal, he undoubtedly has a vision problem. This was indicated in the tests given by the psychologist."

Mark was given special medication and within a short time he was behaving in a much calmer, more acceptable manner. The neurologist forwarded his findings to the psychologist who followed through with several counseling sessions with the parents.

"Cases of neurological impairment," said the psychologist, "are not unusual. Many children and adults have such cerebral damage. And usually we see an improvement in behavior when the doctor gets them on the right medication. Of course, new attitudes on the part of parents and teachers make considerable differences too."

"Well," said his parents, "Mark is like a different boy. And to think that all this time we thought his problem was a spiritual one."

Neurological impairments do account for many problems seen in children, teen-agers and adults. Even marriage problems are sometimes traced to brain injuries sustained by one spouse. So counselors are becoming more sensitive to possible physical causes of behavior problems and they are making referrals to physicians when they suspicion such difficulties.

Another frequent cause of maladjustment and undesirable behavior is a chemical imbalance of the body caused by endocrine malfunction. More and more we are beginning to recognize the relationship of proper endocrine balance to good physical, mental, and spiritual health.

Dorothy V. Clark, M.D., a prominent endocrinologist, made the following observations concerning endocrinology while conducting a seminar for school psychologists:

The glands which make up the endocrine system should be

a balanced group that work harmoniously. Endocrine disturbance in one gland can upset the whole system, thus causing more than one gland to be malfunctioning. Children with poor endocrine systems frequently are unable to withstand stresses and strains of childhood diseases without resulting glandular dysfunction. Puberty is a particular time of stress, and endocrine disturbances occur frequently in the 9-13 age group. Stress may be mental, physical, or emotional. Physical stress may be caused by factors such as surgery, infections, or by changes associated with puberty.

What are some of the basic personality characteristics of children with endocrine dysfunction? Namely these:

Short attention span. These children tend to be restless and over-active. They do not pay attention. They are frequently a nuisance in school because they annoy other children. They often daydream or appear to be bored. Sometimes a normal child may be considered overactive but a truly overactive child almost never sits still, even though he is interested in what he is doing. He is even unable to sit quietly through a half-hour television program which he enjoys.

Poor memory. Children with endocrine dysfunction may have trouble learning to spell. They also have difficulty in remembering dates. Reading is especially difficult for them as these children are weak in visual memory and do not profit as much from instruction through sight methods. However, children with endocrine deficiency may be good students in spite of their handicap. Their best subject, usually, is arithmetic.

Poor coordination. Small children cannot color well, finding it hard to stay within lines. They also have difficulty in learning to "cut out." They are frequently so frustrated trying to tie shoelaces or button and unbutton clothing that they throw tantrums. Due to poor balance these children may experience difficulty learning to ride tricycles and bicycles and in learning to roller skate.

Instability of I. Q. Test scores. Children with endocrine disturbances may be expected to earn different intelligent test scores on a series of tests given at different times. The endocrine imbalance affects the intellectual functioning and regardless of native ability, the child is unable to use his intelligence to its fullest extent.

Emotional instability. These children usually feel inadequate and insecure. They are sensitive, cry easily, and sustain hurt feelings. They are frequently over-conscientious and try very hard. They may try so hard and fail so long that they finally refuse to try at all. They feel badly because they are unable to successfully compete with others. They have difficulty making friends and are often "lone wolves." Although they are frequently shy and timid, they may become aggressive and slap or push other children. They are not usually chosen for teams because they are unable to run fast and cannot throw and catch balls well. They may withdraw because they are not popular and cannot compete successfully in sports.

Can anything be done to help those who suffer from glandular dysfunction? Yes, medical science has discovered that through the use of certain medication, help is available. A thorough physical endocrine examination is given and a clinical impression is confirmed or denied by laboratory work. This work includes endocrine assays on the blood and x-rays of sella turcica (the pituitary fossa) and wrists for bone age. This is followed by weekly check-ups for three to five weeks to adjust dosage. Then the patient is checked once monthly. Unless children are physically or mentally retarded, medication is given by mouth. Injections are used for adults.

Do children ever "outgrow" endocrine disturbances without diagnosis and medication? Usually not, but they may take on different symptoms. That is, they may change, for example, from asthma to migraine headaches. In adolescence, the disturbance usually grows worse.

Bobbie, for example, was eight years old and in the third grade. He had been attending a Christian day school which refused to keep him any longer. He could not play successfully with others and often struck his classmates. He was a nail-biter. His only playmate was one younger child.

Under treatment Bobbie's school marks improved considerably. In six months he played quite well with other children. After a year his teacher said he was getting along well but still was not good in sports. At the end of two years Bobbie had made excellent progress, and the teacher considered him normal.

In addition to neurological and endocrine problems other physical causes may disturb one's emotional balance. This was the experience of Mr. Kay. He was a well-educated administrator in a Christian college. He had served the college several years when he began to feel nervous, upset and easily disturbed by things which had never bothered him before. There seemed to be little explanation for his emotional stress and despondency. Mr. Kay had a lovely wife and family, no financial burdens, and he enjoyed his work. Yet his distress mounted. In time he consulted his family physician who, in turn, suggested he see a psychiatrist.

I, a deacon in the church, see a psychiatrist? thought Mr. Kay. *Never!*

But as time went on his condition grew increasingly worse until he was unable to continue his work. Finally he sought psychiatric care. But after a number of sessions, he felt no better. In fact, he was growing steadily worse.

Mr. Kay then made trips from one specialist to another. At last one physician began to raise the question of undulant fever. Careful diagnosis confirmed the physician's suspicions. So the doctor started treatment for undulant fever. Within a few weeks some improvement was noted and it was not long until Mr. Kay felt much better. In time, and with medication, he recovered sufficiently to resume his normal activities and work.

Yes, poor physical health is often directly related to emotional and mental problems. God's Word teaches us that we are *"fearfully* and *wonderfully* made" (Psalm 139:14). We should register no surprise then, that our physical well being and our emotional and spiritual health are interrelated. Counselors understand that man is a whole being, that whatever affects one portion usually affects the entire human organism. Thus, neurological impairment, glandular dysfunction or other physical ailments can be the basic causes for emotional disturbance. And, of course, a study of psychosomatic illness shows that poor mental or spiritual health can reflect itself in physical symptoms such as headaches, heart ailments, ulcers and many other disorders.

As we view the possible causes of human problems, we see that they are multiple. And it behooves the skilled counselor to become sensitive to *all* the causes of behavior — *physical,* as well as emotional, mental, and spiritual.

16 | MULTIPLE PERSPECTIVE

As seasoned counselors look back over years of experience, they are impressed with this simple, basic fact: *problems usually have many sides*. Even situations that at first seemed to indicate one person was completely innocent while the other was to blame often later revealed that *both* parties were somewhat at fault.

Rev. Hodges found this to be true — but after it was too late. Mrs. Frazer, an active member of his church, came to see him about a serious problem she was having with her husband.

"Oh, pastor," she sobbed, "he's simply unbearable. He drinks, abuses me, and treats the family terribly."

During several sessions Mrs. Frazer filled in the details about her husband's contempt for the church and his unspeakable treatment of her and the children. Although the pastor had never met the husband, he came to resent him.

Mrs. Frazer's story was so utterly convincing that Rev. Hodges agreed that this "dear woman of God" had only one alternative: separate maintenance. With this encouragement she felt justified in separating from her husband, then later suing for divorce.

Time passed. Several years later, while pastoring in another city, Rev. Hodges met Mr. Frazer through a business contact. After continued business transactions they came to know each other quite well. Finally their conversations turned to Mr. Frazer's former wife whom the pastor had counseled some years before. For the first time the pastor began to hear another side of the story. Now he realized that he had acted on only half of the information

—he had made definite suggestions when he had heard only one side. How he wished that he could turn back the calendar and give Mrs. Frazer the opposite advice!

Undoubtedly all counselors have, at times, regretted the counsel they have given. To have had a few such experiences is understandable. But some counselors make this mistake over and over again. They are "fooled" quite regularly.

It is human nature to favor one's own side of a situation. This is even more true when a person is distressed or emotionally disturbed. When he is carrying a heavy burden such as a marriage problem, conflicts with parents or employment difficulties, a counselee is likely to see only one major side — his own. He looks at it from his own viewpoint, his own experience. Since he is emotionally upset everything seems exaggerated. This results in his side looking (to him) like the *only* side. But a full, adequate perspective may be lacking. To see the complete picture, a counselor makes sure that:

*He has sufficient interviews to uncover not one, but many of the basic causes.**

One or even a few counseling sessions may not be sufficient to find the main sources of conflict and maladjustments. Only as the counselee goes deeper into his problem can he begin to see the network of incidents that have brought about a given condition.

He does not permit himself to be emotionally moved by the counselee.

The counselor who permits himself to "cry" with his client immediately shuts out opportunities to view a problem objectively. Furthermore, he discourages his client from seeing points of view other than those he already knows.

He seeks to interview the several parties concerned in the problem.

To see only one person who is involved in a complex problem is usually to understand only one side. If possible, the counselor should keep the way open to counsel with the husband, parent, child or whomever is directly related to the situation.

---

*See Chapter 6, *The Counseling Process.*

He does not think of himself as a referee.

People do not need referees; they need competent, trained counselors. Their problems require someone who can help them discover basic causes; then point the way to concrete solutions. When a counselor places himself in the role of a referee he not only offers little help, but he is likely to give advice based only on the "facts" he has at hand. These few facts are probably not adequate for satisfactory understanding.

*He does not disregard the clear teachings of the Word of God.**

There are times when a solution to a problem may seem like an "exception" to the teachings of the Bible.

"But this case is different," you may say.

This is a dangerous assumption. God's Word is infallible and not to be tampered with. Rather than advise against God's perfect laws, the counselor should wait and withhold definite suggestions until he has gathered more facts on the case.

When a counselor observes the above safeguards, he will avoid "snap" judgments. And as the years pass, he will clearly see that most problems have many significant sides!

---

*See Chapter 31, *The Use of Scripture in Counseling*.

17 | MOTIVES FOR DISCUSSION

The reason people say what they do is often more revealing than *what* they actually say. This is because motives are more basic than verbalization.

Keeping this in mind, a skilled counselor listens carefully. Then he looks behind the psychological curtain for the impelling factors which motivate the counselee to say what he does. Until the motives are clearly understood, the picture remains hazy.

This very process challenged Mr. Hart, an adult Bible teacher, as he talked privately with Mrs. Thompson, a member of his class.

"I think I'm a complete failure as a wife," she said.

The teacher listened carefully, encouraging her to say more. He knew that there could be various meanings behind her confession of failure.

"Why does she say this?" he asked himself. "Does she really feel this way? Is she wanting reassurance that she is *not* a failure? Does she want sympathy? Or does she want my praise for the good job she is doing?"

As the conversation continued, Mrs. Thompson kept talking about what a failure she was, how she had disappointed her husband and her children. Mr. Hart said little but he watched for clues as to what prompted these statements.

"Has she always been made to feel that she is a failure? Has she lost her self-confidence through criticism? Is she building up resentment against her husband? Will she blame someone else for preventing her from being a good wife? Will she offer excuses?"

The key to Mrs. Thompson's motives did not reveal itself during the first interview.

During the week the counselor thought over the things Mrs. Thompson had said. "Does she have unrealistic ideas of what a good wife should be?" he wondered. "Is she judging herself too harshly? Does she resent the restrictions imposed upon her by marriage? Is she too immature to assume parental responsibilities? Is marriage interfering with her dreams of a career? Has she been unable to adjust sexually to marriage? Does she doubt that she is a good mother? Is she unconsciously rejecting her children? Is she having a financial struggle?"

Mr. Hart could have thought of many more possible reasons why Mrs. Thompson said what she did. But he knew that the true motives would emerge if she were given sufficient opportunity to talk.

During the second counseling session Mrs. Thompson began to blame herself for being harsh with her children and argumentative with her husband. As rapport increased she complained about the restrictions of marriage. She wished she had stayed single and gone on with her career as a commercial artist. Eventually, she shifted the blame to her husband. He was the cause of her being "a failure as a wife." *He* was just like her *father*. How could she be a good wife under these circumstances?

The true motivation for Mrs. Thompson's opening statement was now becoming clear. She had started out to blame herself. But actually her self-criticism was a cloak to cover a deep resentment toward her father and her husband. It was this resentment that had to be considered and dealt with before she could receive help. If Mr. Hart had accepted her first discussion at face value he might not have discovered the root of her problem.

Not only do counselors examine the motives for what people say, they also look at the causes for silences — what they do *not* say. What a counselee does *not* discuss is probably as important as what he does. He may speak freely about various matters in his life but in other considerations, he may freeze up. This blocking is an indication to the counselor that somewhere in the counselee's past are experiences or lack of experiences which preclude his entering certain areas to talk about them.

MOTIVES FOR DISCUSSION

Mr. and Mrs. Crawford sought out a speaker at a Bible conference and asked to see him about a personal problem. During their session together the counselor noticed that when the husband brought up the matter of sex he discussed it easily and in good taste. But with his wife it was different. She could not express herself. Embarrassed and ill at ease, she turned the subject aside and talked about other things.

With this clue in mind the counselor suggested at the close of the interview that if they wished he could see them again on the following day, perhaps separately or, if they preferred, together. Mrs. Crawford suggested that they *would* like to talk with him, but that it might be best if they saw him separately. This was arranged. During the session with Mrs. Crawford the counselor learned that her childhood had been marked by numerous experiences that had caused her to feel most uncomfortable about discussing sex. In fact, these experiences were serving to prevent a good adjustment in the marriage.

Although the counselor was only able to see the couple a few times, he did help them considerably. And his success centered mainly in the fact that during the initial session he was alert to what Mrs. Crawford did *not* say. He understood that sometimes people are emotionally *unable* to discuss certain topics. He knew that an important part of counseling is to uncover the motives for what people avoid as well as what they verbally reveal.

Effective counselors cannot afford to skim over the surface of people's problems. True motives often run deep and they must be uncovered before solutions are available. When the reasons "why" have been determined, neither the counselor nor the counselee is left groping in the dark with problems still unsolved.

18 | FOCUSING ON THE CLIENT'S PROBLEM

It has been suggested that the best counselors do not have problems of their own. This sounds good, but it is quite unrealistic. Even the best adjusted people, including counselors, because they are members of the human race, are not exempt from problems. But, by and large, if a counselor is to function at his best he should not be struggling with serious problems himself. Counselors who are contending with unresolved conflicts of their own have this serious handicap: they often attempt to work out their personal problems through and at the expense of the counselee. Unless they are careful, they will use the counselee and the counseling session to resolve their own difficulties.

Those who have serious problems themselves should not attempt to counsel others because their own maladjustments are prone to interfere with the therapeutic process.

Pastor Cook realized this when a lady in his church offered to assist him in visitation work, especially in calling on various members who were having problems.

"I'd be glad to help you, Pastor," Mrs. Bain said. "I just love to visit and talk with people, and I'm sure I could help them."

But Pastor Cook knew that this would never do. He realized that Mrs. Bain had severe problems of her own and he was certain that she would use such contacts as opportunities to talk about them, hoping to find some solutions for herself. So he thanked her kindly but explained that he felt he should make these calls himself.

Minor problems, however, need not interfere with successful counseling. Neither should a counselor who has resolved his own conflicts hesitate to counsel others. In fact, he may be in a better position to understand and identify with a counselee than the man who has not experienced any serious difficulties of his own.

This was the case of Mr. Warren, an administrator in a local school. A young couple came to ask him about enrolling their daughter in a special class. "Martha has a serious handicap," sighed the mother. "She's a spastic."

As they discussed the child's welfare, Mr. Warren assured them that he knew just how they felt. He explained that he, too, had a child who was a victim of cerebral palsy. From that point on the discouraged young couple felt much better. They knew that Mr. Warren understood completely and that he would do everything within his power to bring help to their little Martha.

So it is that when we have passed through deep waters and have come out victoriously, we can often become a blessing and help to others who are passing through similar circumstances. Experience is an excellent teacher. It can make us more sympathetic and understanding. It can give us insights into other people's problems. However, we should guard against offering the same solutions to our counselees that worked well for us. We must keep in mind that we have no patent on resolving problems. What worked for us may not work on Mr. Brown and vice versa.

"But his problem seems to be just like the one *I* had when I was 18!"

Perhaps it is. However, your client's background is different from yours. He has a backlog of his own experiences, values, resources and needs. Yes, the problem *looks* similar. But it has a different setting and it requires its own study and solution.

Ultimately, the counselee must take responsibility for his own problem. You can help him. You can provide the conditions which promote insight and self-reliance. But little permanent good is done by handing out ready-made, pat solutions. Even though the counselee seems to want a direct answer it is our duty as counselors to know that a deeper understanding must be gained if any permanent good is to be accomplished.

Don, a high school junior, was constantly the butt of derision by his classmates. They tagged him "egghead." One day he got in a fight with a boy who had been making fun of him. Don was sent to the Dean. As Dean Archer talked with the boy, he saw how similar the problem was to one he had experienced in his school days. The dean, too, had been ostracized as an "egghead." He had solved his problem and gained acceptance by going out for sports while keeping up his good grades.

Dean Archer, however, did not tell Don about his *own* problem and how it had been solved. Instead, he wisely used his experience to help him *understand* Don's feelings. He encouraged the boy to talk about his conflicts. Gradually Don began to realize the basic reason for his persecution. He was intensely afraid of competition. This prevented him from being a "regular fellow" and earned him the middle names of "chicken" and "egghead." It also kept him out of sports.

In a later counseling session Don began to see that his fear of competition stemmed from his home life. His father was a domineering man who had always rejected and belittled him. As Don discussed his problem he saw that he should enter into more activities. He decided to take music lessons and join the school orchestra. Later he joined a debate club. As he entered into various activities his social adjustment improved.

If the dean had not focused on the problem with Don's own understanding as the basis for the solution, he might have counseled the boy like this: "Nothing to your problem. Nothing at all. Why, when *I* was your age they called *me* an egghead, too. Know what *I* did? I joined the football team. What you need is some good rough competition. Physical contact. It'll make a man of you. It sure worked for *me*. They never called *me* an egghead anymore. Not after I made right tackle!"

Perhaps few counselors would be this extreme. However, a surface similarity in problems can sometimes cause one to overlook some basic differences. Yet, because the dean did not jump to conclusions about Don's problem and because he was wise enough not to offer the solution that had resolved his own difficulty, the dean was able to help Don achieve the insight he needed to solve his individual problem — in his *own* way.

Can a counselor *know* when he is focusing on his own problem rather than on his client's? One of the best ways to avoid becoming too personally involved is to check on the use of the first person singular. When we catch ourselves using *I, me, my* or *mine,* we might ask ourselves, "Am I working on *his* problem or *mine?*"

Giving people advice based upon one's own experience is not the only way a counselor may focus on his own difficulty while counseling. He does not even need to mention his problem or use the first person singular. All he does is to *attach undue significance* to something the client has said or done. He enlarges on it. He builds it up to represent something out of proportion to its real importance to the counselee. He encourages the counselee to talk about it. And, if he can, he may convince the counselee that it is the real source of his problem. The counselor sends him down a blind alley, the counselee thanks him profusely for his help and goes off — *unhelped.*

Of course, no counselor intentionally does this. But it may take place unconsciously when the counselor's attention is fixed on solving his own unresolved conflicts. They are important to him. And by a process of projection he tends to read them into other people's situations.

What a person sets before a counselor during a counseling session could be compared to a psychological smorgasbord. The counselee verbally lays out various experiences and problems. The pitfall? To judge the counselee's problem by his own. When the counselor's attention is diverted from solving the client's problem to solving his own, it is as though he chose potatoes (because *he* liked them) and put them on *the counselee's* plate. If he had waited, the counselee might have chosen carrots instead. Just as he is courteous enough to let a person serve himself, so he should allow the counselee the right to reveal his own problems. When the counselor arrives at his own conclusions and forces the issue, he is in great danger of being led by his own needs rather than the needs of the counselee.

Mr. Clarke, a counselor, listened attentively as Mrs. Jackson poured out her marital problems. She talked about the children, her in-laws, and problems with her husband. In a mood for confession, she discussed, among other things, her guilt feelings over some heavy petting and sexual relations she and her husband engaged in before they were married.

Interestingly enough, the counselor, before he was saved, had engaged in illicit sex relations before marriage and he had never quite resolved his guilt feelings over these episodes. So when Mrs. Jackson mentioned it in passing, his "ears pricked up." He began to question her about it and by his interest in the subject implied that it might be "very significant." The counselor then commented that such experiences could have serious psychological effects and that they were probably the basis of her marital trouble.

The rest of the counseling session revolved about that subject. Mrs. Jackson was discouraged from delving any further into other aspects of her problem — emotional, spiritual, financial and other such areas. This was unfortunate because Mrs. Jackson's marital problem had little, if anything, to do with her premarital experiences. She had resolved that problem long ago. Her present problems revolved around finances.

Mr. Clarke had read into her situation his *own* anxiety about his *own* problem. He had discouraged her from exploring further and prevented her from finding the real cause. Fortunately, some time later Mrs. Jackson saw another counselor who was able to help her find and deal with the root of her difficulty.

If we wish to help others we must first be willing to bring our own problems and sins to God. He asks us to cast all our care upon Him; for He cares for us (I Peter 5:7). If we do this sincerely He will cleanse us and heal us. It will not be necessary for us to try to solve our own problems, especially while counseling others. When we have committed every detail of our lives unto God, then we will be able to focus our attention on the client — not on ourselves.

19 | ENCOURAGING SELF-RELIANCE

The counseling process is a maturing process. It leads a counselee away from over-dependency to greater self-reliance and independence.

One of the responsibilities of a counselor is to help the counselee put away his crutches and stand on his own two feet. This is sometimes referred to as *inner-direction*. It does not mean "without Christ," but rather, "through Christ I will be a mature, responsible person." This is the "growing up" or maturing process about which God speaks in His Word: "Rather, let our lives lovingly express truth in all things — speaking truly, dealing truly, living truly. Enfolded in love, let us grow up in every way and in all things into Him, Who is the Head, (even) Christ, the Messiah, the Anointed One" (Ephesians 4:15 ANT).

Controls from within are truly the best ones because they do not require continual assistance from other people. A man who cannot discipline and regulate his own life is dependent upon others to regulate it for him. The inner controlled person stands independently, but the man who has not developed self-reliance has to lean on others.

Most people are not found at either extreme. They are somewhere in between. Research indicates that parental attitudes often determine the amount of inner direction developed in their children. For example, a mother who continually restricts her child's activities because of anxieties about him may stunt the growth of his inner-direction. On the other hand, when a parent gives a child appropriate responsibilities, personality growth and self-reliance begin to develop.

What has this to do with counseling? This: people come to you seeking solutions to their problems. But they do not need *your* solutions. What they need, through Christ, is to work through their own problems. Naturally, your solutions may be valid ones. And if a counselee leaves your office with your suggestions, then incorporates them in his own situation to solve his problems, well and good. But this is unlikely. Furthermore, if you solve a person's problem *for* him, he will probably return when something else goes wrong — *expecting you to solve that problem too.*

Actually, you do your counselee little permanent good if you keep him on crutches, that is, dependent on *you*. In fact, you may weaken or retard his development. It is important to help him understand and take responsibility for his own problems, to increase his self-reliance and to put him on his own as soon as possible.

As a counselor, you assume the role of a catalytic agent, encouraging and regulating therapeutic process but not causing or strongly directing it. You provide a temporary environment in which the "healing" process can take place. The surgeon cannot heal. Were it not for the fact that God has given the body power to heal itself, surgery would destroy rather than preserve life.

The human personality has innate tendencies toward psychological healing which correspond to the body's physical healing powers. Your responsibility as a counselor is to help the "patient" delineate his problem, face it, find the causes, then take positive steps toward healthy, wholesome, Christian living. It is not the counselor's responsibility to take the counselee's personality apart and remodel it after his own. If he attempts this, he will probably never help the counselee to stand on his own two feet.

Dependency on a counselor may be a subtle, unconscious process. It may creep in without our awareness. Most of us like to believe that others need us. Unconsciously, perhaps, we feel that many people are depending upon us. We may rationalize by assuring ourselves that we merely want to *help* people. They ask for our advice. They pour out their troubles to us. And they keep *coming back.*

"It isn't my fault," you may say, "that Mrs. Brown keeps returning. Some new problem always seems to crop up to disturb her. I helped her solve her other difficulties, so naturally she comes back to me."

But there is more to the picture. Perhaps you have never fully realized the importance of helping Mrs. Brown help herself. You may not have shown her how. Perhaps you really *wanted* her to depend on you.

Effective counselors encourage clients to take an honest look at themselves. We counselors certainly cannot expect them to do this if we, ourselves, insist on feeling needed and indispensable to others. Unfortunately this motive is much too common among seemingly altruistic counselors. Some are guilty of gratifying this selfish desire at the expense of those with whom they counsel. This is not only unfortunate; it is unethical.

Stan, a tall, husky, college sophomore, sat across the desk from the college dean. He began to unfold his anxieties about choosing his vocation. He could not decide whether to continue in his present course, to change his major, or go to another school. As Stan described his problem, the dean thought, "I want to help this boy but I don't want to rob him." The dean was wise. He desired to give the boy support but he did not want to make decisions for him or to prevent him from taking responsibility for his own plans. After two sessions it became evident to Stan that it would be better to drop out of his academic course at the college and enter a technical institute.

Several difficulties then reared their heads. Which technical school should he attend? Would any school accept him this late in the semester? What should he tell his parents? After all, his mother had her heart set on his becoming a physician.

Of course, the dean could have advised the boy immediately. He could have reached for the phone and obtained the information for him. Also, he could have interceded for him with his mother.

But he didn't.

He put Stan on his own. He encouraged him to think the problem through, then he handed Stan the task of working out the details himself.

During these sessions the dean encouraged Stan to answer his own queries. Point-blank questions like, "What do you think I am good at?" or "What should I tell my mother?" were tossed back to Stan to untangle himself. When he concluded his interviews with the dean, the young man had the answers but they were his own. Now he could take each step confidently. He could face the opposition of his family and friends. And, in addition, he could tackle similar problems in the future. He had grown in self-reliance.

Strange as this may seem, counselors should guard against helping people *too* much. Naturally, it is easy to suppose that we are showing brotherly love by doing as much as we can for people. But is this truly an act of kindness? Actually we may be weakening our counselee by not encouraging self-reliance and independent growth.

The counselor should continually ask himself, "Am I helping him gain his *own* insights? Am I giving him enough or too much support? How can I assist him in assuming responsibility himself?" These considerations will not only help a counselor achieve a better balance in his own professional growth, but the results will be seen in the life of the counselee as he begins to take his own steps, then walk.

20 | HANDLING DIRECT QUESTIONS

Mr. Cleveland was a friendly young psychologist, newly employed in a large elementary school district. As he talked with various teachers and administrators they often turned to him for answers:

"Do you think I should just ignore Dick's behavior?" a teacher asked.

"Why do you think Stevie comes to my office each morning complaining of headaches?" inquired the nurse.

"What makes Rose wander around the room all day?"

"What would you do," the principal asked, "if a boy openly defied you in front of the class?"

"Is there any way to teach a girl like Gertrude how to read?" a third grade teacher wanted to know.

"What's the best thing to do for a highly gifted child?" asked the vice-principal.

"What can I do to help a boy like Jimmy who is mentally retarded?" questioned the playground director.

And so it went all semester. Direct questions, like swift arrows, kept flying toward the psychologist.

"Man alive," said Mr. Cleveland to the head of the guidance department, "I didn't know people could ask so many questions. And I'm supposed to have all the answers!"

"Well," replied the guidance director, "people raise many

questions for various reasons. And I think psychologists get more than their share. When I first went into this work, it bothered me some, too. But I finally learned that direct questions did not necessarily require direct answers. Now I think of them as handles —discussion handles. When these handles are offered us, we can take hold of them and use them to fully consider the question. But we need not give direct answers. Sometimes a person doesn't want you to answer the question at all. I think this is one way that we can help people — by taking their direct questions and considering them as opportunities for discussion."

Like Mr. Cleveland, many counselors wonder what to do with direct questions. Actually, people raise questions for various reasons. For example, they may want to talk, and this is their method of getting started. People sometimes ask about a less important subject when actually they want to discuss another. They use the initial question as a wedge into conversation. Then they hope they can soon steer the discussion toward the more urgent problem.

Questions are also used to pry out a counselor's general attitude, his point of view. In this way a counselee hopes to learn whether he should trust a counselor with his particular problem. Most people are sincere in the questions they ask. They have no intention of cornering the counselor or putting him "on the spot." But neither do they actually mean for you to give them a direct answer. What they really want is an opportunity to think and talk.

Since one of the basic objectives in counseling is to *promote insight,* the handling of direct questions offers many opportunities to do just that. Here the counselor considers the possible reasons behind the asking of questions. For example, an upset parent might ask, "Why am I so patient with my Sunday school class and yet so short on patience with my own children?"

Your response should draw out further explanations which will aid the parent in gaining self understanding. Such replies as these are valuable.

(1) "You feel, then, that you are not as patient with your own children as you are with others?"

94

(2) "This is an important point you have raised. Let's talk about it."

(3) "Would you like to explain further what you mean?"

In this way your response takes a direct question and converts it into a helpful discussion whereby the person can clarify his thoughts, find possible causes and gain real insights.

Quite frequently someone may raise a question which the counselor should place in a larger, more meaningful setting. For example, a youth director was chatting with Bruce, a rather unsettled high school boy, when Bruce asked, "Mr. Morris, what do you think about dancing?"

The youth director realized, of course, that Bruce's problem was much bigger than "dancing." So he began to place the question in its larger setting.

"Bruce," Mr. Morris said, "the question of what is right and what is wrong for the Christian has come to the mind of every believer. And I feel that the answer is found in another, much larger question: 'To what extent shall I devote my life to Christ?' Let's sit down and talk about it, shall we?"

This opened the way for the two to earnestly consider the matter of consecration. Yes, the youth director had skillfully taken a smaller question and had developed it into a soul searching discussion of God's claim on the believer's life!

Should one *never* answer direct questions? Should "small" questions always be placed in larger settings?

Naturally, there are many questions which deserve definite, precise answers. But a skilled counselor is sensitive to the motives behind a question. He determines whether it has been asked for the sake of information or whether it represents a need to discuss something deeper, the real problem.

When a counselor keeps these things in mind he will also avoid giving answers which the counselee is not ready or able to accept. Instead, he will use a direct question as a means to explore and find the solution to a more basic problem.

21 | INVOLVEMENT

Mrs. Lance, the minister's wife, called upon Muriel, a teenage girl from the church. But Mrs. Lance was not prepared for the unfortunate condition she found in the home. During the visit Muriel's story came to light. She was unwanted and unloved by her godless father and step-mother, and now that she had become a Christian, they made life even more miserable for her. When the father was under the influence of liquor he would curse and beat the girl. As Mrs. Lance was leaving the home, Muriel stepped outside with her, then broke down in pitiful crying. "I don't know what to do," she sobbed. "Oh, I wish I could die!"

Even after Mrs. Lance returned home, Muriel's pathetic crying kept ringing in her ears. The more she thought about it, the worse it seemed. Mrs. Lance could not eat much dinner that evening — she wasn't hungry. In fact, she felt ill as she thought of the heart-breaking situation she had witnessed that afternoon. However, as she discussed the situation with her husband, Mrs. Lance began to realize that she could not possibly help the girl if she allowed the problem to disturb her to this extent.

This is true in most counseling. We dare not identify so closely with problems that we become ill ourselves. Yet, counselors do need to be sympathetic. There is little place in Christian counseling for cold, calculating attitudes.

Our Lord was sympathetic. He had compassion for the sick and mercy for the sinful. In God's Word we read that when Christ saw the multitudes, "He was moved with compassion" (Matthew

9:36). We read again that He is "touched with the feeling of our infirmities" (Hebrews 4:15). He wept when He came to the grave of His friend, Lazarus (John 11:35), and He mourned for the city of Jerusalem as He poured out His heart over its wayward, indifferent condition (Matthew 23:37).

We, too, should "bear one another's burdens" (Galatians 6:2). This is especially true in counseling. God instructs us to "comfort the feebleminded, support the weak, be patient toward all men" (I Thessalonians 5:14). We also read through the pen of Isaiah, "Comfort ye my people, saith your God" (Isaiah 40:1).

Indeed, Christians are to be sympathetic and understanding toward one another. When a counselor is kind, the counselee is comforted by realizing that someone understands how he feels. This sympathetic relationship paves the way for free discussion of the counselee's problem. People often become reserved or defensive when they feel that others do not understand.

Sympathy is communicated by a gentle approach and kind words. Yet a counselor cannot afford to let his heart run away with his reason. He is of little effect if he becomes so involved in a counselee's problem that he, himself, becomes ill. This only aggravates the situation. In such cases the counselor, as well as the counselee, needs help.

When we become too closely identified with a problem we tend to lose the objective attitude so essential in good counseling. Some counselors become so involved that they vicariously become part of the problem. Naturally, their judgment is colored by their own emotional feelings. When a person falls into a well, the best thing to do is to throw him a rope — not to climb in with him. Occasionally a counselor unwisely sinks into the problems of his counselee instead of remaining on firm ground where he can lift the counselee out of his undesirable situation.

People who are disturbed want a counselor who is well poised. Upset people need someone who can help them gain stability and balance. It is only natural that a counselee tends to pattern his reactions after those of the counselor. This is why it is essential that the counselor maintain his composure. By his quiet, calm example he can help the counselee achieve poise and steadiness. This in itself is a big step toward rehabilitation.

To prevent becoming too deeply involved in someone else's problem, the counselor should consider the following:

Focus your attention on the counseling process.

During each interview concentrate on the therapeutic process. For example, ask yourself such questions as, "Why is he saying this? Does he understand the causes of his behavior? Is he accepting responsibility for his problem? What is his depth of spiritual understanding?" This will turn your attention to the counseling process rather than the emotional involvement.

Realize that a person's unfortunate situation is not unfamiliar to him.

In all probability his problem has developed over a long period of time and has gradually become what it is. Therefore, it is not especially traumatic to the counselee. It may be a shock to you but not necessarily to him. He has undoubtedly seen his problem develop and has conditioned himself to it. Although it may be unpleasant and indeed difficult to bear, he has become somewhat accustomed to it. He has built up defenses against it so that it is probably not a shocking experience to him.

Realize that objectivity is seldom achieved through too close identification.

Only as a person remains some distance from an object can he discern its true perspective — its comparative size. So in counseling, a friendly distance allows more accurate judgment. As a counselor reads books and delves into the art of counseling he will gain valuable insights. He will clearly see his unique roll as a counselor. And through continued experience he will learn to be more objective, remaining a friendly yet healthy distance from the problem.

Commit the problem to the Lord.

He knows and understands and He is able. Worrying about a problem is an indication that the counselor may not be trusting the Lord to meet the needs of the counselee. The Christian counselor can maintain a sympathetic yet objective attitude toward cases by praying about them and committing them to God.

These, then, are ways a counselor can achieve a healthy balance in helping those who have serious problems. A counselee wants help, not hindrance. Unconsciously, he seeks in his counselor an example of poise and composure. It is the privilege of the counselor to be this man or woman.

22 | RESPONSIBILITY FOR REFERRALS

For years Ed Baker had thought about the possibility of seeking professional help for his problem. But somehow responsibilities crowded in and time slipped by.

Why can't I lick this myself? he thought. *A Christian should be able to conquer his problems anyway.*

But the problem lingered on — sometimes greater, sometimes smaller, but always uncomfortable and persistent. Although Ed had casually talked with his pastor about it, the pastor had not advised professional help.

One day while talking to a Christian friend, Ed dropped a little hint about his difficulty.

"Tell me more about this, Ed," said his friend.

Ed was relieved to share his problem.

"I'm glad you brought this up," he replied, "because there is help for you. It's out of my field altogether but if I were you, I'd get professional help right away. It won't be long until you are rid of it. I suggest you see Dr. Peters at the local clinic, or possibly Dr. Rogers over in Clarksvale. They're both specialists and they deal with problems like this nearly every day. Why don't you see one of them right away?"

That was just the encouragement Ed needed. And many people with serious problems are just waiting for a counselor to suggest specialized professional help.

A minister or a Christian worker is often expected to counsel with people who represent a great variety of problems. Yet he may have neither the time nor the training to handle some of the situations. In spite of this, some pastors seem to feel that it is their duty to work with every case.

One pastor said, "When I was young in the ministry, I often felt that I was failing if I didn't help everyone who came to me. Then I learned that certain kinds of problems required training that I did not have. From then on I was on the lookout for capable (preferably Christian) specialists — counselors to whom I could refer people."

Actually, we perform a valuable service when we refer counselees to the right person. Many people do not know the kind of specialist they should see, and, of course, there is a difference even among similar specialists. There is a difference in skill, but even more important, a difference in *attitude*. Some professionally trained men and women, although they are not saved, are at least sympathetic toward spiritual things and would not take it upon themselves to destroy the client's faith in Christ.

The Bible says that Jesus, the perfect man, matured mentally, physically, spiritually and socially. "And Jesus increased in wisdom and stature, and in favor with God and man" (Luke 5:52). People's problems tend to stem from one or more of these four areas.

Man is more than a spiritual being. He is a physical, intellectual, social and emotional being as well and he has many needs in addition to spiritual ones. Although a person's spiritual condition affects all other aspects of his life, he may need diagnosis and help in these other areas. Therefore, a counselor may need to refer his counselee to the person who can help him most.

*Sources of Referral**

In cases where the nature of the problem is suspected to be physical or medical, it is best to refer to a *medical doctor*. A physician will decide whether it is necessary to refer further to a given specialist. In extended counseling it is wise to encourage the

---

*For these and other referrels see Chapter 32, *Terms*.

counselee to have a thorough physical examination. In fact, many psychiatrists and psychologists require a medical examination when they accept a client for counseling sessions.

Sometimes a person who displays psychiatric symptoms is actually suffering from such ailments as endocrine or neurological disorders. Many people who are referred to a psychiatrist refuse to go. They do not want to be thought of as "crazy." This situation can sometimes be remedied by suggesting that the counselee see his family physician or a *neurologist*. In many ways, a neurologist's training is similar to a psychiatrist's. Yet, strangely enough, there is less stigma attached to seeing a neurologist. Everyone has nerves!

Spiritual and psychological help are not always sufficient. Sometimes a person needs legal counsel. Being able to refer him to a capable Christian *attorney* may be necessary.

In some marriages, sexual incompatibility is a serious problem. Referring the couple to a *gynecologist* or *urologist* may reveal a physical disorder which is causing the maladjustment.

Some people need vocational guidance. If so, it is wise to refer to a psychologist who can evaluate aptitudes and interests. Through various tests and inventories as well as interviews, a psychologist can help his clients find their own strengths and weaknesses.

Another person may need counsel concerning his educational plans. He could be referred to a Christian *educator* who has first-hand knowledge about educational institutions, courses of study, entrance requirements, tuition, accreditation, credentials, licenses, certification and Christian emphases.

There are times when a person's problem may be severe with gross personality distortions. In serious cases (psychoses) he will no doubt benefit from hospitalization. In such instances, he should be referred to a medical doctor or a *psychiatrist.**

Many problems are basically spiritual ones. People in their natural state are not at peace with God. The consequences of sin and the curse have left their marks upon the human race. When a person is at peace with God, he enjoys good spiritual health. But

---

*See Chapter 28, *The Mentally and Emotionally Ill.*

there are some types of problems that do not right themselves instantly when one is born again. Although he may improve greatly, a person suffering from physical, mental or emotional ills usually benefits from additional help.

Following Up Referrals

When you refer, make every effort to follow up your referral. This keeps your counselee close enough for spiritual help. It shows your continued interest and it tends to improve your relationship with the specialist to whom you referred the client.

The benefits of a referral service often work both ways. Many times a professional person (especially a Christian) to whom you refer will, in turn, refer his patients to you for spiritual help. This opens the door to a ministry that can bring results for eternity.

Your referral service will also result in associations with people in other professions. This will broaden your knowledge and extend contacts so that you may have the opportunity to lead some of your non-Christian professional associates to Christ.

Brief Contacts

Some Christian counselors, because of the nature of their work, may not be able to follow through on cases but they can perform a valuable service of referral. After hearing a lecture on counseling an evangelist raised this point: "During your presentation I have been impressed with the fact that counseling takes time. You have mentioned the fact that most problems require several counseling sessions. And I readily agree with this. But my question is this: How can I help people effectively when I am in a community or a city for only a week or so at a time? True, many people will come to me with their problems when they would not see their own pastor or any other Christian in the community. But since I can see them only briefly, how can I best help them?"

The speaker then pointed out that although the evangelist might be limited in time he could, nevertheless, make a valuable contribution. "One of your greatest contributions," he said, "is through referrals. I'm convinced that many people are waiting for someone to encourage them to seek specialized help. They may need to see their pastor, a medical doctor or someone else. But you, the evangelist, are the man to give them direction. Your single contact can start them on the road to the help they have long needed."

This is true not only of evangelists but of all counselors. Willingness to refer a counselee to another member of the counseling team is a mark of professional maturity. God gives a variety of talents for various purposes. The physician, the pastor, the youth director and others comprise a much needed team. In fact, the Bible is explicit in describing this teamwork in terms of harmonious functioning of the human body. The source of inspiration and direction (the head) is the Lord Jesus Christ, and every born again Christian is a member of His body. "From whom the whole body fitly joined together and compacted by that which every joint supplieth, according to the effectual working in the measure of every part, maketh increase of the body unto the edifying of itself in love" (Ephesians 4:16).

So it is in counseling. Different specialists make their own contribution in helping a person resolve his individual problem. Many people who need specialized help would never seek it if it were not for your suggestion and encouragement. By referring a person to one who is competent in handling his special problem, you are rendering a much needed service.

23 | EXTENDING YOUR COUNSELING MINISTRY

Every conscientious Christian leader is faced with the dilemma of "too much to do and too little time in which to do it." Pressed with over crowded schedules, he sometimes wishes he could be in several places at once. As he sees the many needs about him, he may almost resent his human limitations. How he wishes he could somehow serve in several capacities at the same time. This search for time is especially critical in counseling. The Christian counselor realizes that for every one he sees, there are many others who also need help.

But many Christian leaders are learning that they can extend their counseling ministry beyond themselves. This extension is usually made possible in the following ways:

By training leaders in the church to assume responsibility for specific types of counseling.

By conducting discussion and study groups, thereby helping many people at the same time.

COUNSELING IS EXTENDED THROUGH CHRISTIAN LEADERS

Through assistants, associates and other Christian workers, a pastor or another leader may reach out to more people and provide them with much needed counsel. Most Christian workers who have counseling ability are only too happy to assist the pastor in such a responsible service. Offered this challenge, they eagerly take the required training and conscientiously apply it in their work.

REACHING CHILDREN

Many children have problems — some of greater and some of lesser severity.* Often these boys and girls can be helped by an understanding Sunday school teacher, the leader of a boys' brigade, or a children's choir director. Many children are being helped every year by dedicated teachers and children's workers. Interestingly enough, the vast majority of these people have never opened a book on counseling. Consider how much their effectiveness would increase if they were given the opportunity to attend seminars in the basic techniques of counseling and the handling of common problems. Throughout the year a pastor, Christian education director or Sunday school superintendent should arrange meetings or "sharing sessions" for small groups of children's workers.

The following are a few suggested topics for discussion in such seminars.†

- Children who are emotionally disturbed.
- Common problems at various age levels.
- Problems of the slow learners.
- Meeting the needs of the gifted child.
- Delinquency: Its early signs and solutions.
- How to lead a child to Christ.

Such a seminar was helpful to Mrs. Wilson, a Sunday school teacher, in understanding Karen, one of the children in her junior class.

Karen had always been an alert girl. Whenever the teacher asked a question, Karen was there with the answers, and invariably she had the right ones. But something happened. Karen began to come to Sunday school unprepared. While the teacher talked, Karen appeared to drift off into a world of her own. The activities in the class no longer held her attention.

Mrs. Wilson had recently attended a study series for Sunday school teachers. At one of the sessions, the discussion centered around, "The Child Who Is Emotionally Disturbed." From what

---

*This applies not only to churches but to Christian day schools, camps, and other organizations.

†Nearly all seminar and study topics mentioned in this chapter are available on recordings which play for approximately twenty minutes each. A discussion guide accompanies the album. See Chapter 33, *Books and Recordings*.

she had learned, Mrs. Wilson realized that she should visit Karen's home.

What she saw there helped to explain the girl's behavior. For ten years Karen had been an only child. Then, a few weeks before the teacher's visit, a baby brother was born. The parents, especially the father, had long wanted a boy. During the ten years since Karen's birth, they had almost given up hope of having another child. But now he was there, the long, awaited son, and Karen was out in the cold. To some children this would not have been serious. But to Karen it was. She had not been told much about the arrival of the "new intruder," and she was uncertain as to how a baby was born. In addition, Karen was left with some acquaintances of the family for two weeks while her mother remained several extra days in the hospital. This, combined with the fact that the parents were now spending all their time with the new baby, caused Karen to resent her little brother as well as her parents. At first she struck out with angry words. Strong discipline only served to aggravate the situation. Now she entered a little world of resentful silence.

Mrs. Wilson decided to ask Karen to meet her at the church two afternoons that week to help prepare for a class party. As the two worked together cutting out paper decorations, the teacher skillfully encouraged Karen to talk and tell how she felt about her baby brother. The second day, after Karen had freely expressed her hostility, she seemed to be relieved. As the weeks passed, her teacher went out of her way to help the child. Now that Mrs. Wilson understood Karen's situation, she could give her the attention and counsel she so badly needed.

REACHING YOUTH

Adolescence is universally recognized as a period of turmoil.* During this period a young person may become vulnerable to emotional and mental illness. Many teen-agers could be spared unnecessary emotional conflict, educational failure, moral tragedies and sometimes even suicide, if adequate counsel were available.

Unfortunately, the pressures of a busy schedule often hinder a pastor from devoting the time required for adequate preventive

---

*See Chapter Twenty-seven, *Counseling with Teen-agers.*

counseling. He is too involved with the serious problems of adults. But often there are youth leaders who are available. These leaders have already gained the confidence of the young people and are doing considerable counseling. Unwilling to discuss problems with their parents, teen-agers often seek out a youth leader whom they respect and consider their friend. Such leaders can function much better when they are adequately trained. Through books, recordings and discussion groups, they can gain much insight into counseling. Those who work with young people not only need to know the techniques of counseling; they should also have a *fund of knowledge* at their command. The following topics are helpful in preparing youth leaders for the important role of youth counselor.

1. Understanding Young People
2. Improving Leadership Skills
3. The Kind of Parents and Teachers Young People Want
4. Helping Teen-agers to Become Mature
5. What Makes a Good Marriage?
6. Educational and Vocational Guidance
7. Knowing God's Will

Jerry was a 15-year-old boy from a Christian family. As he stood before the juvenile judge, the records indicated that this was his first offense. He and two buddies had "borrowed" a car and had driven it around the block several times, each taking a turn. As they were parking the car where they had found it, the owner walked up. Then came a little skirmish with the law. The judge warned the boys severely. Jerry was frightened. He had not expected to get into so much trouble. He could not explain why he had done it. He wanted to talk about it. Yet his parents did nothing but blame and warn him, so he did not feel free to discuss the matter with them. He hesitated to go to his pastor.

Then Jerry thought about Mr. Johnson, the Youth Director. He would go to him. He "understood the guys."

Mr. Johnson did help Jerry, and his effectiveness was due in part to the deeper understanding he had gained through the leadership workshops that had been held in the church. Now as he worked with Jerry, he was able to help the boy gain insights into his own problems.

A pastor can also extend his counseling ministry through establishing a simple plan of *vocational guidance* for the youth of his church. He can train his youth workers to keep a card file on every unmarried young person. Each card should contain such information as name, address, birth date, educational status and vocational plans. Most of the information can be filled out by the young person himself. Through individual and small group counseling sessions, the Sunday school teacher or youth leader maintains notes on each person concerning his educational progress and vocational plans. Periodic interviews of this kind are invaluable in offering vocational guidance which is so desperately needed among Christian youth. In addition it gives young people the opportunity to bring to light many personal problems that otherwise might remain concealed. This systematic plan extends the pastor's counseling ministry to many who otherwise might never have the advantage of talking to him individually.

REACHING ADULTS

The ministry of counseling should also be extended throughout the adult Sunday school classes. Take the case of Jim and Pamela. They were a couple who had attended the young adult class for some time. Then, one Sunday Jim lingered after class for a moment to speak to the teacher, Mr. Stuart.

"Could Pam and I talk with you for a few minutes sometime soon?"

"Certainly," the teacher replied, "how about Tuesday evening?"

"Fine, we'll see you then."

The evening arrived. As the couple explained their problem, it became evident that they were deadlocked over the discipline of their children.

Mr. Stuart listened sympathetically and drew from his experience and training. Although Mr. Stuart had never taken any formal college courses in counseling, he had a genuine interest in people and considerable natural skill in dealing with them. The pastor recognized Mr. Stuart's aptitude for counseling and had encouraged him to develop this ability by reading books, attending lectures and viewing films on the techniques of counseling. Now

109

as Jim and Pam placed their problem before him, Mr. Stuart was better able to help them because he had acquired some training in counseling. Thus a trained adult Sunday school teacher was able to extend the counseling ministry of the church.

As pastors and Christian leaders use this method, they must select their personnel with care. The following are several factors that should be taken into consideration:

First, some people seem to have little or no aptitude for counseling. They may habitually, though unintentionally, rub people the wrong way. They mean well but are not sensitive to other people's feelings. Although extensive training may help, such people rarely make good counselors.

Second, Christian leaders are not exempt from having problems of their own. Although they may have a desire to help others, their own problems can distort their understanding, causing actual harm. They need help themselves.

Third, some people tend to become too officious when delegated an important responsibility. They may think they are protecting the pastor when actually they are sidetracking people who should see him personally.

Fourth, the counseling assistants you choose must be scrupulous in keeping confidence. Every Christian leader knows that an unchecked tale bearer can almost ruin an organization. How much more dangerous such a person is when he has access to intimate personal information about other members! Of course, such people should not be church leaders. But a few edge in — so counselors should be carefully selected.

Counseling Is Extended Through Discussion and Study Groups.

Another effective means of extending one's counseling ministry is through discussion and study groups with the adults and young people themselves. In these sessions (meeting perhaps two to four times) the principal aim is therapeutic or instructive in nature. Such groups might be geared to parents, teen-agers, Sunday school teachers, or other classifications. Many people in need of help would never seek individual counsel but they would attend group meetings. The following suggestions may be helpful in planning these study groups:

(1) Listen to recordings on counseling and other psychological subjects.

(2) Review books on counseling.

(3) View and discuss appropriate training films.

(4) Discuss pamphlets and other printed literature.

(5) Listen to lectures by specialists such as physicians, psychologists, psychiatrists and other Christian leaders.

Group counseling requires free discussion among the participants. The counselor acts as a moderator, encouraging discussion and interpreting significant interaction between members.

In many larger churches, adults may fit into such study groups as:

• Young married couples
• Parents of pre-school children
• Parents of primary age children
• Parents of pre-adolescents
• Parents of teen-agers
• Unmarried adults
• Senior citizens

Discussions could center around such topics as:

• What makes a strong Christian home?
• Children in the Christian home
• Meeting the needs of teen-agers
• After you have said, "I Do"
• Discipline in the Christian home
• Sex education in the Christian home
• Children with emotional and behavior problems

Let us not forget that even Moses, great man of God that he was, needed assistance in leading his people. In Exodus 17:11-13 we read, "Then, while Moses held his hand raised, Israel gained the upper hand, but when he lowered his hand, Amalek won. But Moses' hands grew weary, so they took a stone and placed it under him. He sat on it and Aaron and Hur held up his hands, one on each side, so that his hands kept steady until sunset. Thus Joshua defeated Amalek and his people with the sharpness of the sword."

Indeed, pastors and Christian leaders have physical limitations. And their hands grow weary. But by means of training *other* leaders, and through discussion groups, they can extend their ministries effectively.

24 | THE GREAT PHYSICIAN

The wise counselor never overestimates his counselee's spirituality. We can never take for granted that people are where they should be spiritually. The basic solution to many difficulties is a closer walk with the Lord Jesus Christ.

Although people may have organic and emotional problems which must be dealt with by medical doctors and other specialists, the great majority of their problems stem from the fact that they are not letting Christ control their thoughts and actions. *No one fully realizes what Christ is able to do for him.* There are unlimited resources available for a person who truly seeks God.

Undoubtedly the greatest mistake made by counselors is that they fail to utilize spiritual forces. This is an insidious trick of Satan. Too often things of God are discounted or completely left out. The result? We tend to work on a human level rather than on a spiritual level.

A pastor once confided in a retired missionary about a church official who was having a serious problem.

"I need your advice," said the pastor. "Frankly, I don't know what to do. Have *you* any suggestions?"

"Well," replied the missionary, "as you describe it I'm prone to think that it is a case of a believer who is far from the Lord. Perhaps you have been working *around* the problem. I am wondering if you have called sin by its real name. Have you actually dealt with him concerning his relationship to the Lord Jesus Christ?"

After talking confidentially for a while, the minister admitted that in all possibility this man's difficulty was a case of old-fashioned sin. So he counseled with the man again, pointing out his backslidden condition, then helping him surrender to Christ. In a short time the man's problem was solved.

Such cases are common. A Christian worker counseled with a woman who was seriously disturbed — on the verge of taking her life. Day after day she grieved over an only son who had died just a few months before. Her entire life had been wrapped up in her boy — and now that he was gone, she felt life was not worth living. As the Christian worker talked with her, she clearly saw that her life was centered in the boy rather than in *Christ*. This was misplaced affection. If she had been living close to the Lord, honoring and serving Him, the loss of her son would not have caused her such undue confusion.

However, she was now in a serious condition, unable to sleep or eat, losing weight and entering into serious stages of mental illness. Medication was needed to induce sleep. The counselor spent most of his time helping her spiritually. Within a short time, she rededicated her life completely to Christ. This marked a turning point in her mental and emotional well-being. From then on she started to recover. As she began to read the Word, to study, to witness and to pray, her affections soon turned to the Lord and she developed a completely new outlook on life. Indeed, her problem was a spiritual one. What she needed was spiritual help. Yet, if she had fallen into the hands of an unbelieving psychologist or psychiatrist she might have continued for years without getting the assistance she needed so desperately.

Roy, a man in his thirties, was having serious employment problems. In his youth his heart had been set on becoming a medical doctor. After college he took one year of medical school. Then because of finances, he had to drop out. Several years passed and now his present work in a printing shop was intolerably dull. It affected his relationship with his employer and his associates. It also affected his attitude at home. He developed serious headaches. But after a series of counseling sessions with his pastor he began to gain insight into his own problem.

While in college, God had challenged him to enter full time

113

Christian service. But Roy had his *own* profession in mind and so he closed his ears to the call of God. This stemmed from selfish desire and pride. Now, for years he had been out of God's will. As he talked these things over with his pastor he saw the root of his difficulty. He surrendered his life completely to God and soon he began to achieve a much better adjustment at home, at the shop and in every area of life. Shortly afterward he began to take Bible training. Later he went to the foreign field as a printer. Needless to say, Roy became very happy — *in the center of God's will*.

Another case was that of a Christian man who had pushed himself physically beyond the danger point. He had an insatiable desire for wealth. A Christian? Yes, but not a consecrated one. Satan had tempted him to "kill himself" making money. As a man of unusual ability, he was constantly increasing his bank account. However, he was destroying himself as he grew wealthier. In this respect he was a *poor* man and to be pitied. After several counseling sessions he began to realize that although he was a Christian, Satan was causing him to misplace values in life. Realizing this, the man sought God's forgiveness and surrendered completely to Him. When he did, he was released from the obsessive compulsion to work day and night in order to make more money. As time went on he developed into a well-balanced man of God. He learned the true meaning of stewardship in time, talent and money.

And so the list continues, people needing spiritual help. A counselor cannot assume that a counselee is where he should be spiritually. Even though he may be an official in the church, he may not be walking on consecrated spiritual ground.

Christian counselors also find that some counselees have never experienced a personal relationship with God. They may or may not be attending church, but they have not been born again. Doubtless, *the counseling privilege that dwarfs all others is that of soul winning.** God's Word tells us, "He that winneth souls is wise" (Proverbs 11:30). This still holds true.

Many of the most successful soul winners down through the years have used several simple Bible references. For example: "For all have *sinned,* and come short of the glory of God" (Romans

---

*See Chapter 31, *The Use of Scripture in Counseling.*

3:23); and "For the wages of sin is death; but the gift of God is eternal life through Jesus Christ our Lord" (Romans 6:23). When personal guilt is admitted, the next step is made plain. "For whosoever shall *call* upon the name of the Lord shall be saved" (Romans 10:13).

Soul winning is and should be uncomplicated. The infinite wonder of its composition does not make life hard to transmit. In this respect eternal life is like other marvelous forms of life. While bearing the inestimable value of the Creator-Redeemer, it is transmitted according to fixed laws.

The phase of counseling which deals with soul winning should never confuse birth with growth. Our birth in Christ is the real point of our beginning in eternity. We can take no particle of credit for it. At the same time, we may marvel at the "pre-natal" powers and influences that were disposed in favor of the one who accepts Christ.

Growth is another thing. It appears to have no ending. But growth cannot occur until first there is life. The Christian believer is a *new* species. God can afford to enhance this investment forever. "The path of the just is as the shining light, that shineth more and more unto the perfect day" (Proverbs 4:18).

The motive for soul winning is infinitely greater than many Christian counselors realize. The heroic Moravian missionaries sensed the heart of it. They bore banners of a Lamb on which was written: "To win for the Lamb that was slain the reward of His sufferings." They laid hold of God's viewpoint. ". . . He, for the joy (of obtaining the prize) that was set before Him, endured the cross, despising and ignoring the shame, and is now seated at the right hand of the throne of God" (Hebrews 12:2 ANT).

Suddenly the soul-winning counselor sees his privilege in a new climate. He has a positive role far more fervent than the counterfeit reform of the dedicated communist. He is at once the beneficiary and messenger of God's eternal gift. He cannot languish at this task like a clock-watching junior clerk. He cannot regard his work in the cold, antiseptic manner of a laboratory technician.

Through a lifetime, at any price, against all odds, and under the smile of heaven, he must strive to set forth the glorious claims of the Lord Jesus Christ. Every task he will ever attempt, every word he will seek to speak, every joy he will contemplate, will be subordinated to God's great plan of redemption. The soul winner knows that this truth is utterly hidden from an unregenerate world. Hidden, alas, from most of Christendom, for is not the latter as a pretty, pouting bride, preening over her proud person and glamorous garments instead of rejoicing in her Glorious Bridegroom?

The Lord Jesus Christ is the center and circumference of all our purpose. Strange to our redeemed hearts that Christ should have to make a beachhead landing on this microcosmic part of His creation in order to rescue us. Strange too, that many do not *want* to be rescued. Strange that out of this tiny planet He should take His eternal Bride to reign with Him forever. Strange and wonderful that earth should be the crossroads of space and eternity.

After a man has trusted in Christ he needs more than the counselor's good wishes. He needs to develop a strong program for spiritual growth. This carefully considered plan, blessed of God, will bring spiritual results just as a carefully planted field with adequate rainfall will yield an abundant harvest.

Probably nothing a counselor can do, except to lead a person to Christ, is as important as helping the counselee establish a regular program of spiritual development. The keys to this program are clearly outlined in God's Word. They are generally known to Christians, yet they are often overlooked:

A daily plan of communication with God. This time alone with God in prayer should probably be established both in the morning and in the evening. It is a time of thankfulness and petition. It is the hour of communion and fellowship with God. As we wait on Him He speaks to us and shows us what is best.

A daily plan of reading God's Word. This is the way to know God's will — seeking His guidance through reading the Bible. This plan should include reading in both the Old and New Testaments. The reading should be orderly and meditative, always asking God to reveal what we need for that particular day. A system of marking special verses and of memorization is essential, too.

A plan of regular church attendance. In the fellowship of believers there is strength not known in any other way. Worshiping God, hearing His Word, giving testimonies, singing the great hymns and associating with others of like precious faith truly build up the man of God.

A carefully considered plan of witnessing. This is one of the greatest joys in the Christian life. As a believer begins to learn ways of telling others about Jesus, a new brilliance and luster adorns his daily walk. Through personal testimony, printed material and other means of witnessing, he develops into a mature Christian.

A plan of reading Christian literature. It has been wisely said that every consecrated believer should be in the process of reading a Christian book. Through Christ-centered books, magazines and Christian recordings, a believer brings the influence of godly men and women into his life. They will challenge him to live above the world and to devote himself completely to God.

These five procedures combine to make a strong program for spiritual development. But it is the counselor's responsibility to help each counselee enter into such a program, then maintain it. A little time during each session should be devoted to considering each of these five points. If the counselee experiences difficulty in any area, the counselor can help him gain strength. In time the counselee will make great strides in his spiritual growth and he will overcome, as well as prevent, many serious problems in his life.

The Great Physician! Oh, how He longs to bring spiritual healing to the creatures whom He fashioned and whom He loves! What a privilege is ours, as Christian counselors, to become God's very agents to nurture the souls of men!

25 | SUCCESS IN COUNSELING

A great man once said, "Constant success shows us but one side of the world." This surely applies to counseling. If you have never failed in helping people, you have never done much counseling. But the fact that you fail need not make *you* a failure. Hubbard wrote, "A failure is a man who has blundered but is not able to cash in on the experience." Often failure can teach us what success cannot.

The professional counselor must not be discouraged if a certain percentage of his cases seem to be failures. He knows that all people do not respond. However, inexperienced counselors often tend to *blame themselves* for this lack of response. That is why it is important to look at the reasons why a counselee may not respond to therapy. The following are some of the common causes for seeming failure:

Satan may interfere. God says, "Be well-balanced—temperate, sober minded; be vigilant and cautious at all times, for that enemy of yours, the devil, roams around like a lion roaring (in fierce hunger), seeking someone to seize upon and devour" (I Peter 5:8 ANT). In these days of "scientific enlightenment," many have thrown overboard their belief in a personal devil. This, of course, is exactly what Satan wants. Enemy agents can best carry on their malicious work when the people of a nation are too naive to believe that they are there. And Satan is an enemy agent. He is the arch-saboteur of God's plan of salvation.

God wants people to be born anew spiritually. He would have His creatures find the happiness He has planned for them. He wants them to become dynamically related to Him. From God radiates all goodness, beauty and truth. From Him flows the healing water that brings good mental and spiritual health.

Satan lies in wait to sabotage this therapeutic power, to pollute this beneficial stream. When your counselee begins to make progress, especially on the spiritual plane, Satan may try to interfere. Resist him with the weapons he most fears: the Word and prayer. Above all, do not try to fight him with merely intellectual weapons. That would be like trying to ward off an H-bomb attack with a bow and arrow.

God has given every person the right to choose between serving Him or Satan. In spite of your Christian love, fervent prayer and skillful use of the Word, a counselee may choose Satan's way. Though, of course, you will be disappointed, you should not be discouraged.

A person may not want help. Another reason some people do not respond may come as a surprise for some inexperienced counselors. It is this: some people do not *want* to change. Changing is painful and as soon as they get a taste of the discomfort involved, they decide it is easier to continue with their problems. They are like some obese people who have been advised by their doctors to diet. They start out with good intentions. But after a few days (or hours) they are overwhelmed by hunger pangs. At first they snatch one illicit tidbit. Then another. At last they throw away the diet altogether and resign themselves to being overweight. Changing is painful.

Some enjoy the advantages that accompany illness. They become accustomed to shifting responsibility in the direction of others. People take care of them, sympathize with them and make allowances for them. Being sick has its advantages. Sometimes the sick are actually frightened by the demands of good health.

A person who has a psychological problem may have the same reaction. When counting the cost, he may not really want to rid himself of his problem. Unless a counselee is convinced that doing so is worth the effort and the loss of the secondary advantages, a counselor will probably fail to help him.

Rehabilitation requires time. Like any growth process, rehabilitation does not take place rapidly. One cannot imagine a farmer digging up seeds he had recently planted to see if they had sprouted yet. Or a surgeon reopening an incision several times a day to see if the internal healing was proceeding quickly enough. Yet some counselors are just as impatient about their counselee's progress. If they do not see immediate improvement, they are ready to admit defeat. They are like people who are overweight — they want to slim down fast. But they fail to take into consideration that the excess weight was accumulated over a period of time. It also takes time to lose it.

So the counselor is not to be discouraged if rehabilitation seems slow. Results are often concealed at first. Only those who are patient, harvest the good that they sow. As Longfellow advises,

"Learn to labor and to *wait*."

There may be personality conflicts. At times a counselor cannot help his counselee simply because he is unable to establish proper rapport. For some reason, the counselor does not "click" with his client.

Accepting the fact that we have rough spots in our personality, we must not be discouraged if we occasionally encounter some friction with a counselee. When this occurs we can usually refer the counselee to another in whom we have confidence. If a personality conflict is causing the trouble, another counselor may get excellent results where we would have failed. And vice versa. Some people just rub each other the wrong way!

It may be an incorrect diagnosis. Another reason why a counselor may fail to help a person is that he has misjudged the case. Unfortunately, valuable time may be spent before a counselor reaches a thorough understanding of the causes, then changes his approach. Not infrequently he realizes his mistake only after he has lost the counselee.

A certain percentage of errors may be attributed to human fallibility. The physician faces a similar dilemma. But many mistakes can be prevented by avoiding haste. Do not settle prematurely on the causes of the counselee's problem. Let him talk, then take your cues from him. In a sense, he knows what his problem is — if not consciously, at least on an unconscious level. If you are patient and alert, in time he will reveal the problem to you.

If you are able to help most of the people you counsel, you are a successful counselor. The secret of success in counseling is hard work, professional growth, and divine guidance. What a joy to do our very best, then depend upon God for His blessing!

26 | GROWING PROFESSIONALLY

One mark of a professional person is the desire to improve his understanding and skill. This search for greater competence emanates from the fact that in his chosen field a man desires to do his best. He wants to make his greatest contribution, yet he realizes that no one can be fully prepared for his work by merely taking courses and serving internships. Even if this were possible, he would not continue to be prepared because new developments demand constant study and training. Like a soldier marching with an army, if he does not keep moving forward, he is left behind.

Few fields offer more challenge for professional growth than counseling. This is due, in part, to modern advance in human understanding. New insights continually unfold before us as we gain experience and as we keep pace with the findings of modern research. Also, as Christians, we grow professionally when we develop spiritually. As we gain more spiritual depth, we see life in a truer perspective. It is only as a person increases in godly wisdom that he can work at his maximum ability as a counselor. As he depends completely upon the Lord he gains new insights. But growing professionally is not an automatic process. It is carefully planned, then systematically carried out. The following are ways counselors are able to deepen their understandings and improve their skills:

Taking courses

Today many courses in professional subjects are available. Christian counselors are often within driving distance of a university, college, hospital or some institution that offers helpful courses evenings or on Saturdays. The intellectual stimulation provided by a good professional course is a strong factor in promoting growth.

Take the case of Mrs. Richards, a Sunday school teacher. The teen-age girls in her class had many problems. Because they liked her, they often brought their questions and difficulties to her. Feeling a need for training in the field of counseling, Mrs. Richards decided to take a course in this subject. There was no university or seminary within reasonable distance. But a hospital in the town offered a course in counseling designed for nurses. Mrs. Richards was permitted to attend. Naturally she found that some aspects of the course did not apply in her situation; but many did. As the semester progressed she gained valuable insights which she applied in counseling. She had taken a first step toward professional growth.

Attending meetings and lectures

Pastor Brooks was not as fortunate as Mrs. Richards. No courses were available in the town where he ministered. Yet he felt his need for professional growth. Many of the townspeople brought problems to him that ordinarily should have been handled by a psychologist or psychiatrist, had there been one in that vicinity.

In this situation, Pastor Brooks did the best he could. From time to time special lectures and meetings were held at the county seat a few miles away. Whenever one of these gave promise of helping him in counseling, he attended. Over the years he amassed an abundant store of valuable information which was useful to him in his work. He also made the acquaintance of a number of stimulating professional people to whom he could occasionally refer cases. In these ways he increased his understanding and skill.

Reading in your field

There is one thing that anyone can do to stimulate growth, regardless of the opportunities available in the community. That is to read good books.*

Bob and Frank were roommates in their last year of seminary.

---

*See Chapter 33, *Books and Recordings*.

After graduation, both became assistant pastors in large churches. This involved considerable work with young people. Both were called upon to do counseling. But here the similarity ended. Bob felt that the seminary course he had taken in pastoral counseling was all that he needed. He did little additional reading in the field. As the years went by, he assumed a pastorate of his own. He gave most of his time to preaching and reading books on theology, but opportunities to reach people *individually* in their time of need were limited.

Frank, on the other hand, saw that a large portion of his ministry centered in personal counseling. He began to read books and articles in counseling and related topics. He subscribed to a professional journal and kept abreast of the latest developments in research and techniques. Although he had little opportunity to attend lectures or courses in the field, his conscientious reading and application stimulated his professional growth immensely. Over the years he became more and more in demand by those needing individual counseling. And as he helped people to solve their problems he pointed them to Jesus. Because his experiences in counseling enabled him to make his sermons more practical, his preaching also improved. Now he made his messages relevant to people's needs.

Using recordings

Many professional men and women are recognizing the value of recordings. People are busy and time is often scarce. For many, records meet a need.

In some communities, medical doctors meet during the lunch hour and listen to professional recordings on medical science. Counselors and ministers can also find recordings helpful.

Recordings on psychological topics are available at some university libraries. A variety of recordings on counseling and Christian psychology can be obtained through the Audio Bible Society.* These are appropriate both for leaders and laymen. They lend themselves to individual or group listening and discussion sessions.

---

*Inquiries may be directed to the Audio Bible Society, 1016 Memorial Street, Williamsport, Pennsylvania or to the author, Box 206, Pasadena, California.

Viewing films

Another means of growing professionally is through the media of films. Many excellent motion pictures are available through local libraries, schools, Bible institutes and universities. In most public school districts, the school psychologist or guidance director will gladly recommend psychological films that are available.

Local film agencies are also prepared to furnish titles and sources of effective films. Some motion pictures developed by such companies as McGraw-Hill are not religious in nature and they do not indicate the Christian aspects of counseling, yet they do present some vital information which is helpful to all Christian counselors.

After a pastor, for example, has seen a film which is helpful in counseling, he may wish to use it with other leaders in the church or community. When he follows the showing by a discussion, the pastor will gain much himself from the contributions of various group members.

Investing time and money in professional organizations

Those who are really interested in their profession are willing to expend effort, time and money to advance it. As they involve themselves in counseling as a profession, they grow in that direction.

One of the ways to grow professionally is to join organizations that promote the art of counseling. Naturally, the ideal situation would be to join an evangelical Christian group. However, this is not always possible. Nevertheless, there is much to be learned from a secular organization. Since counseling is a science, surely we can gain from those who have made it their lifetime study.

Through associating with other counselors we have the opportunity to profit from their experiences. A problem may be new to us. But someone else may have worked with many such cases. We can all benefit from the experience and findings of others.

Studying related professions

It is important to be acquainted with related professions. A general knowledge of health and hygiene, basic physiology and principles of neurology and endocrinology can be very helpful. This knowledge enables a counselor to know when a referral is necessary and which specialist would be most appropriate. In addition, understanding related fields sheds light on one's own specialty.

Knowledge in these areas can be obtained by taking courses, reading, attending lectures and meetings or any of the other methods previously discussed.

Carrying on active research

A person does not need to wear a white coat or lock himself in a laboratory to qualify as a research scientist. Anyone who applies the scientific method in an effort to advance human knowledge can rightly be called a scientist.

So it is in the field of counseling. There is always need for grass roots research. And our findings are not only of benefit to others; we also experience valuable growth ourselves.

Some Christian leaders have seen the need for practical, active research and are doing something about it. One pastor decided to take a census of the kinds of problems experienced by the adolescents in his church. The results were rather surprising but indeed helpful in planning a youth program. In addition, the pastor presented his findings at a meeting of the evangelical ministerial association. A few weeks later another minister in the group presented a study of the most common problems in the Christian home. Everyone in the group benefited from these studies. But undoubtedly, the men who did the research gained the most. They compared their findings with the results of other studies. They sharpened their skills of research and did some independent thinking. And they grew professionally.

Writing articles

Many people have a desire to write, to see their ideas and experiences in printed form. Yet few ever manage to fulfill this urge. Perhaps time is a deterrent. But another is the disappointment they experience when they discover how clumsy their unpolished thoughts appear on paper.

Writing an idea down is often the acid test of its soundness. Flaws in our thinking may not show up until they are down on paper. There they are brought into sharper focus. When we put an idea in writing, go over it several times, sharpen it up and then submit it to others for suggestions, it improves greatly. In the light of this close scrutiny, it is easy to see whether an idea is worth defending or whether it should be discarded.

Take the case of Art Williams. Although Art worked as a rug salesman, his real interest was his Sunday school class of young adults. His students had confidence in him and often came to him with their problems. Art had taken a few courses in psychology and he liked and understood people. He also knew his Bible and loved the Lord.

Frequently during the lesson, Art would discuss the significance of Christian living to good mental and emotional health. One day the pastor suggested that Art submit some of his ideas to a Christian magazine so that others might benefit from them. At first he was reluctant. He wondered if anyone would be interested in printing his thoughts. But on further persuasion he decided to try. He conscientiously wrote and rewrote a short article. At last he submitted it. It was rejected — but Art was no quitter. He rewrote it and submitted it again. After one or two more rejections, the article was accepted by a fine Christian magazine. Now that he had learned the desired style and had clarified his thinking, Art had little trouble getting other articles accepted. Did he grow professionally? Indeed he did. And his class also reaped the benefits of his growth.

Teaching

It is truly said that no one in a classroom learns as much as does the teacher. The teacher gives thought and planning to what he is to teach. He reads extensively, considering what others have to say on the subject. He refines and reshapes his own ideas. He examines other points of view. As students raise challenging questions, the teacher considers them carefully, often gaining new insights himself. Hence, teaching courses or conducting classes in counseling or related fields is one of the most effective means of growing professionally.

Evaluating your work

The time-worn advice of the ancient sage to "know thyself" is an appropriate motto for all counselors. This is because one of the best ways to improve one's self is to examine his own work. A counselor can look back at his procedures and techniques with a view toward improving. Perhaps this is part of what the Apostle Paul meant when he said, "If we would judge ourselves, we should not be judged."

Looking at our mistakes helps us to avoid repeating them. Owning up to our weaknesses allows us to find ways to overcome them. It is a wise counselor who recognizes his need for self-evaluation.

The following questions can serve as a basic guide to help you evaluate your counseling:*

- Do you prepare for each counseling session by reviewing information about the case?
- Realizing that counseling is a process and not a lecture, do you arrange for a sufficient number of appointments with each counselee?
- Do you keep distractions at a minimum so the counselee can make full use of the time?
- Do you devote your complete attention to the counselee?
- Do you let the counselee establish his own pattern of divulging information?
- Do you exert leadership, yet maintain a flexible approach to each new development?
- Do you wait for the counselee's "real" problem to emerge?
- Do you encourage the counselee to rid himself of tensions and fears?
- Do you explore the setting of a person's problem?
- Do you accept the counselee as he is, even though his ideas differ from yours?
- Do you continue to focus on the counselee's problem?
- Do you make an effort to help the counselee grow in self understanding?
- Do you help the counselee find the basic causes of his difficulty?
- Do you keep in mind the fact that many problems have physical causes?

---

*Several questions in this section are based upon those in Clifford Erickson's book, *The Counseling Interview*.

- Do you welcome pauses in your counseling sessions?
- Do you endeavor to maintain an objective attitude toward the counselee and his problems?
- Do you keep in mind the fact that decisions must be emotionally as well as intellectually acceptable to the counselee?
- Do you approach problems as having several "sides"?
- Do you help the counselee to accept responsibility for his own problems and solutions?
- Do you make the counselee aware of his and your joint responsibilities in the counseling relationship?
- Do you handle direct questions discreetly?
- Do you recognize problems that are not within your competence or that can most appropriately be handled by others, then refer the counselee to an appropriate resource?
- Do you enlist the cooperation of community resources in assisting you with various types of problems?
- Do you keep a brief written summary of each session?
- Realizing that no counselor is effective with every counselee, do you make allowance for seeming "failure"?
- Do you gain insight into the counselee's spiritual condition?
- Do you use Scripture effectively with each counselee?
- Do you help the counselee to set up a definite program for spiritual development?
- Do you seek God's guidance and wisdom in each counseling session?

"I am the vine, ye are the branches. He that abideth in me, and I in him, the same bringeth forth much fruit: for without me ye can do nothing" (John 15:5).

As we evaluate our own work we find strengths to take advantage of, errors to correct, insights to develop, mistakes to avoid, skills to apply and weaknesses for which to be watchful. Then, with the help of God, we will grow *professionally* as well as *personally* and *spiritually*.

part two

SPECIAL AREAS OF COUNSELING

27 | COUNSELING WITH TEEN-AGERS

Socrates once said that if he could get to the highest place in Athens he would lift up his voice and ask the citizens why they were turning every stone to scrape wealth together, yet taking so little care of their children to whom they must one day relinquish all.

Those who have the high privilege of counseling with young people know what Socrates meant. "Where else," they ask, "can you receive so much for your investment of time and effort? And who could be more interesting than an adolescent?"

Counseling teen-agers is much like counseling *anyone*. The basic concepts and techniques of counseling apply to all age levels. Yet working with teen-agers is just as specialized as working with the aged or with pre-schoolers. Adolescents are passing through a special, significant time of life. This truth results in many unique considerations. And every adult who counsels with young people must give attention to the salient facts of adolescent psychology:

- What are teen-agers really like?
- What are universal adolescent interests?
- How does contemporary life leave its impact upon teen-agers?
- What are some of the basic guides in counseling young people?

These, then, are the considerations that challenge all who are privileged to work closely with teen-agers.

UNDERSTANDING TEEN-AGERS

Although adolescence is, in most respects, an extension of childhood, it does present some unique characteristics. Being neither a child nor an adult, the teen-ager has his own "in-between" interests. He looks at himself and the world about him in his own, unique way. Understanding the teen-ager helps the youth counselor establish rapport and a sympathetic kinship. It enables the counselor to accept teen-age behavior without undue alarm or resentment. The teen-ager, too, senses when an adult understands him, and naturally, he responds to acceptance with frankness and respect.

A teen-ager is a person in transition. He is leaving childhood and approaching adulthood. He is traveling somewhere on the road to maturity. Yet, probably no two teen-agers are exactly at the same place in their maturation level. Besides this variation in growth levels, there is an accompanying oscillation between childhood and adulthood. Sometimes he acts dependent and young, sometimes loftily sophisticated. One girl after attending her first day in junior high school returned home with a newly acquired air. "What's the matter?" asked her mother. "You're acting so strange."

"Well," replied the girl with a toss of her head, "I'm in high school. Can't you tell — I'm completely different!"

This transition yearns for understanding, if not acceptance. The youth leader knows that the teen-ager laughs hilariously one moment, then takes on an air of maturity the next. Popular youth leaders not only understand the fluctuation of teen-age moods but call the changes. As an electrical rectifier can separate and utilize the useful fraction of alternating current for direct current tasks, so do leaders of youth know how to deal with the emotional instability of adolescence. Indeed, such realism is necessary. Youth will continue to link its bright freshness and beauty with frail and disappointing failures. Great gains may be acknowledged by the leader when the teen-ager is assuming unusual responsibility. However, this does not call for a blast of condemnation and rejection when at another time the unfortunate youth proves undependable.

Failure to recognize the teen-age shifts in responsibility is recalled in a missionary anecdote of the Tibetan border. Hyndrew, a brilliant and lovable orphan lad from the Tibetan highlands, rapidly learned to set type in a mission station. He was actually illiterate, though able to speak five languages. But the mission was delighted with his rapid ability to learn the English type case and expected marvelous things of him. A great field of activity was planned. Hyndrew, however, had alternate interests which appeared without warning. His teen-age heart yearned to herd yaks, string crossbows, and procure goats from beyond the snow passes. The missionary, being aggravated with him for his daydreaming and lack of responsibility, scolded him. Hyndrew was grieved by the hard discipline of his white friend and a short time later he left with a detachment of border militia, though his heart truly remained with the mission that had befriended him and brought him to Christ. Understanding the nature of teen-agers could have prevented this loss.

A teen-ager is one whose life patterns are crystallizing. In common terms, he is about to "jell." He is assuming a recognizable life form. But he is still capable of being molded. This lends a sense of urgency about working with teen-agers. If you don't reach them today, they are likely to be out of reach tomorrow. Their patterns are being formed. Like soft cement, they will be hardened or set by tomorrow. They are taking their impression, shape and pledges now. Life commitments are being made today. No one can even venture to guess the difference in world history if the bookish young Indians, Ghandi and Nehru, had been reached with the transforming salvation of Christ when they were teen-age students in England. The same might be said of Stalin and Mikoyan who were one time students in nominal Christian seminaries. This is true of millions of youth at home and abroad whose minds and future influence are going to the most understanding, if not to the highest bidder.

*A teen-ager is a bundle of possibilities.** He is well called our number one investment. It is unthinkable that we should neglect him for infinitely less important concerns. He is not only different

---

*This term is often used by Dr. Henrietta Mears, nationally known Christian leader.

in degree from common securities, but in kind. The pay-off will come to fruition long before the maturity of popular government bonds. According to the investment, the teen-age lad with whom we counsel may, in a few years, become an Edison, Graham, or Moody. He is the adult of tomorrow. His potential demands nurturing as he unfolds into adulthood. The only difference between common bees and queen bees stems from food. When the common larvae is fed a food called "royal jelly," royal traits develop. In the same way the Word of God alters forever the nature and destiny of the impressionable soul of youth.

Even if trite sounding, the teen-ager is our future leader. Not tomorrow — but later this afternoon. He is not only an adult in embryo, but the ancestor of an unborn host. When we invest in a young person, we are investing in one who in a short time may reach a million. He is a factory of potential and a storehouse of power. Like a dynamo that sends its power and light through thousands of factories and homes, the teen-ager also needs starting help and an activation from a purposely designed local circuit. And, in another figure, the one who counsels with teen-agers may be the modest relay switch that pulls the giant power switch in another life, affecting the supply and blessing of a whole nation.

A teen-ager looks through the eyes of an idealist. The teen-ager views the world with optimism. He has the perennial wholesomeness of Whittier's "Barefoot Boy," Mark Twain's "Tom Sawyer," and Mrs. Alcott's classic characters of American girlhood. Youth tends to see the "Big Dream." Joseph Conrad's "Youth" utilizes this teen-age idealism. Longfellow borrowed a cherished figure from Lapland lore when he penned the deathless refrain, "A boy's will is the wind's will and the thoughts of youth are long, long thoughts." Wordsworth spoke of youth as a time when he felt there were "Intimations of Immortality."

Utopia seems practical to youth. He has not yet been hurt with counterfeits that are a hair from the truth but utterly antagonistic to the welfare of man. The advantage he enjoys of looking at the world through rose colored glasses has given him a priceless response to inspiration. His outlook has not yet dimmed. It is the springtime of the soul. It is the dawn hour that invites conversion. It is the crisis hour of spiritual history. "Remember now thy

Creator in the days of thy youth, while the evil days come not"
(Ecclesiastes 12:1).

A teen-ager is capable, but is short on experience. It is a para-
dox that a teen-ager should be endowed with such wealth of
promise and yet carry an enormous handicap. Immaturity and its
twin, lack of experience, have placed obstacles in the path of every
young person. Certainly, it is not youth's fault that he has not had
actual experience. Yet, without experience he may find himself at
a real disadvantage.

A wise counselor takes note of youth's capabilities, then bal-
ances them with a touch of sober wisdom. It is a friend indeed
who tactfully supplies a woefully needed portion of mature judgment to supplement youth's lack of experience.

Unfortunately, some of the mistakes of youth are not easily
repaired and may be attended by ruin or life-time scars. Wrong
friends may be chosen. Poor judgment may be shown in courtship
and dating, for example, resulting in an unfortunate marriage.
A severe economic handicap may be invited by foolish decisions
regarding the youth's education. Without the counselor's firm but
tactful guidance, the fresh beauty of youth may never reach
through to its rich and wholesome goal of fulfillment. Thus, lack
of wisdom, poor judgment, and immaturity are often overcome with
the help of an understanding Christian counselor.

*A teen-ager is one who has a rapidly maturing body and
intellect.* Suddenly the boy of last year begins to wear the massive
frame of a man. The frank loveliness of womanhood is seen in the
bearing of one who was only recently a little girl. Some gracious
allowance should be made for the all-too-evident shortcomings that
accompany such astounding phenomena. There may be notable
awkwardness and poor coordination at this time, especially in a boy.
He is naturally curious about his own physical development, going
to almost any extreme to find satisfying answers to his questions.

An accompanying intellectual spurt may enable him to grasp
ideas easily. But another fact looms before him. He may soon discover some of the limits of his physical and mental development.
This may be difficult to accept. Yet these things must be faced and
lived with. One can hardly change one's height or the shape of
one's head. The bantam weight is not likely to become a heavy

weight. The intelligence quotient is a rather stubbornly fixed factor. Sometimes it may be difficult to accept personal limitations. Nevertheless, within this frame of endowment there are still utterly unexplored possibilities for good. Counselors can help young people realize that God is more interested in dedication than in abundant talent, and that He can make great use of whatever endowments they have.

A teen-ager is someone who responds to a challenge. His imagination is captured by the man or woman who throws out a challenge. The successful college professor realizes this and bears in mind that he is recruiting the scientists and writers of tomorrow. The athletic coach knows that he can often communicate an overwhelming impulse for victory. The sales manager has vision enough to see that he can trigger the sale of merchandise representing a vast fortune.

Unusual resiliency is required of a counselor. Otherwise he may keep visionary young people within the frame of his rather limited horizons of yesteryear. He may have to adjust considerably with the soaring aspiration of the teen-ager. Youth often dreams about serving in new and challenging places. He wants to rally to important, significant causes. He is as interested in obstacles as he is in advantages. He is frankly disappointed when he is not challenged to do things. He may attempt to join Antarctic expeditions, or plan to sign with an oil drilling crew bound for Arabia. He may be challenged to offer his life as a medical missionary in the heart of Alaska, to die carrying the gospel message to jungle tribes that have never heard of Jesus Christ. He may be willing to be identified with an inglorious but equally important job of serving Christ in woefully needy places in the American homeland. He means it, too, and if his guidance is from God and his training and long term encouragement by counselors are directed to a worthy aim, he may do the very thing that has captured his youthful heart. History is full of such achievements.

He is not yet in that back-eddy of human experience where a man, tied to his wife's apron strings, dreams of heroic active roles that turn the destiny of nations, and at the same time, is in a banal struggle to remember the brand dog biscuit his unhappy spouse had assigned him to purchase!

Indeed, youth responds to one who offers a vision and a challenge.

A teen-ager is one who wants to know. The thirst for absolute knowledge is fresh upon him. In common with all human beings, he has an innate desire to learn and find out. This desire appears more pronounced at this age because he is without much experience. Yet, he feels that he must master some skills, for he senses he will soon be in the driver's seat in life, and, naturally, he does not want to make a fool of himself.

Because he lacks experience, the teen-ager is at some time or other almost pathetically open for cordial help or suggestions. Tragedy stalks when his mentors are base and unworthy in their advice, whether they be members of a construction gang or a university faculty. The teen-ager's queries may be tentative since he does not want to threaten his status. He is searching earnestly for a mature viewpoint by talking things through. Even when he falls into questionable activities, it is often a clumsy cover-up for lack of understanding. This has been his ill-fated way of finding out.

He is attracted to those who can capably teach him. He likes the man who has the answers. He is inspired by the rock-ribbed authority of God's Word as it is delivered by earnest, sincere men who believe it and are governed by it. He comes to prize the immovable foundation the Bible offers, and "Thus saith the Lord," satisfies his heart. "The Bible says," is a tag of imperial finality that does not seem inconsistent with a Creator Redeemer who is intimately and eternally concerned about those who belong to Him. He notes that the prophets and apostles were men who said, "I know," in connection with their trust in God and His revelation. The teen-ager who has found this same unchanging authority is challenged to live by it.

A teen-ager is one who craves activity. The teen-ager is a creature of bubbling activity. He is constantly in motion. He must be on the move. Even the most devoted adolescent is apt to regard Mom's and Dad's Sunday afternoon nap as an overture to opening an old people's home. Hatred of sitting at home with "Daddy-O" on the parlor "pad" may be beatnik language but it indicates the passionate unrest of youth.

The impression is given that this is youth's last fling. The teen-ager must take this opportunity to go, go, go! Action is his chief desire. He must get going. He must take part in all he can. In all probability he may be doing more than he should in this frenetic period of life.

Undoubtedly, sports, parties and scores of Christian activities can serve to round out and satisfy the boundless urges of this age of incessant activity.

A teen-ager is a person who needs and is happiest when he exercises self-control. The teen-ager needs regulation. Interestingly enough, this kind of confession and complaint is heard from the boys and girls themselves. This is especially true when they have met with trouble. It is then that they express envy of friends whose parents established well-defined lines of conduct and behavior.

One of the most essential lessons of life is to learn self-restraint. As taught in Proverbs 16:32, it is more important to control one's self than to conquer some distant city. But one's self is not the only consideration. An uncontrolled person may also bring great harm to others. So, he needs to harness himself. For example, an engine without a governor may literally fly apart no matter how marvelously designed. Think of a powerful and intricate machine destroying itself, other valuable equipment related to it, and above all, not delivering the splendid function for which it was designed.

An effective way to help a teen-ager gain self discipline is to give him opportunities for thoughtful discussion. But most important of all, this inner force is strengthened when one is surrendered to the Lord Jesus Christ and *He* has control.

A teen-ager is one who needs God. He has an eternal soul. Boys and girls, as well as men and women, have a God-sized vacuum that nothing else can fill. In the short-time orbit of human life there may not be any closer or more impressionable moment for God than the teen-age period.

The teen-ager not only needs the Lord. He needs Him now. Satan may prevent him from finding Christ later. *Now* is probably the time when he will be the most responsive to the voice of God.

Two teen-agers worked toward their chosen professions; one, dentistry, the other, medicine. Harry played it cunning and would never commit himself concerning the claims of God on his life. He struggled heroically for the success that came to him as an outstanding dentist. At length the warm springtime of life had passed and he found himself cold and non-committal concerning spiritual matters. Salvation did not seem to coincide with the brittle frame of his meticulous scientific scrutiny. Professional distinction was his reward, but no peace of heart. One day a stroke silenced his speech. Loss upon loss of his faculties pathetically followed but there was never any evidence he trusted in God as he hopelessly departed this life.

Fred, on the other hand, was bent on becoming a medical doctor. While he was in high school, he attended Christian youth meetings. During this time he surrendered his life to Christ. The strong tower of assurance that Christ afforded gave rich nobility to his character. He chose a Christian college and met scores of young people, many of whom became his esteemed friends for life. He found that the rewards of acknowledging Christ infinitely outweighed the mute silence that some young people observed in order to escape criticism. God inspired his studies and research in the far-flung frontiers of pathology and medicine. He gave God all the glory for his achievements throughout his fruitful life. He served both his profession and the people of his church with a humble and sweet testimony of Jesus Christ. His promotion to heaven was an event that struck the hearts of many who rose up to call him blessed.

What a striking contrast between Fred and Harry! Yet, like many of the young people we may be counseling today, the destinies of these two men were decided in adolescence.

CAPTURING THE INTERESTS OF TEEN-AGERS

The key that unlocks the adolescent heart is "interest." The Christian counselor who has a fruitful ministry with young people knows that he must never overlook their natural, God-given interests. In fact, all attraction is based upon this phenomenon. Men who have spent a lifetime studying and teaching young people say that interest is the sign that indicates when a person is ready to learn. Until natural curiosity is found or created, the counselor is usually ineffective or even resented.

But capturing the interests of a teen-ager involves more than dangling a few clever ideas in front of him. It is more basic than that. Reaching his true concerns is based upon knowledge about his development, his challenges, and his obstacles. Generally speaking, teen-agers are the same the world over. True, unique, cultural influences establish some guide lines — but for the most part, teen-agers around the globe are akin in their own world of interests. When youth leaders and counselors understand these life-pulsating concerns, they can shape their approaches to them and usually meet with success.

What are these motivations? Most adolescent psychologists agree that they number about ten or twelve.* Serious considera- tion of these basic interests is imperative for success in counseling.

Teen-agers are interested in fun. This is a broad field, encom- passing every enjoyment from nonsensical giggling to delving into a serious, highly technical hobby that may lead into a dedicated life's work. Fun may have such direct natural expression as the caper- ings of a colt, or the playfulness of a kitten. On the other hand it may find cruel and coarse expression through wisecracks and jests on the gang level. Teen-age fun may also have intellectual over- tones in bright and skillful accomplishments. Or it may embrace the serious goal of competing in classic sports. Youthful fun may be revealed in terms of cars, lots of food or many other things. But regardless of the activity, with youth the fun objective is every- where and to them it seems almost like serious business.

Teen-agers are concerned about friendships. They want to know how to win friends, and how to keep them. This enlarging, teen-age experience marks an exchange of esteem, respect, and affection. Perverted, it may result in death pacts for vile and trivial aims or even a relationship of living shame. Yet, potentially, it may have the undying glory of a mutually ennobling comradeship of a David and Jonathan. But whatever its form, the teen-age search for friends is never ending. Acting as if it were almost pain- ful to be alone, most adolescents are looking for a pal — some- one with whom to associate. If he is not able to be one of the gang, the teen-ager asks himself why. Indeed, the pressure of group acceptance is highest during the teen-age years.

---

*See Chapter 33, *Books and Recordings*, for annotations of books and records concerning teen-agers.

Teen-agers continue to be interested in parents! Although some parents may doubt this, nevertheless it remains true for various reasons. Even for reasons of self-interest it pays to get along with mother and dad. Parents still control the financial horizons of most adolescents. Occasionally there is a break-through admission that mother and dad may have gone this way before and might possess some valuable information. Actually, parents are the only intimate connection with a remote ancestry and a rather cold and aggressive world. Learning to live with parents has been found generally rewarding.

"Why don't they trust me?" "They think I'm still a little kid." "They don't understand being young." "Their ideas are so old-fashioned." "Mom, what do you think I should wear?" "Dad, how do you make this thing work?"

Trying to cut the apron strings, yet holding tenaciously to them, most teen-agers live in a world of parental give and take. Whether over-relying on mom and dad or just plain overlooking them, teenagers *are* concerned about family relationships.

Teen-agers are interested in education. "What subjects should I take?" "Why do they require math, anyway?" "I'm going to ask about part-time employment." "What should I major in?" "I think I'll be a teacher."

These, and many other vital questions involving educational plans loom insistently before every high school and college age young person. Many lifetime decisions are being made during the teen years. The engineer is learning that a stiff mathematical training is necessary. The budding professor of liberal arts finds that he must immerse himself in classic and modern tongues as well as in science and humanities. Teen-age decisions on choices of subjects are strongly governed by college entrance requirements.

"Is it true," they wonder, "that the average college graduate earns $125,000 more in his lifetime than does a non-college grad?" "Should I go to a Christian or a secular school?"

More than any other time during his life, a teen-ager is concerned about his education. *Now* he is charting the course that will steer his entire life. It is a period of decisive planning.

The teen-ager is interested in personality development. "How can a person be popular?" Never has there been such fear of being

a "square"! If personality is the totality of a person's characteristics, the teen-age boy or girl wants to take an inventory of the
building blocks.

"What kind of person am I? How can I change? Is personality
something you do or something you say? I like people who are kind
and thoughtful. I wonder what people *really* think about me."

Teen-agers want to know what combination of emotions and
behavior makes for popularity and acceptance. They want to be
that kind of person. They would like to do something about it.
The adult who counsels with teen-agers realizes that many attitudes
and actions are actually cover-ups or compensations for a basic
concern about one's personality development.

The teen-ager is interested in looks. He is very style conscious.
A popular boy or girl may set the style pace of an entire campus.
A certain kind of haircut may become nearly obligatory if the
right boy introduces it. Some sort of European peasant headgear
that American girls would not dream of wearing may become the
rage because several well-liked high school girls began to swath
their pert heads with these colorful scarfs. Campus shops display
clothes which the suave teen-ager should don. After taking a close
look at themselves, teen-agers also evaluate what the youth leader
and the counselor are wearing.

Manners are a serious concern to teen-agers. "Which fork
should one use first?" "What is the proper way to introduce
friends?" The sort and sum of little courtesies that make life
gracious now seem to be desirable equipment. Lack of this means
at least a bashful insecurity. Teen-agers are entering a world
where they are expected to know what to do and when to do it.
They are conscious of the fact that there are rules to follow. In
fact, books have been written about them. "What right have they
to tell us what to do, anyway?" they mutter. Although teen-agers
may grumble about the rules of etiquette, they still want to know
what is proper and polite.

The art of communication is important to teen-agers. How to
start and hold a conversation is a vital question with many. The
explosive egotism of blooming adolescence does not buy everything.
It becomes important to enter into the thinking of others. Rare
and charming is the occasional teen-ager who can promote conver-

sation by drawing out the interests of others. A girl of rather plain face may find herself regarded as a desirable and queenly creature for her ability to make a rough and insecure boy express himself. But a girl with high intelligence and good looks may be avoided if she is unable to hold an adequate conversation. "How do I sound when I talk?" young people wonder. "I hope I can think of the right things to say." In a sense, people stand or fall on their ability to communicate with others. The teen-ager knows this — so he is interested in improving his conversation skills.

Dating is of special interest to teen-agers. The early teens bridge childhood with blossoming manhood and womanhood. An unsuspected aura of heart-warming loveliness has suddenly enveloped a maiden of plain endowments. The shy and squeaky-voiced lad has changed from a "bean pole" to a square shouldered halfback whose bearing and reflexes literally carry the athletic responsibilities and honors of a whole community. He is nearly grown and the first stirrings of mature love are in the making. This is the time for dating.

"I sure wish he'd ask me." "I wouldn't go with him if he were the last man on earth!" "I think I'll ask her for a date." "I hope she doesn't say 'no.'" "What is right and what is wrong?" "What shall we do?" "How far should we go?"

Many are the queries that demand honest answers as young people enter the thrilling world of dating. And these questions *can* be handled adequately and sincerely by someone who is understanding and sympathetic. The respected Christian counselor can be of inestimable influence in this important and interesting area of a young person's life.

The teen-ager is vitally concerned about military service. In our day it has become a probable, if not an inevitable way of life. There is no choice; every young man must face it. Nevertheless, during the past generation it has also afforded a large area of training and opportunity. Recently it has offered much in the direction of college credit and been a stepping stone to further professional training and has opened specialized doors into trades, old and new.

But these questions arise, "Should I join now or later? Should

I volunteer or just wait and let them draft me? Which branch of service should I enter?"

Military service embraces the dream of far-off places, of undying heroic exploits, of comradeship in the vast deployment of our nation's defense or, looking at it from the other side, a deterring waste of time.

Military service also affects young women. Some may join. Although the majority do not, many times their plans are influenced and altered by the direction of their boy friends. Military service often affects marriage considerations as well as vocational and educational plans. Indeed, interest in the armed forces is a live contact with teen-agers.

Teen-agers are vitally interested in marriage. This has always been true. But now it seems particularly so. Whether advisable or not, there are many more marriages per capita among teen-agers than in former times. This is especially noticed in the ages of 18 and 19. An illegitimate expression of this teen-age trend is seen in 5,000 babies born annually to unwed mothers under the age of fifteen, according to reports from the U. S. Children's Bureau. It is also noted that the current practice among teen-agers of "going steady" is linked with earlier marriage plans.

A team of specialists was amazed at the findings they gleaned from a questionnaire distributed to a group of high school seniors. Materials for a course in "Personal Living" called for classroom discussions on "An Approach to Dating." But results from the questionnaire showed that in this sophisticated high school nearly one fourth were already engaged or married.

Teen-agers show a solemn interest in spiritual issues. Analysts might call this a philosophical trend. Genuine interest in what the Bible has to say about salvation and eternity is shown by hosts of young people on the high school and college level. This can hardly astonish even the cynics when the secular world itself has found its imagination and vocabulary bankrupt as to the description of things to come. Worldly orators and writers have summoned up such awesome and wonderful Bible words as "Apocalypse, Armageddon, Heaven, Hell, and Eternity." Youth has not only looked at these words, but has reached through to their absolute, personal, and eternal meanings. In recent decades, Christian youth leaders have capitalized on this emphasis. And young people have responded to the challenge. Multitudes of teen-agers of all backgrounds and intellectual abilities have accepted Christ as Saviour and surrendered their lives to His will. They have made decisions in college clubs, summer camps, week-end retreats, youth rallies and churches. Their sincere interest in things of a spiritual nature is beyond doubt.

CONTEMPORARY CONDITIONS LEAVE THEIR IMPACT UPON TEEN-AGERS

Adolescence covers the period between childhood and full adulthood. During these years of dramatic physical and intellectual growth, boys and girls are expected to learn new ways of responding to others and also come to terms with themselves as individuals. During this time, too, the young person moves toward decisions about his occupation, marriage, family life and spiritual dedication which will influence, if not determine, his future.*

Many swift and turbulent changes in contemporary living have brought youth face to face with new problems and decisions. Conditions over which young people and their families have little control, make growing up today vastly different from that of the past. In current times, the age-old drama of youth seeking to become established is staged against a complex and disturbing background. Some of the towering obstacles looming up before young people today are:

1. Population is mounting not only in our country but throughout the entire world. As schools and communities grow larger and larger, a climate of anonymity often pervades. Facilities are strained and relationships become impersonal. It is harder to be an individual and easier to follow a leader or conform to the mass.

Young people may search in vain for someone to understand them as a separate, unique person. For example, in a large city high school a study was made of every graduating senior. The

---

*Portions of this section are based upon materials prepared by the Division of Research and Guidance, Office of the Los Angeles County Superintendent of Schools.

results told a pitiful and lonely story. Nearly ninety per cent related that outside of their family members, no one in the high school knew them well enough to understand them as an individual person.

Sometimes a Christian counselor is literally one of the best friends a teen-ager may have.

2. The spread of technology and the feverish nationalism of once backward countries have created international tensions. American youth face a future in which their country's position seems somewhat threatened. The resulting anxiety has focused strong pressures upon the education of our young people. Demands to "toughen up" school standards, to extend science and math requirements, and to speed up education, have left their mark on our high schools. In addition, universal military service raises new questions. Each boy must consciously consider how to plan for continued education and when to decide upon marriage and a vocation. Girls, too, feel uncertain about forming deep attachments when long-term separations may be inevitable.

3. In a single generation, Americans have shifted rapidly and have become predominantly a city people. The exodus from rural areas into large metropolitan clusters has uprooted thousands of families from familiar communities and has separated friends and relatives. In the suburban fringes of the large cities, both adults and young people often feel ill at ease and uncertain as they seek to find their place. As families move from region to region in search of new occupations or better ways of living, young people struggle to establish a sense of identity which the youth of former generations found easy.

In years past adolescents were known by most of the people in their small communities. But today the teen-ager may be a stranger in the community where he lives. The Christian counselor realizes this and keeps it in mind as he talks with members of "the lost generation."

4. The changing role of women has raised crucial issues in the lives of both boys and girls. Girls now have more and more choices of occupations open to them. On the other hand, the demands of marriage and family make the timing of these choices

difficult. Boys, too, are often confused regarding their own role as breadwinner and head of the family.

Many girls feel that since they can be readily employed, the door is open for them to marry young without undue financial strain. Yet, early marriages often introduce serious family responsibilities at a time when teen-agers are not prepared to accept them. They are still working on their *own* problems and not able to cope with the problems of a mate or of children.

5. Technology has ushered in a variety of new occupations which were not dreamed of yesterday. Today's youth, both boys and girls, are often faced with vocational choices about which their parents have had little experience or information.

For example, scores of young people are considering the opportunities afforded in such areas as science, space conquest and other relatively unexplored fields. Yet there are few adults with whom they can talk about such aspirations. Too often parents, not understanding these fields themselves, tend to discourage their sons and daughters from entering such areas of unknown endeavor. In a culture that is changing rapidly, young people do not have clear patterns to follow. Without the help of Christian counselors, they must often find their way alone.

6. Secular emphases are surrounding today's youth more forcefully than ever. The spirit of materialism is infiltrating every area of life and leaving its ungodly imprint on all. Like walking through a forest of unbelief, the teen-ager's daily living is shadowed by many forces of evil. In the classroom his teacher instructs from a worldly frame of reference. In the home the adolescent's parents are frequently unbelievers. In community activities the unregenerate set the standards. And all too often, in the church he hears a "do-it-yourself" philosophy which is entirely lacking in the true Gospel of salvation.

Today's young people read books, listen to lectures and view programs that originate in the minds of worldly men. They are enticed to places intended to satisfy those who have never experienced the new birth. In short, they are growing up in an environment that has forgotten God.

Thus, population changes and mobility, the spread of technology, and the clustering of families in metropolitan centers, the changing role of women in our society, the variety of new occupations open to boys and girls, and the influence of secularism all combine to leave their impact upon the modern teen-ager.

BASIC GUIDES FOR COUNSELING TEEN-AGERS

There is an urgency about counseling with a teen-ager. His life patterns are crystallizing and he will soon be remarkably set for life. In many instances it is now or never. A counselor knows this, so he does not regret spending extra time with him, taking full advantage of this crucial period in his life.

During the high school years young people make numerous major decisions which affect their entire lives. Many high school young people are deciding whether to go to college and which one to attend. Other considerations such as marriage, life's work, and spiritual dedication also loom up before them. In view of this, the counselor may give serious consideration to establishing a regular program of counseling with individuals or groups of teen-agers. Time passes swiftly and the boy today is a man tomorrow. The wise counselor keeps this in mind. He also knows that the film of adolescence can never be run through for a second showing!

The first step in helping teen-agers is to gain their confidence. When teen-agers are assured that an adult is interested, approachable, capable and confidential, they are more likely to seek his help. This cordial relationship is *earned,* not legislated. One cannot coerce a young person into a relationship of respect and confidence.

For example, John, a high school student, had noted for some time that there was something refreshingly different about his math teacher. The teacher, a consecrated Christian, first earned John's respect by his competent teaching, then through his understanding and sympathetic attitude. Because he had won John's confidence, the boy felt free to talk to him. This was the beginning of a friendly relationship which eventually led to John's acceptance of Christ.

Wise counselors help teen-agers identify their problems from their own teen-age point of view. It is natural for adult counselors to see problems through adult eyes. But the teen-ager views his problem as it faces *him.* Naturally, he feels most comfortable when he discusses a problem in *his* way and in the terms he is accustomed to using. A teen-ager moves in his own world — one that encircles his own vocabulary, interests, and associates. These are vastly different from those of an adult. So if we are to be effective counselors with young people, we must look behind the teen-age curtain and see the world through teen-age eyes.

Counselors realize there is a problem to be solved; not a sermon to be preached. It is comparatively simple (and natural) for an adult, with his years of experience, to preach to a wavering teen-ager. But such "sermonizing" may only destroy the relationship between the two.

Take Jack for example. As a junior high school student, he had been with a group of boys one night when they stole several automobile hub caps. Finally this bothered him so much that he decided to talk it over with his Sunday school teacher. The teacher, rather than listening and discussing the problem with Jack, proceeded to preach a sermon about the virtues of honesty. The result? Instead of resolving Jack's problem, he built a wall between them. Naturally, Jack did not come back.

Like Jack, most teen-agers need acceptance and understanding. Their problems often require several sessions before insight is gained and solid solutions are established.

A counselor should avoid giving too much advice until he has drawn a teen-ager out sufficiently to understand the problem and its setting. A young person who is guided wisely can often arrive at the answers to his own problem. This self insight is far more meaningful than advice imposed by a counselor. A teen-ager should be encouraged to talk. A counselor should raise questions and reflect what is said. As a young person discusses his problem he will gain much understanding.

Frequently the counselor will gain insight into a young person's problem in an early interview, yet the counselee may not be ready to take action on it. Skillful guidance can lead him to the point where he sees the best course of action. This kind of solution is far more effective than merely "spoon feeding" the answers to a teen-ager. Youth counseling is a process that requires patience and restraint on the part of the counselor, but it pays off in good results.

To encourage an adolescent to talk, the conversation should be slanted toward those things that are of immediate concern to him. The very fact that a young person can talk things out and air his problems may provide help in itself. This means that the conversation must not be dominated by the adult, but rather, by the adolescent. A willingness to listen to him will not only help a teen-ager gain understanding, but also it encourages confidence in his counselor.

Since teen-agers want to be recognized as young adults, counselors should follow this cue and respect their maturity. This can be shown in many ways. One of the most important ways is to take seriously what a teen-ager says and how he feels. If a counselor will think of teen-agers as young men and women, he will find himself talking to them accordingly.

Actually, a person in his middle or late teens is much more of an adult than he is sometimes considered to be. By this age he has usually achieved his full height. He is sexually developed so that he is capable of human reproduction. His intellectual development is leveling off, having approached its maximum. Too, his physical strength is nearing its peak.

Thus, a counselor may justifiably think of the teen-ager in terms of a rapidly maturing, young adult. The counselee will sense this respect and will respond favorably to it.

Individual counseling affords one of the best opportunities to challenge young people. Since adolescence is a time when challenges are desired and accepted, the counselor should not minimize his responsibility to help a young person consider his full potential and to do the seemingly impossible.

Many Christians live bland, mediocre lives because they were never given a challenge in their youth. Through group and individual counseling, a teen-ager may be challenged to realize his potential and take steps to fulfill his BIG DREAM.

Men who have accomplished great things have first had great dreams. During adolescence when this quality of idealism is soaring high, the counselor should take advantage of it and challenge the teen-ager to do worthy and noble deeds.

If a young person has ambitious plans the counselor should not attempt to temper them too much. In all possibility, as the teen-ager grows older his vision will be properly blended with the realities of life. But if he does not sow great plans in the springtime of life, he will not likely harvest abundant accomplishments in the mature years that follow.

Hence, the counselor remains alert to the idealism of youth and turns the teen-ager's eyes toward great exploits for God!

A counselor should help teen-agers accept themselves. One of the marks of a mature person is the ability to accept himself for what he is and to recognize his own strengths and weaknesses. It is a crucial period in a young person's life when he comes face to face with himself as he actually is. It is a time when he must learn to accept his abilities humbly, and his lack of them, graciously.

During childhood a boy or girl dreams of what he will be like when he is grown. But one day he reaches the age when he is nearing adulthood. His full height (be it tall or short) is no longer a question. His nose? Well, its shape is plainly seen. His talents (or lack of them) are no secret. And a dozen other facts about himself are settled. Then he faces a big task: accepting himself! If he does not do so, he will go through life as an unhappy, immature individual.

Counselors have the privilege of helping teen-agers become realistic about themselves. This is a great contribution to any maturing teen-ager.

The family and religious background of a young person has an important bearing on his understanding and actions. The teen-ager is the product of many forces. These forces usually include such things as the home, church, school, friends and reading materials. Much of a teen-ager's behavior is a direct reflection of these areas of influence.

Joan, for example, was a new Christian. She came from a non-Christian home. The youth director at church was disappointed that she continued to take part in certain worldly amusements. But when he looked into her background, he understood. So he did not condemn her: rather, he was patient, encouraging the girl to spend more time in Christ-centered activities. As Joan grew in the Lord, she found the things of Christ much more appealing than worldly activities.

In counseling with teen-agers, the counselor patiently remembers that a young person's attitudes and actions are natural for him. In all probability, they stem directly from his family and home background. These attitudes have been building up for years. It may take time to change them.

Youth counselors cannot overlook the influence of the group upon adolescents. Group acceptance looms up as an important factor to teen-agers. Pressures to conform are stronger in the adolescent years than at any other time of life. Whether in styles, verbal lingo, activities or a host of other things, the "gang" is a powerful force in a teen-ager's life. Why? Because he has not yet found his mature, adult role. He is still groping for a secure place in the world. Conformity to his own group seems to offer him a measure of security. Here he identifies himself as *belonging*.

The wise counselor does not minimize the influence of other teen-agers. Group influences can be extremely beneficial when young people associate with consecrated Christians their own age. Young people take their cues from each other. They are often more interested in what their friends think than in what adults think. It is the counselor's privilege to help teen-agers understand group pressures, then assist them in finding *desirable* groups with whom they can identify. Counselors may also point out the belongingness which believers have with Christ and that occasionally it is necessary to stand alone. This is one of the responsibilities and privileges of the Christian.

Counselors make allowances for young people's lack of information and understanding. Numerous problems which teen-agers face might not have developed if they had been better informed. But teen-agers are young and still tottering on the threshold of adult life. They have just stepped over from childhood and they are relatively inexperienced. Adults must guard against measuring teen-agers by the yardstick of their own knowledge and experience.

When counseling with teen-agers, adults do not show surprise or displeasure at young people's apparent lack of knowledge. Rather, counselors must be prepared to provide sound, practical information which will aid teen-agers in their effort toward maturity. This may be provided in both individual and group counseling.

Christian counselors should encourage young people to take part in many Christian activities.

Every teen-ager needs to participate in wholesome activities. The road that leads a teen-ager to mature, Christian adulthood passes through a variety of first-hand Christian experiences.

It is the Christian counselor's responsibility to encourage teen-agers to participate in social groups which provide wholesome, Christian relationships. They develop as they take part. People learn by doing. This principle assumes added significance in the social development of Christian young people.

Counselors should view teen-age interests in physical development and sex education as normally related to their adolescent growth. Those who work with adolescents know that they are passing through a time of rapid physical development. This brings many implications. The boy, for example, usually turns to physical activities. The girl is interested in becoming more attractive.

During this time young people are also seeking knowledge about how their bodies function. Since this is the period of secondary sex development, they may show an unusual interest in matters of sex. This is natural and should be accepted and utilized by the counselor. Discussions and Christ-centered literature along this line will not only help teen-agers to accept themselves, but will tend to minimize personal problems.*

A counselor should help teen-agers develop self-control. One of the major tasks facing an adolescent is learning self control. When leaving the restrictions of childhood and entering into the freedom of an adult world, a teen-ager is likely to throw all restraint to the wind and do whatever he pleases.

The Christian counselor has a unique responsibility to help teen-agers achieve inner control. Through much discussion and quiet reasoning, a young person can learn the value of regulation. He can accept the fact that with adulthood freedom comes adult responsibility.

One of the most significant contributions a Christian counse-

---

*Chapter 33, *Books and Recordings,* includes an annotation of *Life and Love* which is intended for adolescent sex education.

lor can make to the life of a teen-ager is to point out the power of the Holy Spirit who indwells him. This is the true basis of a well regulated life.

A counselor should not assume that there is a serious problem behind a seeming trivial circumstance, but neither should he overlook the possibility. Those who counsel youth do not look for or expect to find a terrible situation couching behind a teen-ager's problem. However, experienced counselors realize that a teen-ager is capable of committing almost any crime, and that behind a seemingly casual situation, there could be a serious condition.

When counseling with Marie, for example, the youth leader listened to her describe what she thought was a "terrible, terrible incident." In fact, it was so "awful" that she wept most of the time. When she finally sobbed out the story the youth director learned that her "terrible incident" was kissing a boy.

Gus, on the other hand, casually revealed to the youth director that he had been suspicioned by local officers of stealing. But as the youth director drew Gus out, he learned that Gus had not only been picked up for *armed robbery* but for *peddling dope.*

The wise counselor does not suspicion the worst. Nevertheless, he must bear in mind that some teen-agers are hardened criminals, requiring extensive help.

The Christian counselor makes a unique contribution by being a source of balance and stability. The teen-ager is going through a period of ups and downs. At one moment he may be laughing; the next, despondent, "without a friend." One day he thinks he will do this; the next, that. He is juggling many ideas. This is a natural attempt to find himself and to bridge the gap between childhood and adulthood. In this effort he is often thrust from one extreme to another. This is where the counselor assumes an important role.

Those who counsel youth should not be overly indulgent or sympathetic, but neither should they be too critical or severe. Achieving this equilibrium is important, requiring considerable poise on the part of the counselor. His influence may be a stabilizing force that helps a groping young person keep his balance through the turbulent teens. Thus, the counselor becomes a symbol, as well as an example, of stability which the adolescent can emulate.

The counselor should not underestimate the potential of a teen-ager. Even though a boy or girl may be making a poor showing, he should not be overlooked. Poor school work? Irresponsible at church? Perhaps this and more is so. But many unpromising adolescents have climbed the ladder of success and reached the very top.

One teenager, for example, seemed destined to failure. His grade averages for the year were: English 95; history 85; mathematics 50; Latin 30. In fact, he ranked third from the lowest in his class. His records contained written reports such as these by his teachers: "The boy is certainly no scholar and has repeated his grade twice. He has also, I regret to say, a stubborn streak, and is sometimes rebellious in minor matters, although he usually conforms. He seems to have little or no understanding of his school work except in a most mechanical way. At times he seems almost perverse in his ability to learn. He has not made the most of his opportunities."

But even with a record like this, the youth grew up to be successful. In fact, he became one of the greatest leaders the world has ever known. He was Sir Winston Churchill!

There are many things that may prevent a teen-ager from demonstrating his true ability. Lack of encouragement, no definite goals, little challenge, personality conflicts, poor health and many other factors could deter him. But when he finds his "niche" and sees a real challenge, he may develop in a surprising manner. Therefore, a wise counselor will set his sights high for *all* Christian young people, trusting in the Lord to make each teen-ager an effective instrument for His glory.

Patience is a must when counseling with teen-agers. Because they are in a period of transition, vacillating somewhere between childhood and adulthood, teen-agers may make unusual strides at one time, then slip back the next. All too often they may not be counted upon to make steady, continued progress.

A discouraged youth counselor may ask himself, "What's the use? I guess I'm wasting my time." But the counselor who exercises patience, will, in time, be able to look back and see that a "problem" teen-ager has come a long way. This long-term perspective may seem impractical and indeed distant when one is counseling or working intensively with teen-agers. But it eventually brings results. The adolescent years are ones of growth and development and they cannot be circumvented. Patience is a necessary ingredient for those who counsel with youth.

Counselors should help teen-agers build a closer relationship with their parents. Adolescence often brings rifts between teen-agers and their families. During such times counselors may help young people appreciate their parents, even though their parents may be unsaved.

Adults do teen-agers no favor by coddling them, encouraging them in the idea that their parents "don't understand." When we help teen-agers get along with parents, we are helping them to get along with *all* people. The skills needed for living peaceably with one's parents are the same as those used in getting along well with anyone else. Teen-agers must use these important interpersonal skills throughout their lives.*

In addition, the Christian teen-ager should know that even though his parents may be unsaved, he has a Christian responsibility to call upon God's great resources and live a sweet, consistent life before them. This may result in the conversion of his parents. But it yields even more: it builds Christian character and maturity into the lives of young people.

Since the teen-age years are "conversion years," the Christian counselor should make every effort through individual counseling to lead young people to a saving knowledge of Christ. Leading a person to Christ is the greatest contribution any human being can ever make. And it is surely the highest goal in counseling.

A teen-ager may be too bashful to make a *public* decision. But he will usually do so after he has made a *private* decision. A counselor should find opportunities to carefully review the plan of salvation with a teen-ager, then encourage him to surrender his life to Christ.†

Many young people in their teens may come face to face with this spiritual concern: "Am I really saved?"

---

*See Chapter 33, *Books and Recordings,* for an annotation of the teen-age book, *Young Only Once,* which discusses this topic in detail.
†See Chapter 31, *The Use of Scripture in Counseling.*

Although he may vaguely remember making a decision some years before, now that he is maturing, he wants to settle the question definitely. The wise counselor will not minimize this concern. Rather, he will seriously consider the question, show him appropriate Scriptures, then encourage him to make a reaffirmation of his faith.

Doug, for example, was talking to his youth director one day. "Mr. Doan," the boy asked, "how do you know when you're really saved?"

Mr. Doan realized that teen-agers who are crystallizing their beliefs may want to make sure of their soul's salvation. So he took the opportunity to help Doug. Although the boy seemingly had made a profession of faith when he was seven years of age, Mr. Doan talked with him about the assurance of salvation.

When Doug left Mr. Doan's study he remarked, "Thanks a lot, Mr. Doan. Maybe I was saved when I was a little kid, but I just wanted to make sure. Anyway, I do know *now!*"

Thus counselors can help teen-agers make these important decisions and thereby prevent much confusion and doubt in later years.

28 | THE MENTALLY AND EMOTIONALLY ILL

During recent years, reports have repeatedly come before the public about the serious mental health condition in our country. It is a fact that more hospital beds are occupied by those suffering from mental illness than from all other types of illnesses combined.

About one million patients are treated each year in public and private mental hospitals. The cost of caring for these people is over a billion dollars a year. Practically all of this cost is borne directly by the taxpayers, since few individuals can afford to pay the entire cost of the long-term treatment. In addition to those who are hospitalized, it is estimated that there are several million other Americans who also suffer from some form of serious mental disorder for which they must receive professional help. Also, many physical illnesses treated by doctors are greatly complicated by psychological factors.

Mental illness touches many of our homes. There is hardly a family in America that is not affected, either directly or indirectly. Naturally, some cases are much more serious than others. But mental illness in some form or other reaches out and puts its crippling hand upon many thousands.

In the past, good mental health was considered as merely the absence of mental disease. However, today we think of good mental health as a dynamic balance amid the stresses and strains of life. Mental illness is not necessarily a strange malady that sets a person apart as being different from all others. Anyone might temporarily succumb to pressures that would force him to seek psychiatric help.

160

If anxieties and confusion interfere seriously with one's life, he is considered emotionally or mentally ill.

Mental healthiness, then, is a state of personal good health of mind and emotions. This has been described variously as:

- The most effective or optimum development of one's personality.
- The attainment of a level of maturity appropriate to one's age and the society in which he grows.
- The capacity for feeling right about one's self, about others, and about the world around him.
- The state in which caring for others motivates one's relationship to himself, and the majority of his relationships with those around him.

Characteristics of People With Good Mental Health

1. *They feel comfortable about themselves.*

- They are not overwhelmed by their own emotions—by their fears, anger, love, jealousy or worries.
- They can take life's disappointments in stride.
- They have a tolerant attitude toward themselves as well as others; they can laugh at themselves.
- They neither under-estimate nor over-estimate their abilities.
- They can accept their own shortcomings.
- They have self-respect.
- They feel able to deal with most situations that come their way.
- They get satisfaction from simple, everyday pleasures.

2. *They feel right about other people.*

- They are able to give love and to consider the interests of others.
- They have personal relationships that are satisfying and lasting.
- They expect to like and trust others, and take it for granted that others will like and trust them.
- They respect the many differences they find in people.
- They do not push people around, nor do they allow themselves to be pushed around.
- They can feel they are part of a group.

- They feel a sense of responsibility to their neighbors and fellowmen.

3. *They are able to meet the demands of life.*
- They do something about their problems as they arise.
- They accept their just responsibilities.
- They shape their environment whenever possible; they adjust to it whenever necessary.
- They plan ahead but do not fear the future.
- They welcome new experiences and new ideas.
- They make use of their natural capacities.
- They set realistic goals for themselves.
- They are able to think for themselves and make their own decisions.
- They put their best effort into what they do and get satisfaction from it.

EMOTIONS AND PHYSICAL HEALTH

One of the great advances of modern medicine is the increased recognition of the important role one's emotions play in influencing bodily health. This view recognizes that mind and body work together as one (not as separate units), with the body reacting upon the mind, and the mind upon the body.

The knowledge that illnesses must be considered and treated in relation to the whole person forms the basis for psychosomatic (*psyche,* mind, plus *soma,* body) medicine. Much has been written about this concept, but much has been misunderstood. The following discussion deals with some of the ways our emotions directly relate to our physical health:

Emotions We Understand

There are many everyday situations in which all of us have experienced some of the effects produced by emotions on bodily functions. Most of us can recall blushing when embarrassed, experiencing a tight feeling in the chest or a weight in the pit of the stomach before an examination, or having a pounding heart and perspiring hands when excited or afraid. These are normal bodily reactions to specific situations. They are beyond the control of our will power and generally disappear quickly once the cause is removed.

162

These bodily changes occur because emotion is really the trigger for action. Fear, for example, makes some of us tense. When this happens, it, in turn, leads to certain physiological and chemical changes in the body. Adrenalin is released which causes the heart to beat more rapidly. The muscles of the stomach and intestines contract, forcing the blood out into general circulation. The rate of breathing is increased and other changes occur (all within a split second) which are meant to gear the body for action — either to run or fight.

Knowing how these normal, everyday emotions influence body functions, we are better able to understand how, over a period of time, strong and persistent emotional conflicts may disturb the working of body organs such as the heart or the stomach. It is believed that in some cases they can eventually result in an actual change in the organ itself.

Suppressed Emotion

Rapid heartbeat is a familiar symptom of many emotions. In some cases where the emotional tension is prolonged, palpitation of the heart may occur so readily that the person suffering from it may no longer be aware of the emotional stress that originally triggered it. He then becomes filled with new fears, concerned now about whether his symptoms may mean that he has a serious heart ailment. Worry, in turn, can influence the severity and duration of any illness.

Sometimes a person's emotional conflicts are so difficult for him to accept that he represses his feelings altogether and is no longer consciously aware of them. Often what seems to be a purely physical illness stems from a hidden frustration quite different from the one obviously demanded by the situation. The patient himself may also be completely unaware of this. The little boy who vomits before going to a new school or the woman who develops a headache an hour before a tiresome party may well be examples of a subconscious protest against something the individual does not really want to do.

Studies show that almost fifty percent of all people seeking medical attention today are suffering from ailments brought about or accentuated by such emotional factors as prolonged worry, anxiety, or fear. Emotional tensions often play a prominent role in certain kinds of heart and circulatory disorders, especially high blood pressure, digestive ailments (such as peptic ulcer and colitis), headaches and joint and muscular pains, skin disorders, and some allergies.

Some of our most common verbal expressions show that, even unconsciously, we accept the relationship between emotional and physical reactions. "He burns me up," we say. Or, "This is more than I can stomach," "That makes my blood run cold," "You give me a pain in the neck," "Oh, my aching back." These are only a few examples of the awareness we manifest regarding our emotional-physical relationship.

A man developed severe and frequent headaches for which no physical cause could be found. Finally, in trying to establish just when the headaches began, his physician learned and was able to point out to the man that they began about a year before, shortly after a much disliked mother-in-law had moved into his home. The patient had never openly expressed his feelings but had kept them bottled up inside. The tension had to come out somewhere — and it did. It expressed itself in the form of violent headaches which, in time, disappeared after the cause was identified and fully understood.

A woman suffered, more or less, from a continuous heart palpitation and was convinced that she had a serious heart condition, although careful examinations revealed no organic involvement. She had increasing difficulty in breathing; her chest felt heavy. With the doctor's help she was finally able to identify some of her emotional conflicts. Her relationships with her sister (with whom she shared an apartment) had never been harmonious, but the woman felt that she should keep all such troubles to herself. She did have a load on her chest — a load of unhappiness, confusion, and guilt. When this woman was helped to resolve her conflicts, the heart symptoms disappeared and there were no further recurrences.

Discovering the causes of illnesses in which emotional factors are involved takes time and skill. A complete physical check-up, of course, is a necessity, but other kinds of information are equally vital. The counselor needs to know many details about the background of the counselee and his emotional responses to various life situations. With this knowledge the counselor can help him become aware of those fears and worries that may have caused or contributed to his illness. Recognizing the causes is the first step toward recovery.

Because of considerable new knowledge about the emotional factors involved in many types of illness, the wise counselor will encourage his counselee to consult a physician at the first warning sign of trouble. Pains and ailments of whatever origin can now be treated with greater hope of success than ever before if brought to the early attention of a doctor, specialist or clinic. More and more doctors, aware of the relationship between certain physical ailments and the emotions, are able to discover these conditions and to treat them successfully by helping the patient to understand them and live with them peacefully without undue emotional conflict.

Not only is it unwise but it is definitely unhealthy to keep emotional tensions bottled up. Instead, we should look for the most reasonable way to work them out. For some of us, just talking over our problems fully and freely with a sympathetic friend or advisor helps to clear the air. Sound health habits and creative outlets and hobbies which substitute physical or mental activity for emotional "stewing" are important for everyone.

As we reach a better understanding of the common emotional stresses and are able to face them instead of attempting to ignore them, we will not be prey for illnesses that strike out at us through our own inner conflicts.

In our individual way we can all practice an important bit of preventive medicine by applying this new knowledge to our children. Childhood is not always the happy, carefree time of life we like to imagine it to be when we reminisce of the "good old days." Most of us have forgotten many of our childhood tragedies because they were too painful to remember. But we can help our children by becoming more sensitive to their emotional needs and by seeing, insofar as it is possible, that they are not placed under the pressures of undue worry and tension.

It is not the emotions that are at fault when we refer to emotional problems. Rather, it is the way we handle our emotions that often cause the problems. Parents and children's workers know that emotions in themselves are not bad or undesirable. Without them we could accomplish little in this world. It is not our job to teach children to hide their emotions; rather, it is our job to help them use their emotions constructively. We do this when we give children opportunities to express their feelings openly instead of having to bottle them up.

And when we show children love and give them sympathetic understanding, we also help to give them a large measure of protection against many of the disturbing conditions so common among adults today. As good parents are cautious to give their children physical immunization against many of the common childhood diseases, so it is also their parental responsibility to give them, inasmuch as it is possible, a large measure of "emotional immunization" as well.

Interpreting the Symptoms

Even the most bizarre disorders, the complete withdrawal of a person from reality, or the irrational thoughts of a mentally ill person are deeply meaningful. Although the well-trained psychologist or psychiatrist may not understand every detail of the patient's symptoms, he proceeds on the tested assumption that the symptoms of mental illness can be interpreted and are meaningful.

Pastors and other Christian leaders also would do well to start with this assumption and to understand that the symptoms of illness are not "just stupidity" or "bad heredity" or "plain stubbornness." They are deeply significant expressions of a person's inner life.

To say that there is meaning in the symptoms of mental illness does not mean that the patient's discomfort can be relieved by a simple intellectual explanation. However, the distortions in thought and action encountered in mental illness do serve a purpose. They represent a blind attempt to resolve the problems and conflicts that the mentally ill person is experiencing within himself. Christian counselors may often find that what is being said by such a person seems quite irrational. It is important to recognize the cause of the person's unusual symptoms. For example, the reason for his hearing threatening voices is often deep and buried below the surface. All human behavior has meaning, even though the purpose and meaning may be partially or completely obscure.

The person who shows signs of emotional difficulty is letting those around him know that he is ill and troubled. His illness is his way of dealing with intense problems that are too painful, too confusing, too demanding, too filled with decisions and challenges for him to cope with.

Accepting Mental Illness

The most important thing to do is to realize that mental illness *is* truly an illness. Those who are mentally ill are people like the rest of us — people who are troubled, unhappy and who need help. The mentally ill may say and do things that outrage the normal person, but they say and do these things because they are sick. Most people are able to accept this fact, but far too many of us, when face to face with someone who is now or has once been mentally ill, react with superstitious fear rather than with a rational understanding of the medical problem involved.

The attitude of the individual citizen is perhaps the most important factor in determining whether or not a mentally ill person can be rehabilitated. The psychiatrist, the clinic, the mental hospital can diagnose, treat, cure and discharge the patient. Whether or not that person can remain well depends on whether he is wholeheartedly accepted back in his community, by his family, his church, friends, neighbors, work associates, and the other people in his everyday life.

SIGNS OF MENTAL ILLNESS

There are occasions when the inner stress and confusion felt by a person are sufficient to impair his day-to-day functioning. It is almost as if facing his everyday problems were too much for him. He finds communicating with family and friends extremely difficult, functioning on his job is a heavy burden, and he tends to deny reality.

When the person is so overwhelmed and pained by the demands of everyday living that he begins to live in a world of his own, then he has a serious mental illness called psychosis. Some signs of psychosis and illustrations of psychotic behavior are:

167

1. Changes in Behavior

One indication of mental illness is unusual or strange *behavior*. Most people tend to act in a rather consistent, dependable manner. But after one has become mentally ill, his behavior may become quite strange. He may do and say things that normally would be completely foreign to him. This may be noted, for example, in someone who has always been a dependable, respected individual but who suddenly becomes quite quarrelsome, stays out late at night, or takes part in questionable activities that he would have shunned before. One who is generally happy and light-hearted may become seriously depressed. On the other hand, one who was quite serious may throw all care and caution to the wind and become irresponsible. Each personality is marked by a measure of stability and unity. Under normal circumstances we do not expect radical personality changes in short periods of time. The exception is spiritual conversion. In such cases, we often see a wonderful, dramatic change in people.

In most instances, a mentally ill person is not aware of the sudden change in his behavior and may become antagonistic when this is called to his attention. However, his markedly changed behavior may usually be verified by close friends and family members.

2. General Appearance

One who is mentally ill may be so absorbed with his problems that he may not consider how he looks. This is not true of all who are mentally ill, but it frequently is the case.

One who has always been meticulous about his or her dress may, upon becoming mentally ill, lose interest in his personal appearance. Often this is a symptom which signals to people that the person is no longer well organized and that his mental preoccupations preclude sufficient time for good grooming.

3. Preoccupation

Another symptom is self-preoccupation. As one becomes mentally ill he is more and more concerned about himself, and less interested in others. A healthy personality, on the other hand, invests himself freely in others. He gives others a helping hand. But a mentally ill person is so concerned about his own poor health and his own feelings that his thoughts turn inward to himself, but not to others.

4. *Memory*

One who is mentally ill may have periods of confusion or loss of memory. All of us have times of forgetfulness, but a seriously disturbed person may repeatedly forget who he is, that he is married, or what day or month of the year it is. He may even have difficulty in telling you where he is now or where he was a few days ago.

It is not unusual for a mentally ill person to have disturbances of memory. He is so worried and involved with his own problems that nothing else seems to matter. He is too absorbed to notice calendars, whistles blowing, church bells ringing, or even hunger pains in his stomach.

5. *Self Concepts*

The mentally ill person may believe that acquaintances are plotting against him even though such thoughts are completely ungrounded. Or he may believe all activities in an office would cease if he missed one day's work, even though his job is relatively simple and his absence would not at all affect the smooth operation of the company.

Another way of showing his disturbance may be to consider himself a prominent figure. He may think he is a great scientist inventing a drug that will cure the major ills of the world.

6. *Distorted Communication*

Many people, on occasion, talk quietly to themselves when they are alone. However, the psychotic person may talk vigorously to himself even though there are many people around him. He may tell you with utmost sincerity that he is responding to a voice that is talking solely to him. Some persons, when having such experiences, stare suddenly off into distance, or they may interrupt a conversation or an activity to respond to the voice that they think they hear. Attempting to convince the ill person that there are no such voices usually does little good. In all probability he will persist in hearing these voices and may strongly resist the suggestion that it is a figment of his imagination.

7. *Suspicion*

In the early phases of some mental illnesses, a person may be extremely sensitive and feel that his movements are being watched and that the people in the church or community are discussing him. Sometimes he may walk down the street, pass a group of people and be certain that they are talking about him. Or he may be convinced that others are staring at him. Although there is no truth in these ideas, he genuinely feels that he is justified in his suspicions. As the illness develops, he may become increasingly convinced that his ideas are valid and that more and more people are involved.

8. *Sensory Stimuli*

One who is mentally ill may have irrational reactions to what his senses experience. This person may tell you that he sees things that obviously do not exist, or that there is a sickening odor in the room. He may complain of a terrible taste in his mouth caused by poison being put in his food. Since these thoughts are very real to him, a rational attempt to prove them false is rarely of any avail.

9. *Physical Concerns*

A seriously disturbed person may complain of physical disorders that do not exist. He may think that his heart is actually not beating, or that he is suffering from a fatal illness. He may believe his face is disfigured or that he is immune to pain and other sensations. These complaints are so real to him that he may repeatedly go to a doctor. However, simply reassuring the patient without offering other skilled help is rarely of any avail. The mentally ill person suffers from his imaginary ills just as much, or nearly as much, as though they were actually caused by some disease.

10. *Repetitive Acts*

One who is mentally ill may suffer from the need to perform certain acts many times over. He may have a morbid fear of germs and spend an inordinate amount of time in such acts as hand-washing every time he touches a book, a doorknob, a dollar bill or any object handled by other people. He may be possessed with the terrible thought that he will do harm to a member of his family. There are innumerable repetitive acts or foreboding thoughts that may preoccupy the mind of a person who is mentally ill. He becomes terribly upset if he is prevented from carrying out these acts and finds it nearly impossible to eliminate morbid thoughts that haunt his mind, regardless of what he is told by others.

11. *Depression*

Almost everyone at some time feels "blue" or discouraged. These are normal reactions, most often following some loss. Pastors meet many such normal periods of discouragement in their ministry to the bereaved. However, some depressed persons are mentally ill. They suffer from a far greater, more profound disruption of personality than people who enjoy good mental health.

One may sit for hours, not speaking or moving, with his head hung down in an attitude of complete dejection. When he speaks or moves he may do so with marked retardation — heavy, plodding steps and drooping, pained countenance. If he is able to express himself in words, he may indicate that he feels he is unworthy and completely undesirable, or he may think that he has committed some unpardonable sin. Occasionally one encounters a person in great agitation and excitement, talking freely about these same complaints — his overwhelming worthlessness. These persons are also severely ill. Members of the family and acquaintances who have been close to such extremely depressed people are often able to recount a number of recent near-accidents or injuries.

The pastor or Christian counselor who attempts to cheer this person, to get him to look more positively at the world, is almost certain to fail. A rest, a vacation from responsibility, even little kindnesses are more likely to aggravate than help. The person who is in such a severe mental state of depression is seriously ill and needs skilled, professional diagnosis and treatment. When a counselor encounters a person whose severe depression has begun to "lift" without treatment, he should bear in mind that this period of early recovery is often a time of danger, especially in regard to suicidal attempts.

12. *Dangerous Acts*

Although the number of such instances is slight, a mentally ill person may decide to harm some person whom he feels is persecuting him. An individual suffering from this type of mental disorder may tell a convincing story of how he is being abused by another, even though there is repeated assurance that this other person is in no way involved and could not possibly do such a thing. Still, the disturbed person will undoubtedly refuse to be convinced.

Although the mentally ill person may previously have had good, sound judgment, now that he is ill he is illogical. This does not mean that he is illogical in *all* of his thoughts. There may be times when he is perfectly rational. He may be sound on certain subjects but confused on others.

These, then, are some of the symptoms frequently noted in those who are mentally ill. In addition, clinical tests given by psychologists, psychiatrists and various medical specialists reveal many other clues to mental illness.

Pastors and other Christian counselors are undoubtedly aware of persons in their local community who seem to display one or more of the symptoms described above. It is well to remember that many of these people may have been living with some of these symptoms over a long period of time and do not require special attention. It is when the symptoms become exaggerated or when there is a sudden onset of other symptoms that there is reason for concern. When this occurs, one should seek professional help.

CAUSES OF MENTAL ILLNESS

Today's extensive research is expanding man's knowledge concerning the causes of mental illness. Although much evidence is still to be gathered, specialists in the field have been able to furnish some basic facts about the origins of these illnesses which affect so many lives.

We know that constitutional or hereditary factors predispose some persons toward certain forms of mental illness and toward certain ways of dealing with stress. There may be physiological conditions, as yet not understood, which make a person susceptible to mental illness. If so, the stresses and strains of living help determine whether or not such a person might develop a mental disorder.

Further, there is evidence that each person acquires in childhood a characteristic mode of response to stressful situations and the anxiety that accompanies them. This characteristic mode of response is further influenced by teaching and by general cultural forces. Studies show that unfortunate experiences, especially during early years, may precipitate mental illness or may be the basis for serious emotional disorders in later life.

It has also been demonstrated that disturbed relationships with the family, the school, the job, the church or a military unit may limit further the capacity of a person to respond to stressful change. These difficulties can be minimized through trusting in Christ. We know that much stress in life need not be absorbed by the born-again believer. When we accept Christ as our personal Saviour, then trust in Him daily, He gives us unusual peace. This fortifies us against much emotional distress.

Physical factors may also enter the picture. For example, damage to the central nervous system or the gross malfunctioning of a gland like the thyroid, may also impair the ability of an individual to withstand stress. Some mental illnesses are the result of brain damage due to accidents, infections, or advanced age. However, in most instances of mental illness there is no detectable change in the structure of the brain.

Whatever the source of stress and whatever the individual's capacity to cope with it, there are occasions when stress is so severe that it becomes overwhelming. In such unfortunate circumstances, a person may not bounce back but, instead, break down. These, then, are some of the precipitating factors in mental illness.

The Christian Counselor's Responsibility to the Emotionally and Mentally Ill

The pastor or Christian counselor is often in a position of unique helpfulness to persons in emotional distress. He is traditionally involved in the normal life crises of birth, marriage, sickness and bereavement. In addition, he has the rare privilege of visiting among his people and, in most instances, has established a relationship of trust and confidence that is of inestimable value during a period of illness.

As a spiritual counselor to individuals and as a leader of his congregation, the minister is often the only person in the community, aside from the immediate family, who has sufficient background and knowledge about an individual against which to measure changes in behavior. Thus, the pastor occupies a unique position. He can differentiate in individual instances between the transient reactions of normal personalities to stresses and strain as against the profound disruptions of mental functioning that are manifest in serious mental illness. This is not to suggest that it is the role of the pastor to determine whether or not a person is mentally ill; that is a medical responsibility. However, the minister who can detect the symptoms of a serious mental illness can perform an important function in helping his people seek early professional care.

When the pastor becomes aware of individuals who show serious or prolonged signs of mental illness, he should contact the person who is most properly concerned — usually a member of the family. The pastor should then attempt to help the interested relative understand that professional treatment will undoubtedly be necessary.

Frequently and understandably, the relative is not able to accept the fact that someone close to him is mentally ill. He may consider it a disgrace because, to many people, there is still "shame" in connection with illnesses that affect the mind.

In some instances, the relatives may try to deny that their loved one is mentally ill because of fear that they are the cause of it. However, the counselor who is sensitive to the underlying reasons why relatives are unable to accept the fact that a loved one is mentally ill can help them accept the need for professional attention. In many instances, even after the relatives have accepted the need for psychiatric care, the counselor may be asked to discuss the need for treatment directly with the mentally ill person. The relatives are, perhaps, too emotionally involved to handle this major crisis effectively.

The first and most logical source of assistance is the disturbed person's physician. Where there is no particular physician, the counselor may find help by calling the local medical society. It may not be easy to help the mentally ill person obtain treatment. On many occasions, he is too disoriented even to discuss his need for treatment. In these instances, it will be necessary for the counselor to ask a doctor, a social worker, or a person from one of the related professions to help the family in getting the patient to the appropriate treatment sources. Sometimes, the mentally ill person, although confused, anxious and suffering, may welcome the tender guidance of a pastor or other Christian counselor and voluntarily seek psychiatric assistance.

It is always best to be honest with the sick person about his illness and where he is being taken. It is well to remember that the patient will one day be well, ready again to continue his relationship with the church. If his own pastor or some other trusted Christian leader is not truthful, it may prove a real stumbling block to him. On the other hand, if the counselor has been honest with him in these things, in all probability he will respond to spiritual leadership. He appreciates the sincerity and discretion with which his situation was handled. Thus, his confidence in the counselor increases.

A minister should know about the treatment resources in his community if he is to effectively help the disturbed person receive psychiatric help. State hospitals in his community and their various admission procedures should also be familiar knowledge to the pastor. In addition, he should acquaint himself with the guidance clinics, the mental hygiene clinics, the family service agencies, and private psychiatric clinics and hospitals in his area. With this background and understanding, a pastor is often able to do what others cannot.

Mrs. Hall, a lady in her forties, had been in and out of the mental hospital for years. Her case had everyone puzzled. Each time she was granted a leave to go home she would return in a few days in a seriously disturbed condition. In the hospital she had proven herself over and over again to be ready for dismissal. But evidently there was something at home that kept her upset — something with which she could not cope.

Mrs. Hall wanted to be home; she longed for it more than anything. She wanted so much to be a mother to Ronnie, her seven-year old son. Ronnie was a bright, energetic boy, who needed his mother, too.

Her husband, Mr. Hall, gave every evidence of devotion to his wife. He visited her regularly, sent presents and wrote now and then.

When questioned why she had trouble staying home on her leaves she would only say, "I don't know. I only wish I did know!"

The mystery began to unveil itself about the time Mr. Hall took his vacation. He prevailed again upon the doctor to give his wife another leave of absence — to come home with him and Ronnie.

"I'll be home to help out and see that everything goes all right," he said.

Pastor Hudson, a friend of the family, heard that Mrs. Hall would soon return home again. Wanting to help all he could, the pastor called the hospital and talked with the psychiatrist. The two agreed that Rev. Hudson should visit Mr. and Mrs. Hall shortly after she was released. "I wish you could determine," said the psychiatrist, "what prevents her from staying with her family. There's no reason why she shouldn't be able to live at home." With this encouragement, Pastor Hudson made it a point to greet her shortly after she arrived home with her husband and son. After a brief visit the pastor suggested that if she started to feel upset Mr. Hall should bring her to the parsonage first before taking her to the hospital.

"I want to help keep her out of the hospital this time," Pastor Hudson explained to the husband.

Just four days later they brought her over to the parsonage, disturbed, unable to express herself. Pastor Hudson took the husband to one side and began to explore just what had happened. At length he asked, "Why do you think she should be back in the hospital?"

"I can't have her scaring Ronnie like she does," answered Mr. Hall.

"Scaring Ronnie?"

"Yes, when she gets one of her spells he gets scared and I don't like it. I don't think it's good for him to be scared like that, do you?"

"Perhaps not," said the pastor. "But you must talk in front of him about his mother, or he wouldn't be scared. You know as well as I do that she loves him and wouldn't think of hurting him."

Mr. Hall did not answer.

The pastor then suggested that Mrs. Hall stay with them for a few days.

"We think so much of your wife, and we would be happy to have her with us. Perhaps she will quiet down and not have to go back to the hospital."

Mr. Hall agreed to the suggestion. Since it was satisfactory with Mrs. Hall, the husband returned home.

An hour or so later Mrs. Hall began to relax. Then the pastor's wife put her to bed where she slept for twelve hours!

Since she had done very little sleeping since leaving the hospital, she was exhausted. When she awakened she was bright and cheerful much like her old self again. Then the pastor began to talk things over with her. When the subject of Ronnie's fear arose she said, "I believe they unconsciously put him up to it. They don't try to explain anything to the child. They talk too much in front of him. My husband means well, but he listens to his sister too much."

"Listens to his sister?" the pastor inquired.

"Yes," she continued. "You see, she helps take care of Ronnie when I am in the hospital. She has no children of her own so she wants to keep Ronnie. I heard something on the extension phone, something I wasn't supposed to hear. They were talking about my being home, and my sister-in-law said I was crazy — that's all there was to it — that the sooner my husband made up his mind to leave me in the hospital the happier everyone would be — that it wasn't good for Ronnie to have me coming home because I upset him and everyone else."

This explained volumes to Pastor Hudson. Mrs. Hall's family all considered her "crazy." Her husband was being influenced by his sister who, possibly sincerely, thought she should have the boy. Naturally Mrs. Hall was breaking because she had no way to change their attitude toward her sanity. This threatened her entire future and even her son's acceptance of her as his mother. She was convinced that they really didn't want her.

This is not an uncommon problem for those who have been

treated in a mental hospital and who have recovered sufficiently to be returned home to family and friends. It is the type of a problem that a gospel minister can frequently help to solve.

Mrs. Hall was ready to leave the hospital, but her family could not forget her symptoms.

A few days later Pastor and Mrs. Hudson invited Mrs. Hall and her son, Ronnie, to go with them on a few days outing with the young people of their church. Mrs. Hall helped with the cooking. It was a perfect time for her son to renew his confidence in his mother. And how Mrs. Hall feasted on the attention of her son!

After the camping trip Mrs. Hall and Ronnie went home. Since the pastor and his wife had displayed confidence in her, Mr. Hall found it easier to trust her too. He no longer threatened her with "returning" or with close scrutiny of all that she did. Ronnie came to depend on his mother. Having her son's confidence, she also had more faith in herself. Since Mrs. Hall had found Jesus Christ as her Saviour a few months previously, she was able to trust God to deliver her from her fears and to help her further.

A month or so later upon seeing Mr. Hall downtown Pastor Hudson asked, "Well, when are you going to let your wife come and visit us again? We'd surely like to have her, you know."

Mr. Hall began to smile and said, "Oh, I don't know. Ronnie won't let her out of his sight now. He won't even eat my cookin' anymore!"

Mrs. Hall was discharged from the hospital three months later. Every day she gained more self-confidence. Her dream of being a mother to her son, and a wife to her husband, literally came true!

COUNSELING WITH THE EMOTIONALLY AND MENTALLY ILL

Although counseling with the emotionally and mentally ill is of special psychological and psychiatric concern, it is not always the highly skilled, professional person who brings the best results. Christian counselors can also offer untold help. In fact, it is not only our privilege but our responsibility to visit and to help those in mental distress. The following are some basic guides to keep in mind when counseling with the emotionally ill:

1. *Accept his illness as a natural condition for him.*

Whenever you talk with a person who is emotionally or mentally disturbed, realize that his behavior is caused. What he does, and how he thinks, is a natural outgrowth of what has been happening to him. If you could gain an accurate picture of this person's inner self and grasp all of the experiences that have come into his life, you would realize that his illness fits into his life's pattern. If you could know his true physical condition, you would readily understand why he thinks, talks and reacts as he does. Although you do not have access to all this information (and neither may his physician know all the facts) you can conduct yourself on the basis that there *are* real causes for his illness. This attitude will prevent you from being overly perplexed and confused about the experience through which he is now passing. In turn, you will be more at ease with him. He, of course, will sense your understanding and will respond to you more readily.

2. *Do not argue with a person who is seriously disturbed.*

This is an emphatic way of telling him that you cannot accept him. He already senses that he is different from others and, when you disagree with him, it only serves to isolate him more than ever.

When we talk with someone we do not understand, it is natural to argue. In fact, it may seem the only way to make a person "see the light." However, argumentation will not help him to change his attitudes. Discounting his feelings offers no solution. Disagreement only breaks bonds of confidence and friendship.

It does little good to argue with a person who is well — much less to argue with one who is suffering from mental illness. He senses that not only is he seriously troubled, but that you, a so-called friend, do not understand him. This is something more than he can bear.

3. *Encourage the patient to express himself.*

People who are mentally ill may hold strongly to their ideas. These ideas need to be relieved and aired so they will not persist. The road to a person's recovery begins by voicing how he feels. Talking things *out* is one way of thinking them *over*.* We think as we talk. By talking we clarify our feelings and get new directions in life.

---

*See Chapter 8, *The Value of Discussion.*

179

One of the best ways to encourage a person to talk is to reflect what he has just said and ask him to tell you more. For example, if he should say, "I feel terrible. Sometimes I feel like I would like to die." Then you might reflect what he has just said by saying something like this: "You feel sometimes, do you, that life is not worth living?" Naturally this leaves the door open for him to make further statements. At this point he may say, "Sometimes I don't feel so badly, but sometimes I just feel terrible."

You might encourage him to continue talking by saying, "At times you feel better, but other times you don't." Then he is likely to say more. By using this effective technique you will find that a mentally ill person will talk a great deal. He soon senses that he is free to say the things that are burdening his mind. Furthermore he will discover hidden feelings that are affecting him.

Pauses are also extremely important. It is not necessary to keep the conversational ball rolling all of the time. One who is mentally ill may need some silent moments to think about things. Then he is ready to talk again. So patience and pauses on the part of the counselor are necessary.

4. *Do not expect a mentally ill person to respond in a normal fashion.*

The counselor must keep in mind that the strange response of one who is suffering from mental illness is an indication that he is not well. So, if his answers and ideas seem to be unusual, accept them as they are. If he pays little attention to you, just realize that this is normal for a person in this condition. After he begins to get well he will react more enthusiastically to your visits. Some people visit those who are mentally ill, but because they do not receive a cordial or normal reception, they do not return. Unfortunately, this indicates that such people do not understand the nature of mental illness. When counselors visit someone who is mentally ill, they cannot expect the same normal reactions as from a person who is healthy and well.

5. *Reassure the patient that he will get well.*

One who is mentally ill may think that recovery is impossible. By expressing confidence that he will get well the counselor helps immeasurably. Sometimes it means the difference between hope and despair.

One of the best medicines known to men is encouragement. It helps when a patient realizes that others have suffered from the same difficulty and that they have recovered completely. Counselors need to reassure the ill person that undoubtedly he will, in time, feel much better. The counselor can give this encouragement with confidence because research shows that most mentally ill people do recover with proper treatment.

6. *Show a genuine interest in the person.*

Sometimes we make the mistake of not telling people how much we really do care for them. Yet it is important that we do. This is especially true of those who are mentally ill. When we visit a friend who has an illness of this type, we should let him know that we are interested in him, and that we *do* care. This counteracts the almost unbearable isolation which he may feel. Such remarks as: "We've certainly been missing you, Bill. Your friends at church are praying for you, and we are all anxious to see you get well again," bring much encouragement.

When you visit him, remind him of your friendship. This offers an important bond which he will cherish from one visit to another.

7. *Encourage the patient in his treatment.*

People who have been receiving psychiatric care sometimes come to dislike their doctors. They may become discouraged, feeling that the doctors and nurses are not doing all they should. They may even transfer their hostilities from family members or from others to their physicians.

It is your responsibility to help the patient gain more confidence in those who are treating him. Encourage him to express himself, but assure him that the doctors are doing the best they can, and that they *do* have an interest in him.

Sometimes a patient blames a doctor for "hospitalizing" him. These resentments can be very deep. So your encouragement to follow the doctor's orders will help the ill person to place more confidence in those who are treating him.

8. *Be sensitive about the demands you place on one who is mentally ill.*

Sometimes Christian counselors do not feel content unless they leave a sick person's room having "assigned" considerable reading materials. However, an ill person may not be up to this. He just wants to rest. He is not able to tax himself to the extent of picking up books and reading. During each visit you may want to read to him from the Bible. You might say for example, "Bill, recently I read a wonderful portion of God's Word and I thought you might like to hear it." Your reading will help and comfort him.

A woman who had recently been released from a mental institution was talking to her pastor about Bible reading. "I don't feel well enough to read much," she said, "But I like to hear the Scripture if someone reads it to me." She said that during her illness, listening to the Scriptures meant much to her, that it helped her to recover much more quickly.

9. *Be discreet in the use of Scripture.*

True, God's Word is important to those who are mentally ill. But remember that they may not be able to absorb too much at one time. So when you are visiting one who is mentally ill, use only a few verses at a time. Continue to repeat them as the months go by. One time a man who had been in a mental institution asked the pastor if he had ever had the experience of being mentally ill. The pastor replied that he had not. Then the man said, "Let me give you a word of advice. When you counsel with people who are mentally ill, don't throw the whole Bible at them. Use only a verse or two at a time, then keep using the same Scripture week after week." And the man continued, "When I was in the hospital, there were groups who came to our ward. But they used too much Scripture. They got us confused. However, there were others who used only a few verses week after week and month after month. Finally these verses of Scripture began to sink through to us and did us some good."

The man was right. Many who have been mentally ill give testimony to the fact that such patients usually prefer only a few verses of Scripture rather than large portions. This simple plan of repetition is not over-whelming and it leaves a single spiritual impact.

10. *Use devotional materials.*

If a mentally ill person feels well enough to read, there are many Christ-centered devotional materials which will help him. The Moody Colportage series contains a number of excellent booklets by such authors as Anna Lindgren.* These devotional materials are short and easy to read. They are from the heart, and they bring new hope and victory to those who are disturbed.

Those who counsel with the emotionally and mentally ill should visit Christian bookstores and carefully select materials that are especially suitable. In addition to reading materials, splendid devotions are available on recordings. These combine music, Scripture, speaking, poems and prayers in a combination ideal for those who are not well.†

11. *Emphasize God's love and comfort.*

The greatest comfort is *God's* comfort. He is the author of all love and mercy. As much as people may care for one another, human love can never equal God's love. When people are mentally ill they sometimes feel that God has forgotten them. So when you visit them, tell them about God's love. Give them Scripture verses such as, "Casting all your care upon Him for He careth for you." Let them know that God is truly interested in them.‡

12. *Do not cut your visit short.*

People who are ill do not like to be rushed. So give them enough time. This tells them that you are genuinely interested and that they are worthy of love and respect. It also allows sufficient time to talk things out. This added time will help them share their true feelings. Patience on your part will help you gain a better understanding of them — and thus contribute to a faster recovery.

Mental illness! It can strike anyone, anywhere. It is not only the Christian counselor's duty but his privilege to visit and counsel with the mentally ill. As a former patient wisely advised his friends, "Your visits and understanding may very well mean the difference between recovery and further prolonged illness."

---

*Moody Colportage booklets are available from Moody Press, Chicago, Illinois.
†See Chapter 33 for annotations of suitable recordings.
‡See Chapter 31 for lists of appropriate Scripture verses.

29 | BASIC GUIDES IN MARRIAGE COUNSELING

Helen was a young, part-time actress who joined a fashionable Eastern church. She began attending youth retreats and in time professed faith in Christ. Then, she met John, a warmhearted Bible student whose whole life purpose was to serve God and win souls. Through his clear-cut testimony, Helen was challenged to leave her acting career. Despite opposition from Helen's mother, she and John fell in love and soon the wedding bells rang. The marriage seemed to be blessed. Three lovely children came into the home.

John was a valued member of a small engineering firm. His work held promise of continued promotion and adequate income. Not content to live on a modest income, John took extra jobs to help the family budget. Work, work, work. Eventually John became a drudge by day and a baby-sitter by night, since Helen had decided to continue her society connections and supplement their income with enough work to keep her acting career alive. Some of the roles, John felt, were morally doubtful. He begged her to remain home and care for the family.

Helen's mother resented John because he was "religious" and because she felt he had destroyed her daughter's career. She tried openly to break up the marriage. Year after year she awaited her opportunity. Then when the marriage seemed heading for tragedy, the mother stepped in with a strong hand. She belittled John, sympathized with Helen, and offered her financial security and care for the children if she would commence divorce proceedings and renew her career of professional acting.

"Why, Helen," the mother would say, "can't you see what's happening? John doesn't really care anything about you. A fanatic like that never gets ahead and he'll not be content until he drags you down with him. You're just his slave."

John attempted desperate measures to hold the marriage together. He tried to pray but God seemed far removed. Actually, his heart was cold toward spiritual things. For too long he had tried to meet Helen's image of success. He had even tried social drinking to impress her professional friends, but they had only pitied him. He knew that he was emotionally and spiritually bankrupt. The end came after an unbelieving marriage counselor whom they had consulted, arranged for them to spend vacations at separate resort hotels. This, of course, drove them further apart. Backed by an insistent mother, Helen left the children with her and started divorce action on the routine charge of "mental cruelty." She covered her guilt with the excuse that the marriage had been a mistake.

John was broken with a sorrow worse than death. He knew God alone could renew his life as a fruitful Christian.

Tragically, there are many couples like John and Helen who are renouncing their marriage vows, running to divorce courts and dragging their children with them. With aching hearts, shattered dreams and broken personalities, many of these unhappy victims are finding their way to the pastor's study or to the quietness of a friend's home. Perhaps in no field is there more need or more opportunity than in marriage counseling.

Pastors and Christian workers know, however, that marriage counseling should begin long before the marriage vows are ever repeated. Young people who know Christ as their Saviour, whose lives are surrendered to Him, who want only God's will in marriage, and who refuse to be "unequally yoked together with unbelievers" are not likely to present desperate marriage problems later on.

BASIC GOALS IN MARRIAGE COUNSELING

Because of the complexities of marriage there are many causes of friction and unhappiness. The marriage counselor, therefore, considers each case individually and patiently assists the couple in understanding the basic causes of their problems.

As a counselor seeks to help married couples, he keeps several basic goals in mind. These goals are not accomplished simultaneously, and in many cases not all of them are reached. But he realizes that without them he cannot build consistent direction in his counseling.

Expression and Release of Strong Feelings

Before a person can quietly and intelligently discuss a problem he must air his feelings. Since marriage problems are commonly laden with strong emotion, it is the counselor's responsibility to encourage the counselee to express himself without restriction. In some cases this requires only a part of one session. In others, it may take several sessions. The inexperienced counselor may feel that this is a waste of time, or that he must counteract all that has been said. But this is a necessary part of therapy and, indeed, a basic goal in marriage counseling.

Acceptance of the Fact that Adjustments in Marriage Require Time

The counselor is left virtually helpless unless the marriage partners recognize that they must allow sufficient time to work out a good adjustment. During the initial sessions the counselor must help the couple to see that their marriage is worth the effort and time required to improve it.

Many Christian counselors make the mistake of attempting to solve serious, complex marriage problems in two or three appointments. However, this is quite unrealistic. Actually, the best results are obtained when a counselor takes time during the initial visits to show the couple that although solutions to their difficulties will require considerable time, possibly several months, their marriage deserves it. The counselor must emphasize the importance of taking no legal action until sufficient time has been devoted to initiate and carry out a thoroughly sound plan of rehabilitation. If, after sincere efforts to enlist cooperation, the couple is still not willing to devote time to work out their problems, the counselor is not responsible for their refusal to cooperate. He can help only those who *want* his assistance and are willing to spend the time required to bring about the desired solution.

The Client's Understanding of Himself

Before a man can truly understand others he must have at least a measure of self understanding. And this is one of the goals in marriage counseling — to help a husband or wife come to grips with his own attitudes, his own feelings, his own capacities, his own drives and his own shortcomings.

Most people go through life behaving in a certain manner without realizing just how they do act, or why. They seldom ask for a true-to-life mirror. They look at others, but they have little opportunity to turn their eyes inward.

The counselor's office is one of the best places for a counselee to experience self-evaluation. Through patient reflection, the skilled counselor helps his client take a candid look at his real self. In fact, the counselor continually checks for the following. "What insight does he (or she) have about his own life? How can he best be helped to examine his own motives and drives? Is he ready to come face to face with his own potentials and weaknesses?"

For example, it is inevitable that some of each spouse's childhood attitudes will be carried over into marriage. Since this is so, a counselor can lead the spouse to see that the bickering in his marriage may actually be an unresolved childhood conflict with a brother or sister or some other family member.

As the client comes to understand himself, his attitudes will become more mature and many conflicts in his marriage will automatically disappear.

The Client's Understanding of His Mate

One of the chief goals in marriage counseling is to help each party achieve a realistic assessment of his or her spouse. This means recognizing and accepting limitations as well as strengths. Insights which the counselor gains may be somewhat hidden to either or both spouses. For example, the counselor may come to realize that the wife has limited intelligence. But the husband, not being conscious of this, merely feels that she is "stubborn." The husband, on the other hand, may be muscularly strong, yet a man who tires easily and demands considerable rest. How does the wife see this?

"He's lazy," she says.

And so the list grows — intelligence, physical abilities, social competencies, emotional health and spiritual development. These and other factors must be understood by the counselee, both about himself and his marriage partner. When such mutual insight has been achieved, the couple is ready to scrap their competition and start building cooperation. In this way they will achieve their common goal — a happy, successful marriage.

Understanding of the Counseling Relationship

Clients are frequently confused about their relationship to the counselor. They are prone to place him in the category of a judge, referee, father confessor or husband image. It is natural for these thoughts to arise in the mind of a counselee. Thus, during the first few appointments, the counselor must lead the counselee to understand that he is none of these. Rather, the counselor is an unbiased, understanding, professionally trained individual who is there to help the counselee gain understanding and to seek out desirable solutions to his problem.

If you, the counselor, even *seem* to be partial, you may find yourself inadvertently cast in the role of father or mother, deciding which "child" shall be spanked and which consoled. Obviously, if you are once cast into this role, it is hard to throw off your parental garments and take another part. Worse still, you will unwittingly stimulate childish, regressive forces in the personalities of your counselees instead of nurturing mature forces which alone can overcome their problems.

Better Understanding of the Roles Each Spouse Assumes in Marriage

As the human body is more than the sum of its parts, so a marriage is more than the two people who comprise it. Apart from a personality problem that either partner may have, the *roles* which each plays in the marriage are important to their happiness and adjustment. An organ of the body may itself be intact and healthy; yet, if it is *out of place,* it may contribute to disease and even death. Some roles in marriage are the natural result of one's sex. The husband has his responsibilities, and the wife hers. Other roles emerge from the culture in which one is raised. For example, the man may do the outside work and the woman care for the home. Still other roles grow out of certain conditions in each individual family unit; since the wife is a piano teacher and gives lessons during afternoons and evenings, as well as on Saturdays, the husband takes the responsibility for buying groceries each week.

But there are other roles — psychological ones. For example, a man may unconsciously think of his wife as his mother. On the other hand, a wife may unknowingly think of her teen-age daughter as her younger sister who was always favored and spoiled at home.

With this in mind, the counselor will help each partner examine the roles he assumes, those he wishes his partner to play, and the part his spouse is actually fulfilling.

Marital problems often stem from a confusion of the roles of spouse and parent or some other family member. Each partner should be encouraged to ask himself (or herself), "To what degree do I *expect* my spouse to be someone else — for example, a substitute for one of my parents? And to what degree *is* he (or she) filling such a role?"

When one of the partners has experienced a prominent child-parent relationship in his childhood (when the normal loosening of ties to his parents has been either unduly retarded or abrupt), he will often have an excessive need for his spouse to play parental roles. Such a marriage may work for a while, but eventually this confusion of roles will undoubtedly lead to conflict.

Full Surrender to Christ

The goal in marriage counseling which exceeds all others is that of leading a client to a personal knowledge of the Lord Jesus Christ. When a marriage partner learns to trust Christ as his Saviour, he is endowed with a new nature, a new power, and a new capacity to grow and change.* This, in turn, will affect his entire marriage.

During the initial sessions, the counselor should observe the counselee's spiritual status. If he is unsaved, it is the Christian counselor's responsibility to show him his need for spiritual birth. When the counselee sees his own spiritual lack and accepts Christ as his personal Saviour, he will have a new and more solid basis on which to build a better marriage.

---

*See Chapter 24, *The Great Physician*, and Chapter 31, *The Use of Scripture in Counseling*.

Christian Maturity

One of the high privileges of the Christian counselor is to help each marriage partner enter into a closer fellowship with the Lord Jesus Christ. This is accomplished week by week as the counselor continues his contacts with the couple. Besides the five basic steps in Christian maturity discussed previously,* the counselor can stress the relationship of the client's problem to his need for spiritual growth and maturity. In time, the counselee will recognize the influence of godly living on his own marriage. This can actually transform these unhappy experiences into a blessing because they can become a means of drawing the couple closer to God — and to each other. When a couple turns to the Lord, He not only gives them strength to cope with immediate needs, but He will fortify them against pitfalls in the future.

Translation of New Understandings into Appropriate Action

Perhaps one of the most important contributions a counselor can make is to help a couple translate their counseling sessions into practical living in the home. Without this essential step, they may become proficient in verbalizing an attitude without actually applying it. For example, consider the case of a husband who, through counseling, begins to realize that his wife was raised in a home where she was continually criticized by her parents and her older sister.

The counselor then raises such questions as, "How might this past experience be affecting your wife now? How might she interpret criticism of acquaintances or relatives? How might she feel about criticism coming from her own daughter or even her husband?"

After much discussion on these points, the counselor should take the next step and raise the following concepts for discussion: "In addition to eliminating criticism this week, let's substitute something encouraging. What are some of the things she does best? How might you and your daughter compliment her? What are some of the possible ways she may be expected to react? Why may she react in these ways? If she does, what should your attitude be?"

---

*See Chapter 24, *The Great Physician.*

In the succeeding counseling session, the counselor can follow up this practical emphasis with more workable suggestions. With these insights to guide the counselee's action, he will, in time, see a significant change in his marriage.

Motivating the Client

The following ad actually appeared in a large city newspaper: "Private Detective. Shadowing, suspicion verified. Also marriage counselor."

Evidently this is at least one person's concept of a marriage counselor! But it is a far cry from the professionally trained man or woman whom the counselee admires and trusts. Experienced marriage counselors know that success is largely dependent upon the counselor's ability to win the respect and cooperation of the client. Although this is true in all counseling, it is especially so in marriage counseling.* Problems involved in marriage are usually personal in nature. Unless the counselee respects you and places confidence in you, he will not cooperate in explaining the dynamics of his problem, nor will he accept your suggestions.

A person with a marriage problem may have difficulty getting along very well with anyone. The fact that he is unable to adjust to his mate and others in the family may be concrete evidence of this truth. If so, he may not have the interpersonal skills to relate easily or well to a marriage counselor. This need not be attributed to the counselor's lack of ability, but to the fact that this person has not yet learned the skills of getting along with people in general.

As rapport is being established, the successful marriage counselor concentrates on effective ways to motivate the client. This can be accomplished in several ways:

Focus on the marriage. This is one of the best ways to secure maximum motivation for the effort the counselee is expending in securing marriage counsel. Keep in mind that the counselee came to improve his marriage, not to have his personality made over. So concentrate on the marriage. He may fear that you will try to change him and indicate that he is wrong. Focusing on his marriage adjustment will alleviate his fears.

Encourage him to find useful and enjoyable action with his

---

*See Chapter 2, *"To Whom Do They Turn?"*

mate. This offers no threat and helps the counselee to feel that he is getting what he came for. In addition, it is a step toward better mutual understanding.

Motivate the counselee to change by concentrating on what he can do to change his spouse. For example, in reference to her faults, say, "Perhaps you can help her by doing so-and-so." When a person assumes the role of assisting his mate, he is not likely to criticize her.

Have confidence in the counselee's ability to improve the marriage. The fact that he originally won her affections, then successfully won her in marriage is an indication that he can also achieve a good adjustment in marriage.

Encourage him for any effort toward improvement by giving him recognition and praise. When the counselee feels he is making progress, he is motivated to continue his efforts.

Counselors should keep in mind that people do have good marriages even though they have personality problems. Furthermore these may tend to disappear when husband and wife start working cooperatively on a program of improvement. Everyone has at least some idiosyncrasies. But happy marriages are not built on what people are not. They are established on strength: what people *are.* Counselors help marriage partners to look for and appreciate strengths in their mates.

The Initial Interview

The counselor should make certain that the first counseling sessions are as satisfactory as possible.* This calls for a mutually satisfactory time and place. One pastor told of an experience which has undoubtedly been duplicated by many other ministers and Christian leaders. At nearly one o'clock in the morning his phone rang persistently. When he answered, one of the women in his church tearfully implored him to come over immediately. She said that her husband had come home drunk and was now beating up the children as well as herself.

"Come as soon as you can," she begged. "I'm just afraid he'll kill one of us."

The pastor wisely advised her to call the police if she felt

---

*See Chapter 5, *Counseling Arrangements.*

any member of the family was actually in danger. Yet, many counselors have unwisely gone to a similar scene to do marriage counseling. But is this the role of a counselor — settling quarrels or refereeing fights? No, it is hardly appropriate for a counselor to involve himself in domestic disagreements or family rows.

Effective marriage counseling can best take place when both the counselor and the counselee are free to discuss quietly a problem. This requires a suitable time and place. When optimum conditions exist, the counselor takes the next step — structuring the sessions sufficiently to win the interest and cooperation of the counselee. To do so, the counselor may wish to keep several of the following suggestions in mind:

• By the end of the first session arrange for the counselee to have some definite project to work on. Decide what can be done now and what should come later; what is an emergency and what is not. This helps the counselee feel that he is making progress. It also opens the door for him to take additional steps.

• Help him to become oriented to problems in the marriage rather than "who is at fault." Human nature tends to shift blame. But this offers no solution. When the counselee explores his problem he will see its ramifications and will not be so prone to place all the blame on his mate.

• At times it may be necessary for the counselor to begin with symptoms rather than to plunge into the problem before the counselee is ready to accept it. After rapport is established it will be easier to work on the heart of the problem.

• Begin with situational problems then work toward personality difficulties. Interestingly enough, actions often change when conditions change. When couples are mellowed by the seriousness of their situation and have gained some degree of understanding, they will probably be more willing to consider personality suggestions.

• Plan to give the counselee some tasks at which he can be successful. Success is the world's greatest encourager. When a person experiences a measure of success, he is happy to continue striving at other tasks.

• Evaluate the counselee's spiritual condition. This is especially important since many maladjustments are spiritually oriented.

When married couples have the right relationship with the Lord, many problems are prevented.

• A marriage problem may stem from poor health. If mental illness is suspected, the client should be referred to a specialist. Many marriage problems stem from serious physical or mental conditions. It is difficult to take the "rough spots" in life when a person is not well. It is wise to encourage a medical check-up to establish or to eliminate the possibility of a significant health problem.

COUNSELING WITH ONE OR BOTH SPOUSES

Many marriage counselors find that it is usually best to counsel each spouse separately, at least during the initial interviews. This allows the husband or wife to speak freely without fear of interruption, contradiction, embarrassment or injury. For example, Mrs. Jones wanted to discuss something about her husband that was extremely repulsive to her. However, she never felt free to talk about it in his presence. Yet, this one thing was causing her distress which seemed almost unbearable. When the counselor saw her alone, she summed up enough courage to discuss it in detail. With this relief, Mrs. Jones felt much better. And with this knowledge, the counselor was able to work through the problem with her husband.

Like Mrs. Jones, most people feel much freer if the spouse is not there to criticize or oppose. As one man put it, "When my wife and I went to the marriage counselor he saw us together. But nothing was accomplished because we just continued our quarreling in his office. And yet we had to pay him. It would have been cheaper to have had our arguments at home."

However, as counseling sessions progress, the counselor may wish to see both spouses together. In fact, some marriage counselors try to bring the couple together rather early because they feel that much can be accomplished by seeing both marriage partners at the same time.

One experienced marriage counselor states that one advantage in counseling husband and wife together is that this is the only time both marriage partners can speak plainly to each other without fear of intimidation or without the other leaving the room.

Together, in the counselor's office, they can learn directly how each feels about many matters.

"Well, I didn't know you felt that way about it," one might say.

In addition, the atmosphere of the counseling session often provides a climate that makes it easier for the couple to apologize to each other for misdeeds or misunderstandings.

Occasionally, because of fear, one of the marriage partners may feel that he needs the protective environment of the counseling session to enable him to express himself to his mate. Take Mr. Smith, for example. He was a small, quiet man who would do almost anything to avoid a conflict. Finally in his individual counseling sessions he reached the point where he was able to discuss certain personal matters fully. But it was not until he had the moral support of the counselor that he ventured to bring them up and tell his wife how he really felt. Mrs. Smith, an aggressive, competent woman, never imagined that he felt so strongly about things. But when she was faced with the situation in the presence of the counselor, she agreed to consider her husband in such matters.

Counseling a couple together requires much tact on the part of the counselor. He must be extremely discreet inasmuch as there is danger of harming the marriage relationship should the couple be psychologically unready for dual counseling.

When counseling both spouses together, the counselor makes sure that he does not favor either, but enables both to express themselves. At times the counselor may aid communication by paraphrasing or interpreting what is said, particularly when there is evidence of lack of understanding or when the session is filled with too much emotion.

The question of counseling each mate individually or together is not determined by a rigid rule. It is based on the type of problem involved, the spouses themselves and the preference of the counselor. But most marriage counselors favor seeing the husband and wife individually before an attempt is made to counsel both together.

DYNAMICS OF MARRIAGE COUNSELING

Although the dynamics of marriage counseling are much the same as in all types of counseling, some understanding and techniques apply specifically to marriage problems. The following guides will help the counselor to function in a more effective manner:

Encourage a comprehensive review of the major complaints against each other. In this way grievances are brought out in the open where they can be viewed objectively. Tensions may be alleviated by encouraging the counselee to express his feelings and thereby get them "off his chest." Help both the husband and the wife to elaborate, clarify, and identify his and her own feelings. Encourage them to express themselves in such areas as the following:

a. Do they accuse each other unjustly?
b. Do they provoke each other?
c. Do they act out their irritations — become sulky, sullen or bitter?
d. Do they become anxious?
e. How long does it take either to "make up"? Who does it first?
f. How have they reconciled differences in the past?

Analyze each "situation" which is used as an excuse for anger. Point out that each partner may constantly provoke the other instead of finding a solution. Many couples continually bring out the red flag of disagreement when they should be flying a truce flag. It always takes two to make a quarrel.

Mentally note and encourage each as he or she ceases blaming the other and begins asking himself *why* he became so upset.

Suggest release of tensions in constructive rather than destructive ways. Speak of the word "tension" rather than "hostility." The counselee may find release in "acting out" his tension but it should not be directed against the spouse. It can be sublimated.

Note when difficulties may be due to lack of knowledge or experience. Many people have little or no background in practical matters regarding budgeting, household management, sexual behavior, masculine and feminine roles, problems of dealing with the care and/or treatment of children or of aged parents. Instruction and guidance in such matters often alleviates many tensions. If instruction concerning marriage helps young people before they marry, how much more it may benefit them after taking the vows!

The counselor avoids excessive didacticism, and remains keenly alert to the need of being impartial and objective with both marriage partners.

Assess the counselee's personal, social, intellectual, physical and spiritual strengths and weaknesses. Make allowances for these and formulate your plan of counseling.

Various tests and inventories yield significant information which is especially helpful in marriage counseling. Although some of the most valuable tests are highly clinical in nature and are administered only by credentialed personnel, some tests and inventories may be given by counselors who are not psychologists or psychometrists. Information about tests of this type may be secured through local colleges and universities, from test publishers, and from counseling clinics and bureaus.*

Help the counselee to understand his spouse by explaining his role in unilateral counseling and what he can expect in return.

Increase the counselee's objectivity in all areas. Help him analyze his own attitudes with family members and neighbors.

Encourage the counselee to change his spouse's attitudes through his *own* efforts — by doing things himself.

A husband or wife will often try to gain favor with the counselor at the other's expense. The counselor must be alert to this and not show partiality. The counselor's respect for the other spouse will help the counselee to respect the spouse also.

With very hostile mates, the counselor should enjoin them not to discuss the counseling sessions with anyone except the counselor.

Realizing that deep spirituality is most important in marriage, the counselor will find many opportunities to help the wife and husband develop into mature Christians.† When the counselee

---

*Information about appropriate tests and inventories may also be secured through the American Institute of Family Relations, 5287 Sunset Blvd., Hollywood, California.
†See Chapter 24, *The Great Physician,* and Chapter 31, *The Use of Scripture in Counseling.*

is a Christian, it is especially valuable to use a few minutes in each counseling session to pray with him.

FREQUENT CAUSES OF DISSATISFACTION

What are the common causes of marriage unhappiness? Most marriage researchers group complaints into six or eight major categories.

Sociologists Judson and Mary Landis questioned 409 couples about their marriage adjustments (see Figure 1).* The percentage agreeing that they had reached a mutually satisfactory adjustment in certain areas was as follows: Sex relations, 63%; management of children, 71%; social activities, 72%; religion, 76%; management of income, 77%; in-law relations, 77%; mutual friends, 82%.

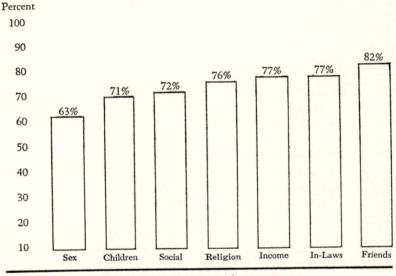

Figure 1. Marriage Adjustments

Each of the areas mentioned in this study should be explored, beginning with ones which interest the counselee and which he feels free to discuss. The counselee will find it easier to consider

---

*Landis, Judson and Mary. *Personal Adjustment, Marriage and Family Living,* Prentice-Hall, Inc., 1950.

the more personal problems of marriage after he gains confidence in the counselor.

One facet of marital conflict which is often erroneously assessed is a couple's sexual maladjustment. A counselor should encourage each partner to discuss such questions as: (1) "To what degree is sexual maladjustment a factor in our difficulty?" and (2) "Is this maladjustment a *cause* or a *result* of the basic problem?"

The role of sexual maladjustment in marriage problems is often either exaggerated or unduly minimized by counselors, depending on their own point of view. To avoid this error, it is best to consider each case individually.

Many people harbor grossly distorted ideas about sex because of fear or lack of sex education. Some even consider sex relations within marriage a shameful concession to man's lower nature. A wife may think that only the man is to enjoy sexual activity. Such notions may beget shame, resentment and infidelity. Because of these attitudes and other factors, some marital problems cannot be solved without dealing with basic sexual conflicts. Although sexual incompatibility may be symptomatic of a deeper psychological or spiritual problem, it must not be overlooked as a basic cause itself. A counselor should not underestimate the value of counseling sessions devoted to matters of sex. Many husbands and wives have found much help through only one or even a few such sessions. Although the counseling may not have been extensive, it enabled the counselee to gain significant new attitudes and understandings.

INTERPRETING CHILDHOOD EXPERIENCES

A marriage partner is often unaware that his pattern of life may stem from events that transpired in childhood. He may not understand the relationship between early experiences and his present attitudes and actions.*

The counselor can help him trace his present feelings to their early origins. He can skillfully bring hidden influences to light by evaluating childhood experiences:

Does the client use the spouse as a "strawman" to repeat the grievances of childhood? What effect does this have on the

---

*See Chapter 14, *Tracing the Origins.*

client's health? On his "peace of mind"? On friends and on other family members?

What was the family pattern in childhood? With whom did he identify? Did he copy or change the pattern?

Is he transferring childhood attitudes of dependency or resentment to his mate or other family members?

Transference is most frequently defined as the distorted perception of the present in terms of the past. In this respect the individual associates people in his current life with the attitudes and emotions of those in his early family constellation. As a result he will behave toward someone as though he were some particular individual in his childhood. For example, the wife who says, "I hate my husband," may unconsciously be saying, "I hate my father." These feelings may have been appropriate in the past but are not justified in the present. Gaining insight into this concept may open doors of understanding.

Close examination might reveal that the counselee may also be relating to the counselor as though he were a child, a peer, or a parent. Although not in an obvious way, he may see the counselor through eyes of hostility, submissiveness, or some other childhood attitude. The counselor can best relate to hostility (either manifest or concealed) by demonstrating a consistent, maximum, positive regard for the counselee. However, one must avoid giving excessive praise and personal attention. These may be manifestations of unintentional countertransference.

IMPROVING COMMUNICATION SKILLS

Oliver Wendell Holmes once wrote, "Talking is like playing on the harp; there is as much in laying the hands on the strings to stop their vibrations as in twanging them to bring out their music."

And how true this is, especially in marriage! There are times when silence is golden and times when conversation brings a world of understanding. Marriage counselors, like personnel managers in industry and like public relations specialists, know that free interchange of thoughts through discussion is the cure for many misunderstandings and hard feelings. Indeed, lack of communication is one of the greatest roadblocks to a happy marriage.

As a marriage counselor works with a couple, he continually helps them to open lines of communication. The following suggestions to the couples themselves will help bring this about:

When talking to your husband (or wife) use non-directive approaches. Rather than arguing, ask him to tell you more about the way he feels. For example, don't say, "How absurd! Mother isn't running our lives at all." But do say, "You feel then that Mother is interfering too much in our marriage?" This gives him an opportunity to drain off his bitter feelings. In addition, it makes him feel that you respect him enough to let him express himself.

Read books or articles together. This allows communication which does not carry high emotional content.

Concentrate on points which permit agreement; postpone others.

Avoid unpleasant discussion at wrong times such as early morning, bedtime, before dinner, when either one of you is tired, or during times of stress.

An overly talkative spouse must deliberately try to cultivate control. An unusually quiet spouse must face his obligation to participate.

A regularly scheduled short period of family discussion (family council) is beneficial.

Respect each other's right to express his own opinion — even if it is wrong!

Learn to listen attentively to what your spouse has to say. It is not very inspirational to talk with someone who is only half listening. Also, do not interrupt. Let him (or her) feel that he always has the privilege of finishing whatever he is saying.

Recognize male and female differences in outlook and values. Neither is necessarily "wrong." But because of his sex and his experiences, he (or she) may see things differently from you.

By learning to understand motives behind ideas, you can more easily accept each other's attitudes.

THE ETERNAL TRIANGLE

Only satanic activity can account for some problems that come before Christian counselors. When God is not held in first place, and sin is not recognized and confessed as such, fantastic distortions may enter the lives of men and women. No less crazed than Homer's sailors passing the Isle of Circe are those who allow themselves to become infatuated with someone they have no right to love. The Bible word for it is adultery. No amount of argument or romancing can make it anything else.

Take the case of Fred and Alice. Fred had invited a jobless friend to his home for a few days. His wife, Alice, had tried to be polite to this outsider in addition to caring for her family of three. The visitor was a clever seducer who remained in the home, then gradually persuaded Alice that she was a "neglected queen." Incredibly, the young woman was bewitched until she made plans to run away with him. At this point Fred learned of their intentions and was frantic with grief. Although he and Alice had been virtually out of touch with Christians a desperate sense of loss brought Fred, blind with weeping, to the altar of a community church. There he talked with the pastor.

Alice finally consented to meet with the pastor, too. When told that her new love had won and abandoned other women, she remained unmoved. She felt he *needed* her. She said she had counted the cost of leaving her small daughters. Fred looked at her as one stunned with disbelief.

The pastor continued to counsel with Fred, who then placed his life entirely in the hands of God. The seducer left the home and left the city. Several weeks later the delusion passed from Alice's life, and she ashamedly and remorsefully turned again to her husband. The family established daily worship and prayer and made their way regularly to church. Even the little girls had learned to pray and thank God for their Christian home.

Unfortunately such family ruptures repeat themselves all too frequently — and often it fails to resolve in the "happy ending" of Fred and Alice's experience. True, Satan motivates such a situation by striking at the "weak spots." Since these vulnerable areas in a person's life are usually his downfall, it behooves the counselor to take a deep look into the reasons behind the action.

When another man or another woman appears on the marriage scene, it is rarely because of an overwhelming love; but rather, because of an overwhelming need. What are the needs which are urgent enough to make a man or a woman unfaithful, either in thought or action? The need not only to *be* loved, but to *feel* loved; not only to *be* needed, but to *feel* needed.

A man may seek acceptance from some other woman when he feels that his wife does not accept him as he is but expects him to be something he neither is, nor can be. The wife may indicate this either by verbal or implied criticism.

The counselor should search, not for what is lacking in the wife, but for what is lacking in the husband himself. What promise remains unfulfilled? Why does he need constant reassurance as to his success as a husband or a father, his physical and intellectual stature, his personal charm? At the same time the wife should ask herself what she has given her husband during the marriage. How much of herself has she given and how warmly has she received what he has had to give in return? The same is true if the wife has sought satisfaction of her needs away from home.

The counselor should help the injured party to recognize certain types of action as unwise. Some things only tend to heighten the severity of the situation rather than rectify it. Advise the counselee against the following:

Contacting the other woman (or man) and begging the party not to destroy their home. This displays her own vulnerability and adds to the other's self-assurance.

Walking out of the home, especially if there are children.

Assuming a moral, judicial attitude. The other marriage partner is doubtlessly aware that he is wrong. To be told by his spouse only puts him on the defensive.

Punishing with silence. Lack of communication is probably responsible for much of the trouble in the first place. More silence only aggravates the situation.

A triangle may be the excuse for a divorce, but it is rarely the cause. For that reason a counselor can do much to help the injured party face the situation for what it actually is and to seek a solution by changing his own attitudes and behavior. In many cases this was what the husband or wife was trying, consciously or unconsciously, to achieve.

A Christian counselor should never endorse divorce unless it is within the teachings of the Word of God, and then only if the husband or wife demands it.

For Biblical references to divorce, see: Matthew 5:31, 32; Matthew 19:3-12; Mark 10:2; Luke 16:18; and I Corinthians 7:10-17.

SUCCESS IN MARRIAGE

A person's attitude toward marriage is of utmost importance. He must possess a determination to make his marriage a success.

A counselor can strengthen desirable attitudes by pointing out that (1) the will to make the marriage succeed is a vital factor; (2) any marriage must have care and attention; (3) a good marriage is a growing marriage. These are some of the attitudes that will promote success. The counselor is wise to center his attention on these areas. By pointing out the real values of marriage, he can encourage and strengthen these aspects.

The marriage counselor should discuss with the husband and wife something of the structure of a good marriage. For example:

Each partner accepts the appropriate role of his or her own sex.

Both husband and wife understand the desirability of good health.

Marital happiness depends, to a large extent, on companionship, working together as a family unit. These are more important than money, prestige, and most other factors.

Both marriage partners have satisfactory opportunities for expressing and developing their own personalities and abilities.

Children may be a blessing, but they do not automatically bring happiness to a home. A childless couple can be very happy. But children coming to a happy couple usually enhances that happiness.

Full and constructive use of special family times helps to involve the husband and wife and make them feel their marriage is more meaningful and satisfying. Family meals, conversations, outings, holidays, anniversaries, projects, sports, pets and other "together times and things" improve the climate of the home.

Spiritual conversion and dedicated Christian living are essential in a radiantly happy marriage. Deep spirituality is the "glue" that holds a marriage together. No marriage reaches its zenith until both husband and wife are humbly serving the Lord. Deep spirituality adds lustre to any marriage. In a sense, happiness is not "things" or "places." It is a Person — the Lord Jesus Christ.

Success in marriage interprets various meanings to different people. But unfortunately, to many it means a rather romantic realm in which one gets his own way most of the time. The marriage counselor is in a unique position to help couples re-evaluate their concepts of marriage. He can help them gain a more realistic perspective of success in marriage and what each can do to realize this goal.

Marriage counselors, like all other counselors, do not expect complete rehabilitation in every case. It is enough if you are able to get the couple started on the road to constructive, happy living. You need not lead them all the way. If they can learn to co-operate rather than compete, to work together for a goal that transcends themselves and, above all, to give their full allegiance to Christ, they will not lose their way. In the words of Paul, they must "be submissive to one another out of reverence for Christ" (Ephesians 5:21, Berkeley Version).

30 | PROBLEMS OF SEX

The pastor listened attentively as one of his parishioners poured out a story about her unhappy home life.

"Yes, we're both Christians," she said, "but we've had trouble from the very beginning of our marriage."

As the woman continued her story she revealed the fact that much of her marital unhappiness stemmed from a personal problem — sexual incompatibility.

The same day, in another church, a teen-age boy talked confidentially to the youth leader. The boy hesitantly mentioned his problem of habitual masturbation. The youth leader encouraged the boy to talk about his problem, knowing that in this way they could seek out the causes and arrive at helpful solutions.

Late that evening in another city, a pastor's door bell rang. As he opened the door, he immediately recognized a young man from his own congregation.

"Pastor," said the young man nervously, "can I see you alone for awhile?"

The pastor invited him into his study where they could talk in privacy.

"I have a serious problem," the young man began. Then, burying his face in his hands he painfully sobbed out an unsavory story of homosexuality.

In still another community an evangelist listened as a young lady, one of his recent converts, revealed the fear and anguish that gripped her heart.

"It's so awful," she said, "that I didn't think God could forgive me. But two nights ago I gave my heart to Christ and I'm sure He has forgiven me now. Yet, I know I am going to have to suffer the consequences of my sin."

Within a few minutes she began to tell her story — how she had become intimate with a man whom she had met at work, and now she was afraid she was pregnant.

"I couldn't tell my parents," she sobbed, "and the man has gone to another city. In fact, I don't know where he is."

And so the list of problems grows: sexual incompatibility, masturbation, homosexuality and fornication. Yet they represent only a few of the scores of sex problems people are continually bringing to Christian counselors.

THE SOURCES OF SEX PROBLEMS

Why are there so many serious sex problems? What are the causes? To learn the answers to these questions is to gain a great measure of insight into counseling procedures. The following considerations are basic in understanding the reasons why sex problems exist:

Many sex problems grow out of the fact that sex is a vital force in life.

Some life urges are much less strong. They are not characterized by the insistent, burning passions that accompany sex drives. Other desires in life may be rather easily deterred or sublimated, but not so, sex. God has given man and woman strong attraction toward each other with a desire to fall in love and cohabitate so that they may replenish the earth. It is this intense force which, if not directed to honor God, surges like a mighty river, leaving untold problems in its wake. Multitudes, young and old alike, because they have lacked the necessary restraints and controls, have given way to the powerful drives of sex. With most people, it is not enough to be told that they should not indulge in illicit sex relations. A new spiritual nature, implanted by God, and dynamic Christian growth are especially important in self control.

Some sex problems arise from the integrative nature of sex.

Sex is not confined to just one aspect of life. It extends to all of a person's being — intermingling with his emotions, his intellect, his physical attributes and his spiritual development.

True, sexual functioning is considered physical, but it can not be separated from man's emotions. The way he feels determines to some extent his sex desires. And conversely, his sex life partially determines how he feels. This two-way influence is seen in other aspects of life as well. Thus, the relationships of sex and other areas of life are like a complex network of wires in a complicated electronic machine. One facet is controlled by and reflected in another.

What has this to do with the causes of sex problems? This: if sex were a single factor not affecting another part of a person's life, its maladjustments would be much more simple. But since it is integrated with the entire person, it can produce and influence a host of attendant problems.

For example, a Christian who transgresses God's laws regarding purity soon has guilty feelings which are not only severe in themselves but which also may influence body functions, thus causing physical symptoms. Too, one who is not walking close to Christ may be influenced by Satan so that he continually dwells upon things of sex. Although he does not commit overt acts, his thought life may affect other areas of his life such as his employment, school work, and family relationships. It also results in further spiritual weakening.

When a Christian counselor works with a person who has sex problems, he may expect many accompanying problems which have a bearing on the counselee's sex difficulty. A sex problem seldom stands alone.

Since sex acts often result in human reproduction, many serious problems follow illicit relationships.

Many problems of life have a somewhat simple solution. For example, a man may steal an object. Although this is serious, it many be handled with expedience without undue, involved problems.

But this is not so in human reproduction. When a man and woman unite in sexual relations and a tiny new life results, these two have brought into being an immortal soul, a soul who will live somewhere — heaven or hell, forever! Immediately a host of problems may present themselves: Whose child is it? Was it conceived lawfully, according to the plan of God? Who will care for it? Who will provide for the child? Who will train it? Who is responsible for its eternal destiny?

These and other questions have caused untold anguish and even loss of life. If human reproduction were not intrinsic in the sexual functioning of the human body, it would not carry with it the possibility of so great a number of problems. If one could look into the minds and hearts of those who have transgressed God's laws of life, he would see scores from every city and community whose consciences are torn and racked by the memory of their deeds. This, in itself, leads to numerous problems.

Many sex problems stem from great variation in sex drives.

A marriage counselor once said, "If everyone had equally strong sex drives, married couples would have fewer problems." Indeed, there is a measure of truth in this statement. People do vary greatly in their sex drives. This is not because one is right and another wrong, but rather, because no two people are alike in any way, and certainly not in sexual functioning. One need only to sit at the desk of a marriage counselor, psychologist, psychiatrist, medical doctor or minister to be impressed with the wide variation in sex desires and capacities of those who come for consultation.

These natural differences tend to result in serious conflicts in marriage and are often blamed for the scores of "incompatibility" cases that crowd the divorce courts daily throughout the land.

Actually, many of these seemingly fixed differences would not exist if couples sought professional help. Still other cases would be resolved to a point of satisfaction if the person were helped to understand his own feelings and those of his mate. But since many couples refuse to seek professional help, these sharp differences continue, causing a multitude of problems.

Sex problems often stem from lack of wholesome sex education.

Most children grow up in homes and classrooms where they can ask almost any question and get forthright, honest answers. "What makes a kite fly?" "How long is forever?" "How far is it to the moon?" These and countless other questions are raised by boys and girls and answered by their parents and teachers.

But questions about sex are different. When a child innocently asks a question about his or another's body, adults often react with such surprise and shock that the child wonders if there is something wrong with his question. After a few attempts like this, a youngster senses that he should not ask questions about "those" things.

Typical of experiences many people have is this: A young man, apprehended for a sex crime, told a psychiatrist that his parents had never talked to him about sex matters.

"I can remember," he said, "when I was just a little shaver —I guess I wasn't more than five or six years old. One day I came in the house where my dad was sitting in an easy chair. I went over to him and asked him where babies came from. After looking at me half stunned for a moment, he stammered out a few words and then told me to go ask my mother. So I went into the kitchen where Mom was mixing a cake. When I asked her where babies came from she became so upset that she dropped the cake batter right on the floor. Then she told me I shouldn't ask such questions, and to go outside and play. I did. And I never came back to them for any explanations. From then on I got my answers in the gutter."

It is unfortunate that parents feel uneasy about explaining matters of sex to their own children. In a prominent seminary where students filled out a questionnaire, over 90% said that their mothers and fathers had never given them any sex education. Little wonder, then, that Christian counselors are continually faced with counselees whose sex problems stem in part from lack of wholesome sex information. Although most people get some kind of answers as they grow up, they are often erroneous ones or, at least, twisted and placed in a vulgar setting.

Every human being is entitled to understand how his body functions. He should also learn his responsibility to God in that his body is the "temple of the Holy Spirit."

Counselors must keep in mind, therefore, that many people, both youths and adults, suffer from lack of sex education, thus causing their present problems.

Faulty childhood impressions and unwise handling by parents have profound effects, sometimes causing sex problems later in life.

Many sex difficulties can be traced back to childhood impressions inasmuch as experiences in early life and in the days of youth frequently persist into adult life. All too often, unfortunate circumstances taking place in one's childhood cause serious sex problems to develop as he matures into adulthood. Even seemingly unnoticed or forgotten impressions of one's early days can be at work in a person's life, thereby causing maladjustments in matters of sex. For example, a young man came to a counselor deeply disturbed because he thought the hair on his chest was the result of masturbation. He had been told this when he was a young boy, and now it was difficult for him to erase the erroneous impression.

Many times parents are not aware that they are doing or saying things that are profoundly affecting their children. A young married woman's nerves went all to "pieces" when she discovered that she was pregnant. As the psychologist discussed her difficulty with her, it came to light that the young woman's mother and aunt had talked so much about the pain of childbirth and the sickness of pregnancy that it caused her, as a young child hearing this, to grow up with the dread of having to bear a child.

All too often children are victims of unwise handling by their parents and other adults. When parents, for example, do not know what or how to explain matters of sex to a child, they may feel that they have to frighten him in order to "settle" the issue. For example, one man who suffered from severe sex problems told a counselor about a series of incidents which occurred during his childhood. On several occasions his mother and father found him masturbating. This disturbed them greatly and in order to impress the boy that he must not do such a thing, they punished him severely, then told him that if he did not stop, he would never grow — that he would always be a "runt." His father also went so far as to tell him that he would have to cut off his sex organ if the boy ever did it again.

"I was so scared," the man said, "that for years I lived in horror. I guess it was only natural that I developed almost unbelievable attitudes toward sex. In fact, I doubt if I have ever completely gotten over some of the things that happened to me when I was growing up."

Although incidents of this type may seem extreme, there are countless individuals whose attitudes toward sex have been warped and distorted because of unwise handling by parents and/or other adults.

Realizing that many sex problems have their roots in early experiences, the counselor should provide ample opportunity for the counselee to uncover these incidents and rid himself of their present influence. This is the first step toward rehabilitation.

Physical causes may be significant in sex problems, predisposing one toward maladjustments.

Modern science continually reminds us that humans are integrated beings. Man is not divided into such parts as intellectual, physical and emotional. He is all one piece. And, as such, when one area of his life is affected, he may react in other areas also. For example, when a person is affected physically he may manifest it emotionally. So it is that certain attitudes about sex may actually find their origin in a physical difficulty. This fact is especially significant to the counselor.

In some instances a sex problem may stem *directly* from a physical cause. Injury to or disease of sex organs, for example, may bring about certain problems. We realize, too, that there are natural physical differences among people. For example, one person, by nature, may have especially strong sex drives while another may not. One husband, for example, may have a high sperm count while another does not. These and many other physical differences must be recognized when counseling about sex problems.

However, an important factor to remember when considering the physical causes of sex maladjustment is this: *an apparently unrelated physical problem may indirectly predispose one toward having sex problems.* Mrs. "Smith," for example, had a physical problem which indirectly affected her attitude toward sex. She was a large, overweight woman who had come to hate herself for her obesity. Try as she might she could not seem to lose weight. When she first began to gain, her husband made little remarks about her "getting fat." Mrs. Smith was sensitive about this but she did not say much. As time went on she grew heavier and heavier. Finally her husband made fun of her openly. Although he did this jokingly, to his wife the sting was no less severe. It was only natural that in the course of time she came to think of herself as a "big, fat woman," unworthy of love and affection. She was envious of friends and neighbors who were slim and attractive. Whenever her husband even mentioned any lady in his conversation, Mrs. Smith immediately thought that he was comparing her unfavorably with the other person.

These strong feelings affected nearly everything Mrs. Smith did. She became a poor marriage partner, one who was unable to respond to her husband's affections. Finally she "gave up" completely and during frequent quarrels with her husband, told him he ought to marry someone else.

Later, as she revealed the problem to her pastor, she began to realize the relationship between her over-weight condition and her attitudes toward sex.

There are scores of physical difficulties which affect, either directly or indirectly, a person's ideas about sex. These cannot be overlooked in professional counseling. They are often the clues that aid the counselor in helping solve problems.

Sex problems are also created and/or aggravated by the elements of a secular society.

In a secular, mundane society there is undue emphasis on sex. In fact, it is almost impossible to go about one's daily living without being bombarded by the suggestive influence of our modern, godless culture. Nearly every billboard, magazine advertisement, radio or television commercial uses sex media to attract potential buyers. Much of today's amusement is centered around unwholesome sex attraction. Low, coarse music, suitable for sex orgies, fills the air waves. Suggestive dress, designed to attract the attention of the opposite sex, often sets the styles. Lewd, sexy literature floods the news stands and is picked up daily by millions. The common use of alcoholic beverages has also seriously affected the moral standards of our nation. The alcoholic content of such beverages affects the central nervous system immediately as it enters the body, often giving a person a pseudo feeling of well being and leaving him uninhibited and without his natural reserve in matters of sex.

It is little wonder, then, that adults as well as young people have developed unrealistic and unchristian attitudes toward sex. Sex is built up to an importance which it can never actually achieve. This constant "sex bombardment" by a secular society results in unnatural stimulation to the exclusion of fine, wholesome activities. But such an impact of sinful influences is natural for a society of sinners. Little more can be expected from unregenerate natures. Even "fine" people, raised in "fine" families often succumb to the influence of Satan because by nature, the human race is sinful.

Alert to the many subtle or flagrant influences of sex in modern society, counselors help their counselees to evaluate the impact of these influences upon their thinking. Counselors, then, help them gain a more wholesome viewpoint regarding sex. A desirable perspective is basic if a person is to overcome a sex problem and achieve a good adjustment in life. It is the counselor's privilege and duty to lead the way.

Homosexuality

There are many types of sex problems with which the counselor is called upon to deal. But because space is limited in this presentation, only one has been selected at this point. Since homosexuality is a far too frequent problem and one that is often not understood, it is briefly discussed here.

The term "homosexual" designates individuals who identify themselves as such, and whose patterns of sexual desires and overt behavior are predominantly or exclusively directed toward members of their own sex. A homosexual is inordinately attracted to, and sexually stimulated by those of his own sex, and not especially attracted physically to the opposite sex.

Upon hearing that her daughter was "married" to another girl, one mother said, "I was shocked to learn that people did such things. I never heard of homosexuality before."

To those who have followed a normal path of development, sexual deviations do seem strange. Yet, it is not unlikely for some people to express their psychological problems through sexual functions just as others may do through a different behavior. Thus, the desire to hurt or be hurt may be expressed through sexual *sadism* or *masochism* respectively. The urge to humiliate or be humiliated, to display or pry may find expression in *exhibitionism* and *voyeurism*. Any of these desires and others as well may emerge in the costume of *homosexuality*.

Actually, clinical experience shows that people vary all the way from normal heterosexuality (normal attraction to the opposite sex) to the extremes of homosexuality. There are an infinite number of degrees in between, and many people are "borderline" cases.

Those continually engaged in overt homosexuality are usually so repulsed by the thought of heterosexual relations that their only sexual contacts are with those of their own sex. Some are not only exclusively homosexual in their sex object choice but even adopt, to a large degree, the mode of thinking of the opposite sex. Males may assume girls' names, wear make-up and don women's clothing. Some male homosexuals, not going this far, wear women's under-garments beneath men's clothes.

Those in the extreme category of somatic homosexuality, in addition to the above, are physically more or less like the opposite sex. Occasionally, a male may have such a markedly feminine body and psychological make-up as to deceive nearly everyone except the examining physician.

They may join homosexual cliques and, on occasion, "marry" homosexuals (those of the same sex) and set up housekeeping. Sometimes, a male homosexual, to affect respectability, enters what looks like a normal marriage with a female homosexual. However, such a couple have no sexual contact with each other. Instead, each leaves the other free to run with his own group.

His full development as a homosexual comes only when he identifies himself as a homosexual. His recognition of himself as a homosexual has a special term in the jargon of this society: it is called "coming out."

Every large city has its homosexual world with its rendezvous, events, parties and "celebrities." This world has its own language quite incomprehensible to outsiders. It has its own literature, group ways, and code of conduct. It is a world where its members find a measure of support, sympathy, and fellowship. The group attempts to identify certain famous men, past and present, as homosexuals, thus providing a justification of their own aberrant ways of life. A person remains a homosexual not just because he is fearful of heterosexuality but because the rewards of the total homosexual way of life (and these, not just primary sexual gratification) are to him, compelling ones. His skewed psychological development finds some expression and response in this unnatural society.

Whatever its variation, there is a mixture, for most "homos," of disgust, shame and hatred, with pleasure and relief in finding that one is not alone and that there are others who look on the homosexual way of life as a "superior" way.

Within the group there may be disruptive forces of hatred of others and disgust of self in what is often a highly competitive, open sexual market. Long enduring relationships are rare and partnerships or "marriages" are frequently dissolved. Change, not stability, is the rule. Deep satisfactions are not found in such groups because their ways are running cross current to the ways God intended His creatures to follow. Pitiful, indeed, is the man (or woman) who spends his youthful days in homosexuality, then faces middle and old age as a debauched, psychological human wreck.

Causes of Homosexuality

What are the causes of homosexuality? Although all of them are not known, it is evident that certain factors are significant. Research indicates that the following situations contribute to this deviation:

Dominant mother: When the mother is a woman who stifles and belittles her son's budding masculinity, he may lose confidence in his own sex. He may also fear women in general because of his mother. He may dread the thought of marriage or any intimacy with a woman. A dominant mother may have a strong, masculine component in her personality. Thus she may rival her son for the father's affections. She may also have desired a daughter, being disappointed at the birth of a son. By many subtle means, as well as overt actions such as dressing him in frilly clothes, keeping his hair long, making him play with girls, she may subconsciously try to make her son fulfill the place of a daughter. By the time the boy reaches maturity he may find it natural to play the role of a girl.

Weak father: Often a dominant mother is paired with a weak father. This intensifies an unhealthy situation. The son cannot look to his father for moral support in his fight to become a man. He loses respect for his father and for his own sex. A daughter may lose respect for men in general because of her father's weakness. She may be seduced by her strong-willed masculine mother. Thus the dominant mother - weak father combination can result in confusion of a child's sexual identification. Fortunately many children are spared such confusion because they have normal sex models (uncles, teachers, friends) available outside but near the home.

Overindulgent mother: Every bit as bad as the dominant mother is the overindulgent mother. She spoils her son — often in the prolonged or permanent absence of the father from the home or when marital relations are strained. She tries to make her son a substitute for a husband. Psychologically, she seduces him. Sometimes, the boy's attachment grows so strong that he cannot break away. Lacking an understanding father, he is helpless. "No girl could ever measure up to mother; so why leave her to get married?" The heterosexual relations of marriage are repugnant—"that would be like having sex relations with mother!" (Mothers sometimes encourage this idea, making sex appear dirty, degrading, unnatural.) The heterosexual door being closed, the door is open for the boy to turn to homosexuality.

Cruel father: When a father is continually cruel and arbitrary — often beating his children while drunk — his son may come to fear competition with men. Many young boys wish desperately to be accepted by other boys. But various experiences and conditions keep them from doing so. As they grow into adolescence they may find the "male world" even·more difficult to penetrate. These longings, coupled with powerful, awakening sex urges, make such adolescent boys easy prey for homosexual practices. Not reasoning it out, yet feeling it just as strongly, a boy realizes that if he cannot have close wholesome relationships with men as a man, he will break into the male circle by letting them do anything they wish with his body. Once this pattern is established and friendships are acquired, it is not only important but pleasurable to him. Since winning a wife usually calls for some competition as well as a self concept as an adequate male, he may fear the challenge of adult heterosexuality.

The daughter may see herself in the role of her abused mother and say to herself, "No thanks, I'll stay single rather than risk suffering that." Generalizing her hatred, and transferring her fear of her father to all men, she may become fixated in girlhood homosexuality. Girls who engage in homosexual practices are often the victims of lack of love. Having parents who may not understand or care for them and being unable to attract boy friends, girls conveniently turn to *any* person, male or female, who will afford them companionship, status, and close affection.

Initial sex experiences: A certain amount of both homosexual and heterosexual experimentation is common among children. Other things being equal, children are rarely harmed by this. The danger lies in their continuing such practices or being exposed to seduction or attack by an older man or woman who is a pervert. Such experiences may arouse sexual desires and anxieties before the child is old enough to interpret and cope with them. The situation is worsened when there is a lack of understanding and frankness on the part of the parents. This lack of understanding only serves to foster guilt feelings and anxieties in the child over his own awakened sexuality. Secret shame and disgust with sex can lead a child toward a perverted sexuality. Parents can prevent this through quiet discussion and wise handling.

Glandular causes of homosexuality are the least understood. A study of 102 male homosexuals by Myerson and Neustadt revealed a relationship between homosexual behavior and the amount of sex hormones (androgen and estrogen) in the blood. Microscopic research has discovered female cells in the testes of some male homosexuals and male cells in the ovaries of some female homosexuals.

But some specialists question glandular therapy. For example one endocrinologist told his psychiatrist friend about real success with several cases of homosexuality.

"How long do you usually work with them?" asked the psychiatrist.

"Anywhere from six months to a year," replied the endocrinologist.

"Well," said the psychiatrist, "they came to you *wanting* help. Furthermore, I imagine your weekly counseling sessions did more for them than did the medication."

One of the most significant research studies on homosexuality now being sponsored by the National Institute of Mental Health of the National Institutes of Health, Public Health Service, indicates that there is little or no relationship between glandular malfunctioning and homosexuality. This study indicates that glandular functioning affects sexual *power,* but not sexual direction. Direction, according to this scientific study, is caused primarily by psychological factors.

Genetic causes have been hypothesized but conclusive evidence is lacking. Nevertheless, studies of identical twins by Sanders, Lange, Henry and Kallman suggest a hereditary influence in homosexuality. Many people who engage in overt homosexual practices claim that they were "born that way." This is an understandable point of view since surely, they did not "ask" to be this way and since undoubtedly, in most cases, the influences that turned them to unnatural paths came so early and gradually that they were not aware of them. Even in adulthood they may not be conscious of such influences. These early childhood and youth experiences (such as lack of normal parental conditions, lack of love, undesirable personality development and many other factors) have entered into and shaped their lives until they were rendered unable to follow normal paths of development. It is understandable, then, that many homosexuals think that they are victims of heredity.

One adult woman, for example, came to a psychiatrist to discuss her homosexual tendencies. In each session she reiterated the fact that she was that way by nature. But as she had more sessions, she came to see that what she thought was "nature" was actually early, subtle influences which she had never fully understood.

Spiritual causes of homosexuality cannot be overlooked. In a godless, secular society it is not surprising that God has given men and women over to their lusts.

In Romans 1:24-27 (ANT) we read:

"Therefore God gave them up in the lusts of their [own] hearts to sexual impurity, to the dishonoring of their bodies among themselves, abandoning them to the degrading power of sin.

"Because they exchanged the truth of God for a lie and worshipped and served the creature rather than the Creator, Who is blessed forever! Amen — so be it.

"And the men also turned from natural relations with women and were set ablaze (burned out, consumed) with lust for one another, men committing shameful acts with men and suffering in their own bodies and personalities the inevitable consequences *and* penalty of their wrong doing *and* going astray, which was [their] fitting retribution."

A consecrated relationship to God is a safeguard against many types of deviations and perversions. Just so, getting right with God can be an asset in effecting a cure. Many men and women who have been engaged in overt homosexuality have become convicted by the Holy Spirit as they have surrendered their lives to Christ. Many have found wonderful relief as they contritely renewed their fellowship with Him. God intends His creatures to live wholesome, normal lives. All that He offers them through conversion and dynamic Christian living, leads them in normal directions.

Case Studies in Homosexuality

One effective way to understand homosexual behavior is to study and analyze those who are participating in it. The following are several cases which furnish a variety of important insights:

Case number 1 is a teen-age girl who professes Christianity. She tells of her relationship with another girl, and the attitude her parents would take if they knew this condition existed.

I am a Christian, but a girl friend and I have really fallen in love with each other. At first we didn't realize it was wrong in any way. But we slipped into it before realizing what had happened. She is also a Christian, but both of us are away from the Lord now.

I fell in love with her right after I led her to Christ. Our relationship has never gone any further than a kiss, and there has never been any desire to go beyond this. But we have been warned that there would be. We have been told by a Christian youth worker to stay away from each other (I just mentioned a little bit to him), but that advice is hard to follow when you love someone.

The way it is now, both of us are afraid to make any further move because we do love each other. But sometimes when I am near her I want to hold her so badly I almost go crazy. It's almost impossible to stay away from each other because we go to the same church.

We can't get professional help because we can't say anything to our parents. We don't have any money ourselves. Her parents would literally disown her — she does not feel close to them at all. The same with my parents. My father has just been released from a mental institution and I'm afraid if he knew it would send him right back to the hospital.

It is interesting to note the following:

- The two girls may be saved but they admit being "away from the Lord."
- They "slipped" into this unnatural relationship without realizing it.
- Their relationship began immediately after a close, personal contact of soul winning.
- They have started kissing each other.
- A youth worker warned them to "stay away" from each other.
- One girl desires to embrace the other.
- Both are afraid to "make any further move."
- They do not have money to seek professional help.
- Neither girl has a desirable, wholesome relationship with her parents.

221

Case number 2 is a Christian man who is seeking help and who is bewildered about his feelings.

I find that I am not attracted to women. Rather, a handsome boy captures my interest and admiration. No matter how hard I fight against it, I cannot prevent this strange feeling. Why do my feelings take this direction? As far as I can remember I have always felt this way. Did God create me like this?

I am not effeminate. I do not dress like a woman. (I can think of nothing more disgusting.) I do not molest children. I do not go to bars. I do not lisp. I do not have limp wrists. In appearance, I am like anyone else. I dress like anyone else. I walk and talk like anyone else. I doubt that anyone even suspects that I am different, except that they must wonder why I do not go out with girls.

What about David and Jonathan in the Bible? Were they homosexuals?

I know what society thinks of people like me. They hate us! But why? I have done nothing to offend anyone.

I mentioned my problem once to my mother, but she did not understand. She thought of it as a dirty habit I could just give up. My father is an alcoholic. If I told him he would only hate me.

I was once tempted to go to my minister, but before I did I heard him lash out against homosexuals, saying that they should be arrested. I was only grateful I learned how he felt before I had revealed my secret to him. Since then, I have been in terror of being discovered as even my minister, who is kind and sympathetic and charitable in all other matters, would only hate me and turn against me.

I am alone and cannot speak to anyone.

I wonder if I am sinful, perverse, perverted; a crime against nature, an abomination in the sight of the Lord. I have heard all these charges. Will even God cut off His love for me because of what I am, even though I cannot love a woman no matter how much I try? If I really believed He hated me too, like everyone else, life would be pointless.

It is interesting to note the following:

- This young man believes that he acts and looks like normal men, yet he is attracted to men rather than to women.
- He is sensitive to the attitudes of society regarding homosexuality.
- He is confused about the relationship of David and Jonathan.
- His mother does not understand his condition.
- His father is an alcoholic with whom the boy has a poor relationship.
- His pastor speaks out against homosexuals and is unable to offer any help.
- He is "alone and cannot speak to anyone."
- He is in terror of being discovered.
- He does not know what made him as he is.
- He believes that Christ understands and cares.

Case number 3 concerns two young women who through the years have had normal sex attractions. Recently, however, they have turned to each other for stimulation and gratification.

Another girl and I have a problem with which we need help. It is hard for me to talk about this problem but I think that something should be done before it goes any further.

To begin with, we two girls have an apartment together. We are especially close to one another. In fact I think more of her than any other living person. My parents have passed away but I was never very close to any of my family.

We are both regularly employed. The other girl has never dated in her life. I have dated a little but not a lot. We are both saved.

Our problem is this: In the last three months she and I have come to think of each other in a way that two girls shouldn't think of each other.

First it began with holding hands in bed at night, then snuggling up to each other, then kissing each other. Once in a while we held our kisses a bit longer which only stirred up our emotions.

Then a couple of weeks ago we began lying on top of each

other and about three nights ago we started putting our tongues in each other's mouths when we kissed, as this made us feel closer to each other.

We said we guessed there wasn't really anything wrong with this so long as we weren't acting funny in public and weren't hurting anyone else. We thought we both had a right to be happy as much as a person who was married.

We didn't realize that our emotions could get so out of hand until last night. We just couldn't let each other go or get close enough to each other and we wanted each other so much it hurt. We are both afraid that we might go further and do things that would ruin us as well as our Christian testimonies. We seem powerless to stay away from each other.

I hope that we aren't what is called homosexuals. I have never wanted girls to even touch me. Neither has she. We both would like to marry some fine Christian fellow and have a home and a family. Our affections for the opposite sex are as normal as they should be.

I hope that you won't tell us to separate because we would both be very unhappy and lonesome. Why our affections have changed in the last few months, I don't know.

Something must be done. Can you help us?

It is interesting to note the following:

- Although this young woman desires help, she finds it difficult to discuss her problem.
- She lives with another young woman.
- This person has never been very close to her parents.
- Her parents are now deceased.
- One girl has never dated in her life, the other only a little.
- Although their physical advances were gradual at first, they have now become very strong and alarming.
- They attempt to justify their actions by saying that they are entitled to happiness, just as married couples are.
- They express fear of "going too far" and ruining their testimonies.
- This person does not want to be considered a homosexual.
- Until recently, neither was attracted to other women.

- Their affections toward men are normal, desiring marriage.
- They do not want to separate.
- They do not understand why their affections have taken this turn.

Case number 4 is a young man in the armed forces who is concerned about his unnatural feelings toward men. As a new Christian he wants to be normal, get married and serve the Lord. He offers some interesting information about his childhood.

I am a born again teen-ager, having been saved about two years. I had hoped conversion would cure me of homosexual tendencies, but our Lord must want me to help myself because I still have these thoughts. However, I have not engaged in homosexual practices since I was about fourteen years old.

I was around twelve years of age when these unwholesome relations first started. At twelve I had a friend whom I looked up to very much. He started playing with my body, and I, not wanting to offend him, went along. Since the sex urge was just awakening in me, it was easy to keep doing it although I didn't care for it too much.

As time went by, it had such a hold on me that I began to enjoy it. I also had crushes on strong muscle men. I never had sexual relations with anyone except three of my closest boy friends, all of whom grew out of it and are now happily married with children of their own. I, too, want to get married like others do.

Right now I have a good friend. He hates "homos" and is just as normal as the average man. I noticed him because of the remarkable resemblance he had to a close buddy with whom I had had relations. I met him in the service and during the past year have grown to like him in a friendly, normal way. I seem to try and be just like him in everything, because I do like him — a sort of hero worship. He has helped me come out of my shy, backward shell. Because of this, I want to get rid of this misguided, maladjusted feeling I have.

One day I was asked to give him a rubdown on his back and shoulders because they were hurting him. I said, "all right," thinking only of doing him a favor.

While giving him an amateurish rubdown, I began admiring his muscular build, wishing I had such a build too. I discovered that I was getting aroused sexually. It surprised me because I had no more thought about sex or homosexual acts than I did of flying to the moon. I curtailed the desire by talking and by entertaining thoughts far removed from the human anatomy.

This all set me to thinking seriously. What is wrong with me? Can't I even have friends and give a person a rubdown without this happening?

Even sex dreams involve men where once they were women.

So after much prayer and soul searching, I decided to come for help. I would like to solve this riddle and get back on the road God intended me to travel and serve Him.

It is interesting to note that:

- This boy has been a Christian only two years, part of which has been spent in the armed forces.
- He was introduced to sexual practices when he was twelve years of age; then continued for two years.
- He did not like the initial experiences, but "went along" because he admired the boy who introduced him to such.
- As time passed he began to enjoy homosexual experiences.
- His present Service buddy reminds him of a boy with whom he had relations previously.
- He does not understand why he was stimulated when giving his buddy a rubdown.
- He curtailed his feelings by thinking of other things.
- His sex dreams now involve men, rather than women.
- This young man desires help and wants to serve the Lord.

Case number 5 is a young man who, after moving to a new community developed confidence in his pastor, then went to see him about a problem of homosexuality. This case gives some information about childhood sex experiences, adolescent experiences, then spiritual conversion and Christian growth.

I'm not sure how I got started in this mess, but I will tell you what my theory is. My mother is a good Christian but I don't think my father is saved.

When I was young there weren't any boys my age around our home, so I spent pre-school days playing with a girl cousin. I had a male cousin who was a couple of years older who always dominated me and beat me up. He introduced my girl cousin and me to intercourse when we were about five years old. My parents weren't around much. When I started school, I had an awful time. The boys all made fun of me because I liked dolls and hated sports. I played mostly with girls. What made it worse, I had straight A's in almost all my subjects and the boys were jealous of me.

When I was thirteen I started to high school and learned to dance. I bought records of exotic and sexy dance music. About this time my cousin (male) began to induce me into homosexual practices. When he came over I would dress up like a girl, then we would go through these orgies, I guess you might call them. My cousin was rather good looking and he had a good build. When we were alone I wore make-up, wiggled and slithered around him until he got aroused and then I would undress him and we would go to bed together. I got so I looked forward to this eagerly. We carried on like this for three years. He is now married and is normal in sex matters.

I had an awful feeling of inferiority because I wasn't good in sports and so when I danced out of school I would dance as sexy as I could. People always watched me when I danced. I loved that. I wanted attention. I collected packs of male movie stars. I also bought those physique magazines and would look longingly at the terrific men in them and desire to have them with me.

Then I met a boy who became my best friend. We did everything together, we had the same likes and dislikes. We both were, as I later found out, interested in homosexuality. We walked the roads at night and yelled comments at men that passed by.

That same year I fell in love, so I thought, with our band director. He was nicely built and he was very nice to me. I wanted him so badly that I wrote letters to him, asking him to take me out some night but there never was any response. He let me fall flat.

About this time also, I started going to church. This put me in touch with clean kids. We went to youth meetings every month. I also went to church twice on Sundays and I was pretty active in all church activities.

I also had devotions at home. I prayed and read the Bible every night before going to bed. In other words, I got saved and started living for the Lord. All this time I was beginning to develop an intense dislike for my father. I felt rebellious, a true sign of teen-age years.

Just a few weeks ago I went to spend a few days with two boy friends. The first night I was there, the one boy started undressing me. No one else was home. We went into the bedroom and he started kissing me under the chin and fondling me. I thought he was crazy. I hated it! He wanted us to have relations and I couldn't even stand the thought of anything with him. I refused to go along with him and after he left the room I prayed for us. The next night the boy with whom I slept, aroused me. Yet I felt sick about it.

It seems I'm changing. I believe I'm capable of being normal. And I'm sure my new life in Christ is purifying my thoughts and changing my desires. But I still have a long way to go.

As one reviews this case he is impressed with the following:

- This young man spent much time during his early years playing with a girl cousin.
- His older, domineering male cousin often beat him up, and also introduced him and the girl to sexual intercourse.
- The boy's parents did not offer him much supervision in his play.
- When he began school the boys made fun of him.
- His excellent grades separated him from the boys.
- At thirteen his sexy dances attracted much longed for attention.
- At thirteen his male cousin introduced him to homosexual practices, then carried them on for three years.

- He bought physique magazines and cards of male movie stars.
- Later in high school he met another boy with whom he had sexual relations.
- He fell in love with a man teacher who paid no attention to him.
- At the end of high school he became interested in spiritual matters, found Christ and began to grow in the Christian life.
- Recent homosexual experiences proved distasteful to him, and now he feels that his new life in Christ is purifying his thoughts and desires.

Implications for Counselors

1. Counselors should remember that those engaged in homosexual practices need to be accepted as human beings who need help. The man's statement (Case 2) "I am alone and cannot speak to anyone" is the classical expression of nearly every person engaged in homosexual practices, who sincerely desires rehabilitation.

2. Help the counselee to see that he is not a homosexual by nature, but rather, a person whose life experiences and other factors have caused him to turn to unnatural patterns.

3. Although homosexuality is a somewhat unique type of problem, nevertheless, a counselor deals with it much as he would other problems.*

4. Realize the value of complete discussion. This brings needed relief. When a counselee is able to see his problem in its true perspective and to seek out the basic causes, his homosexual impulses begin to lose their hold.

5. Encourage the counselee to gain new and different friendships — those of well-adjusted Christians rather than those who would encourage his homosexual tendencies.

6. A counselor should be alert to referral possibilities such as psychologists, psychiatrists, endocrinologists. Yet, a skillful Christian counselor should not minimize his own effectiveness. Sometimes he makes referrals to someone much less effective than himself. A counselor need not feel that he must have a complete

---

*See Chapters 1-26 for basic concepts and techniques of counseling.

knowledge of a man's problem to "stay ahead of him." Rather, he should be willing to work patiently through a problem, usually for several months, encouraging the counselee to discuss and to find the roots of his problems, then work out definite measures for rehabilitation.

7. A counselor should allow a long period of time for rehabilitation. These complex situations have been years in the making, and can not be resolved in one or two counseling sessions.

8. Make sure that the counselee has had a genuine experience of conversion. This is basic. Then help him to establish a strong program of spiritual development. (See Chapter 24.) Allow for occasional regression, but do not neglect to point up his progress and improvement.

GUIDES IN COUNSELING ABOUT PROBLEMS OF SEX

Guides in counseling about sex problems are much the same as for all types of counseling. However, some are especially appropriate, growing out of the basic causes of such problems.

Think of sex problems as attitude or personality problems.

Most problems of sex are reflections of personality maladjustments, of specific attitudes, or of spiritual problems. A person's attitudes are commonly evidenced in matters of sex. For example, a wife confided to a marriage counselor that she disliked the "sex" part of marriage. Yet, as the counselor discussed the problem with her it became apparent that the basis of her difficulty was not sex. Rather, it was an unhealthy attitude she had retained from her early years regarding men — all men. As she gained these insights and discussed them thoroughly, she was released from the impulses that had insistently bound her.

People reveal themselves in all they do — including matters of sex. Sex problems are often symptoms of deeper personality conflicts. To find the causes of these problems, a counselor helps the counselee look at his total life to evaluate the relationship between his present problem and his life experiences. A person's problem may not be a "sex" problem as much as a "life" problem.

For example, a boy may come to a Christian counselor to talk about a problem of habitual masturbation. If the counselor is wise he will not consider this a "sex" problem as much as a "life" problem. He will set up several sessions to discuss the problem, helping the boy to look at his school life, his family life, his spiritual life and his social life. The counselor will encourage the boy to consider his friends, his own personality, his leisure time, and possible sexual stimulants. Realizing the importance of sex education, the counselor will discuss body functions, asking the boy to discuss with him the significant points which he reads in an appropriate book.* The counselor will encourage the young man to establish a program for spiritual development. Thus, the counselor sees the problem of masturbation, as well as other problems, as outgrowths of larger, more significant situations involving one's life and total personality.

Realize that discussion of sex problems promotes understanding and new attitudes.

Until a problem is brought out into the open it cannot be considered. Whether confessing sin and asking God's forgiveness, or contemplating an everyday problem, nothing is solved if it remains hidden.

A counselor should help a person feel free to discuss his difficulty thoroughly. This is usually not achieved in one session. In fact, it may require several sessions even to approach a problem that is very personal in nature. Dr. Rheems, for example, remembers the time that a Christian lady came to his office complaining of "not feeling well." After the initial session, the good doctor surmised that the lady might have something else which was bothering her. In the second visit to his office she hinted at the real situation. The doctor left the way open for her to come again. It was not until her third visit that she felt free to discuss her highly personal problem. In the ensuing visits she received the help she had long needed and wanted. Although she could have been helped before, she had not found a counselor in whom she wanted to confide, nor had she found a counselor who was willing to "wait" for the true problem to emerge.

Airing a sex problem permits a person to see its true signifi-

---

*Several chapters in the book, *Life and Love* are commonly used for this purpose. Also see Chapter 33, *Books and Recordings.*

cance — its seriousness, or its relative unimportance. It gives emotional release. And often, just putting a problem "out on the table" and discussing it in detail brings sufficient release that a person is able to live with his situation with no special ill effects.

Consider sex education as an important part of rehabilitation.

Education characteristically plays an important role in helping a person with his problems, regardless of their nature. When one understands a situation or a difficulty he is in a better position to overcome it. As he gets the facts, he views the problem in a new perspective. Ignorance, of course, never aids in subduing problems; rather, when problems are wrapped in mystery they usually multiply themselves.

Education is especially important in counseling about problems of sex. This is true because sex involves complex organic functioning as well as psychological phenomena. Sex education deals with bodily functioning, and particularly sexual functioning. It also involves attitudes and psychological implications of sexual acts. A Christian counselor can help his counselee gain insights and wholesome information regarding sex by helping him understand how male and female bodies function. Much help is gained by eradicating false beliefs. All this can be accomplished by showing appropriate films, giving a person well chosen books and articles to read, and then discussing these facts frankly, yet discreetly.

"Bill," a young man, asked the church youth director if he could see him about a problem. During the first session the two moved into a discussion of courtship and marriage. During the second session Bill openly admitted that his problem centered in the fact that he was going to have to give up his girl friend. As the youth leader drew Bill out through discussion, he learned that Bill felt it was impossible for him to produce a child, therefore it would be unfair to ask his girl friend to continue dating him, leading her to believe that some day they would be married.

"I'm sure she'd like to have children," Bill said. "But since I am not capable of fertilization, it would be wrong to keep on dating. She likes me and I like her, but I think it is only fair to call it quits before it goes any further."

The youth director wondered why Bill thought he was sterile.

In answer, Bill said that he *knew* he was, because during the past year he had not experienced any nocturnal emissions. The youth director then explained that lack of nocturnal emissions need not have any relationship to sterility. Then he gave Bill a helpful book and suggested that he read the chapter on impotence and sterility. He further suggested that if Bill wanted added verification, he could see a local urologist and have tests made. Thus, through education this young man found a solution to his problem.

Like Bill, most people with sex problems need added understanding and enlightenment about matters of sex. With this education they can be more readily helped to achieve a good adjustment.

Seek the cooperation of both husband and wife in marriage problems.

In many instances sex problems involve both husband and wife. In such cases maximum help is received when both marriage partners are willing to consider the problem. Naturally, much may be gained even when only one spouse desires help. But the Christian counselor should bear in mind that if a problem involves both parties, the counselor is limited in what he can do if only one cooperates in seeking solutions. He should not interpret, however, lack of cooperation on the part of a couple as rejection of the counselor. Rather, he should simply realize that some people are not ready for help. The counselor knows that problems which are produced by, or which find their solutions in two people, must be considered by both parties if an effectual adjustment is to be reached.

Emphasize spiritual conversion and Christian growth.

Probably nothing helps a person overcome sex problems more than spiritual conversion and dynamic Christian living. This is true because spiritual conversion and dedicated Christian living reach out into every area of thinking and living, bringing about a profound adjustment in a person's life.

Since most sex problems are tied in with life problems and attitudes, the Christian counselor can expect beneficial results as the pure Gospel permeates the heart and mind of an individual. When one is saved, sex no longer looms up as the controlling factor

233

of the universe. It begins to assume its rightful, normal place as an essential part of healthful Christian living. It no longer presents itself as a panacea for unhappiness. For example, before "Jim" was saved his life centered around sex. He felt that the most important thing in the world was the sex drive, and interestingly enough he blamed most of his unhappiness on lack of sex gratification. Yet, nearly every "desirable" sexual relationship he had experienced left him dissatisfied. Sex was never able to fulfill the important role he assigned it. But after Jim was saved and began to grow in the Christian life he saw sex from an altogether different perspective. He began to realize that although it was an important function ordained of God, sexual gratification could never, under any circumstances, give him the abiding peace and joy for which his soul had yearned.

But this is not all. Spiritual conversion and Christian growth do more than show a person that sex is *not* the only basis of a happy life. A close relationship with Christ also enables a person to control himself in such a way that his own sex life is enriched and enhanced. A consecrated walk with the Lord takes many kinks and knots out of one's personality, making his total adjustment to life much better. Because of this, he is more effective in *every* area of living.

It is important that Christian counselors realize the relationship between dedicated Christian living and good sexual adjustment. It is their responsibility to make certain that a counselee with a sex problem knows Christ. After the question of salvation has been settled, then the counselor can help the counselee develop an effective program for spiritual development which, in turn, will have an important effect on his problem.*

---

*See Chapter 24, *The Great Physician;* and Chapter 31, *The Use of Scripture in Counseling.*

part three

THE USE OF SCRIPTURE IN COUNSELING

APPENDIX

31 | THE USE OF SCRIPTURE IN COUNSELING

"This book has all the answers," exclaimed "Big Jim," as he leafed through his Bible. Jim, a rough and tough hydraulic engineer, had just stepped into an amazing new world. He had just been converted. Immediately behind him lay an empty life of profanity and alcohol.

Jim had never dreamed such a transformation possible. One week before, the name of Christ had been known only as a swear word. The Bible had been of no interest whatever. He had not even inquired about God, much less a book of guidance.

No one but Pete, the converted Russian, had talked to Jim about his soul. But Pete had boldly opened the Bible to him and shown him he was a sinner. On the face of it, Jim had thought it made little sense. But Pete had engaged him in pleasant conversation, then he had asked him to read, "For all have sinned and come short of the glory of God" (Romans 3:23). There was hardly an answer to such a statement. Then, he had read, "But as many as received Him, to them gave He power (the right) to become the sons of God" (John 1:12).

In a way far beyond any ability to describe it, Jim had found himself saved by a Person who was set forth in a Book. The Lord Jesus Christ was now his Saviour and dearest Friend. And the Book marvelously held the answers for life's problems!

Jim had not heard the modern cavil that you could think "too highly" of the Bible. He had been blind and lost. Now he was saved and transformed by God's Word! It was the Written Word, the same as the Living Word who had come from heaven to die for his sin.

In contrast to "Big Jim," Dr. Haroldson, a top man in science, also heeded the call of the Gospel. Vacationing at his country home, he strolled over to a nearby Bible conference one summer evening and there he heard the claims of Christ. God's Holy Spirit spoke to the heart of this brilliant man and that night he confessed his sin and invited Christ into his life. This was the unfolding of a completely new pattern of living.

Neither Jim nor Dr. Haroldson had ever considered the Bible before. But from the day of their conversions, both gave the Word of God their complete allegiance.

Through the centuries devoted believers have recognized the true source of their strength. Martin Luther said, "It will be easier to transport a rock from the Alps than to remove me a finger's breadth from the Word of God!" John Bunyan's "Evangelist" counseled well with men because, "The best of Books was in his hand."

Again, Luther was so exercised concerning the place the Bible should have in the counseling of lives that he declared: "I am much afraid that the universities and schools will prove to be the gates of hell, unless they diligently labor in explaining the Holy Scriptures and engraving them in the hearts of youth. I advise no one to place his child where the Scriptures do not reign paramount."

Frederick William Faber, the noted Christian writer of the nineteenth century, stood in awe at the power of the Bible over the English reading peoples. "It lives on the ear like a music that can never be forgotten, like the sound of church bells which the convert scarcely knows how he can forego. Its felicities seem often to be almost things rather than words. It is part of the national mind, and the anchor of the national counsciousness . . . The memory of the dead passes into it. The potent traditions of childhood are stereotyped in its verses. It is the representative of a man's best moments; all that there has been about him of soft and gentle, and pure, and penitent, and good, speaks to him forever out of his English Bible. It is his sacred thing which doubt never dimmed and controversy never soiled; and in the length and breadth of the land there is not a Protestant with one spark of religiousness about him whose spiritual biography is not in his Saxon Bible."

Dying, the great Sir Walter Scott wanted no counsel from his vast library except the Bible. He called for "The Book."

Some ministers and Christian leaders are left bewildered by the whirlwind advances in medicine, psychology and related fields. They wonder if much use remains for Scripture in professional counseling. They need to know that no sound technique or valuable discovery of science will ever be contrary to, or complete without, the revelation of God's Word.

The Bible is always up-to-date. It is not merely the Word of God in the measure that it is accepted, understood and enjoyed. It is beyond this. Whether we are nurtured by it or avoid it, it is still the objective and eternal Word of God. The Lord Jesus Christ pinpointed the problem of mankind when He said, "Ye do err, not knowing the Scriptures, nor the power of God" (Matthew 22:29).

We are not wringing our hands over a doubtful conflict. The Bible does not need the championing of brilliant but fallen men. The Huguenots, racked with seas of sorrow and loss, when the flower of France was being destroyed or deported by religious persecution, remained gloriously confident in their motto:

"Hammer away ye hostile bands,
Your hammers break; God's anvil stands."

The Bible is not merely a bland background or a lace cap for scientific discovery. It is the glorious authority for life itself. It not only sets forth the only hope of our redemption and life eternal through Jesus Christ, crucified and risen; it is the glorious manual and guide book of our daily lives.

Doubtless it has been the work of our enemy, Satan, to further the idea that the Bible is now only a feeble supplement to modern living, a soothing syrup for those who cannot afford antibiotics, a second class narcotic for those who are too poor, too old, or too ignorant to have anything better!

But the Bible is an unmovable mountain on the landscape of eternity. "Heaven and earth shall pass away," said the Lord Jesus, "But My Words shall not pass away" (Mark 13:31).

The fact is this. Among the men who are pushing back the frontiers of human knowledge, there are devoted men of God who know and honor God's Word. There are those in psychology, psychiatry and other professions who consistently use the Bible in their counseling. They attest that the Bible advances itself ahead of every generation and continues to be the most effective tool and remedy in the hands of any counselor.

Why do some men *not* use God's Word in their counseling? This is a fair question with several pointed answers.

In the first place, it is possible to be professionally trained in many arts and sciences while remaining unconverted. This results in spiritual ignorance regarding the person and work of Christ and of His Word. As for solving life's basic spiritual problems, it is a case of the "blind leading the blind" with both falling into the ditch.

Concerning the blindness or lack of spiritual understanding on the part of the unconverted, the Bible says: "The natural, non-spiritual man does not accept or welcome or admit into his heart the gifts and teachings and revelations of the Spirit of God, for they are folly (meaningless nonsense) to him; and he is incapable of knowing them — of progressively recognizing, understanding and becoming better acquainted with them—because they are spiritually discerned and estimated and appreciated" (I Corinthians 2:14 ANT).

The remedy for this lies plainly in the counsel of Jesus Christ who told the Jewish ruler, Nicodemus, that he must be "born again." "Marvel not — do not be surprised, astonished — at My telling you, You must all be born anew (from above)" (John 3:7 ANT). Lack of this experience has caused such brilliantly educated but floundering men as the Unitarian, David Starr Jordan, to describe Biblical theology as "systematized ignorance."

Secondly, a counselor may actually know the Lord as his Saviour, but have little experience in the use of God's Word in growth and practical living. This unfortunate condition is not without blame. But it is more like spiritual deformity due to malnutrition, than scorn of God's Word. Those who have fed only on the "milk" of God's Word are described by Paul, in pitying words: "I fed you with milk, not solid food, for you were not yet strong enough to be ready for it; but even yet you are not strong enough to be ready for it" (I Corinthians 3:2 ANT). The remedy is growth. When a counselor has matured spiritually himself, then he is in a place where he can help others.

A third reason why some counselors do not use God's Word is that they attempt to do a superhuman task in their own strength. This is as stuffy as trying to push a wheelbarrow to the moon with only the aid of axle grease. If man can make moderately successful electronic controls for space missiles, God can do infinitely more than this for the aid and guidance of the distressed human heart.

Since God made humanity in the first place, we cannot afford to ignore Him and His Word. For example, if complicated German printing machinery broke down on an American Indian reservation, who would be more welcome in all the world than a providential visitor from the very factory that made it! How foolish, then, for a counselor to attempt to work things out in his own way, when God, Himself, is waiting and anxious to help.

The Nature of God's Word

It is an infinite comfort and joy to know that the Scriptures originated in the mind of God. It is just as wonderful to reflect how He arranged for a human authorship and compilation that occupied a widely representative group of men for about 1,600 years. That the result should be in perfect harmony was a miracle. That this harmony came from no conscious collusion is beyond all possible human design.

Each writer had a particular part. Yet each contributed to the whole. And the whole was Jesus Christ, the eternal God who became flesh, who died for our sins and rose from the dead. He was the One of whom Moses, Joshua, Samuel, David and many others spake. John identified Him: "In the beginning (before all time) was the Word (Christ), and the Word was with God, and the Word was God Himself. He was present originally with God. All things were made and came into existence through Him; and without Him was not even one thing made that has come into being. And the Word (Christ) became flesh (human, incarnate) and tabernacled — fixed his tent of flesh, lived awhile — among us; and we (actually) saw His glory — His honor — His majesty; such

241

glory as an only begotten son receives from his father, full of grace (favor, loving kindness) and truth" (John 1:1, 2, 3, 14 ANT).

Indeed the Scriptures are not mere climaxes of human philosophy. Paul wrote Timothy: "Every Scripture is God-breathed — given by His inspiration — and profitable for instruction, for reproof and conviction of sin, for correction of error and discipline in obedience, and for training in righteousness (that is, in holy living, in conformity to God's will in thought, purpose and action)" (II Timothy 3:16 ANT).

No counselor need be ashamed, therefore, with that which emanates from the eternal God and is indestructible, reliable, incomparable, and beyond competition. It is God's revelation. It is different in essence from every other writing. It invites examination. It commands utter confidence.

God's Word is practical. It applies itself immediately to the problems of life. It reaches men and women and boys and girls where they are. The human soul is starved for the wholesome authority of God's Word. Personal problems bog down in a hopeless marsh of confusion and doubt. The laws of life and the very meaning of words have been so rounded off by selfishness and despair, that all seems relative, and nothing solid. The danger is that the bar keeper and the intellectual snob may finally accept their unhappy, tangled little worlds as the norm of living. Even the passionate seeker after truth is astonished to find a blank at the end of the way.

The Christian counselor possesses a great and a mighty primary fact. The answer to life's riddle lies with God. It was He who took the initiative to save us and to meet our basic needs. "In this is love, not that we loved God, but that He loved us and sent His Son to be the propitiation (the atoning sacrifice) for our sins" (I John 4:10 ANT).

Truth is not a pile of glittering trash glued together by philosophers. Truth is a Person, the God-Man who came from heaven to be our Saviour and Guide.

God's benefits are boundless, yet the method of obtaining them is channeled through Christ alone. Satan may cause the befuddled sinner to think that God's terms are dictatorial, capricious and arbitrary. This is a dark moment on the threshold of knowing God and the splendor of His person and counsel through eternity. Unbelievers flatter themselves in the delusion that they may work their own way to Heaven. But Christ, the very Son of God, has forever said, "I am the Way, the Truth, and the Life: no man cometh unto the Father but by Me" (John 14:6).

The Word of God! Pure and perfect, penetrating man's heart and bringing him peace — this is the counselor's greatest resource!

The Unique Contribution of God's Word in Counseling

What are the vast helps in using the Word of God in counseling? They are as many in number as the sum of all human needs. Reaching out to every race in every part of the world, God's Word penetrates the heart and brings help to every person. It matters not what field of counseling it may be: the Bible's message is the foundation for every human adjustment.

When you introduce God's Word, you bring into use a powerful dynamic. It has no equal. And the counselor who fails to use it is overlooking the most important element in all the world.

In God's Word there is no speculation. It is Divine truth. What God says He will perform. And His Word will not return unto Him void. "So shall my word be that goeth forth out of my mouth: it shall not return unto me void, but it shall accomplish that which I please, and it shall prosper in the thing whereto I sent it" (Isaiah 55:11).

Human advice, at its best, is filled with many inaccuracies. But in the Scripture lodges no error. It is the eternal, perfect Word of God.

The Word of God Convicts Man of Sin

"Missing the mark" is the original New Testament meaning for the word, "sin." An archer draws his bow on a target but he misses the bull's eye. A man comes to a great ravine and attempts to bridge the gap by leaping across. But he misses the other side and falls disastrously into the chasm below. Because of sin, all humanity has fallen into the deep abyss that leads to death and separation from God. "For all have sinned and come short of the glory of God" (Romans 3:23). Man *has* missed the mark!

The universe is Christocentric, or Christ-centered. But ever since Adam's fall, man has been eccentric, or out of orbit with

God. This massive ruin extends to the mind and spirit of man. This unpleasant truth is often rejected by those who are wise in their own conceit. But the first three chapters of Romans leave no doubt. Man is out of fellowship with his Creator.

The Bible reveals man's own *personal* guilt. "Thou art the man!" God declared to David through the prophet, Nathan. David had been blinded with adultery and murder. But at those words, the horror of his sin appeared to him. From conviction followed repentance or godly sorrow. There was much evil that David could never repair. But his restored fellowship and his deep sense of gratitude for God's forgiveness resulted in the glorious treasure of the penitential Psalms, of which Psalm 51 is typical.

It is imperative that each person come to grips with his own sin. Until he realizes this, he is deceived about his depraved condition. *Sin is a reality and it must be dealt with in a real way.* Until sin is sought out, confessed and forgiven by Christ, it continues to linger like cancerous tissue, affecting the entire person. This is why so many people do not actually achieve a good adjustment. They have never dealt properly with the initial fact of sin. They are building on a false premise. It is shaky and cannot endure.

Sin not only brings maladjustment; it brings death. God says, "For the wages of sin is death; but the gift of God is eternal life through Jesus Christ our Lord" (Romans 6:23). "Then when lust hath conceived, it bringeth forth sin: and sin, when it is finished, bringeth forth death" (James 1:15).

What can convict the human race of sin? God's Word! The powerful, convicting essence of the Word was well described by the Apostle Paul when he wrote: "For the Word that God speaks is alive and full of power — making it active, operative, energizing and effective; it is sharper than any two-edged sword, penetrating to the dividing line of the breath of life (soul) and (the immortal) spirit, and of joints and marrow (that is, of the deepest parts of our nature) exposing and sifting and analyzing and judging the very thoughts and purposes of the heart" (Hebrews 4:12 ANT).

The Christian counselor knows that many serious problems are rooted in sin. Until these sinful roots are removed by asking God's gracious forgiveness, problems will continue to crop up and plague the victim. God's Word holds the only real remedy. And when sin is reckoned with, many of its resulting problems will resolve themselves.

The Word of God Brings the Message of Salvation

The next use of the Bible in counseling is to point out the message of salvation. The Word makes the exclusive announcement that the Lord Jesus, the Messiah, the Anointed One, is the Saviour of the world. God delivered the Law to Moses at Sinai but it only revealed man's utter failure. Yet, God's standard could not be altered. So He sent His only Son from heaven to be born under the Law that He might fulfill its complete requirements — the only one who was ever able to do so. And, since mankind was still helpless and hopelessly lost, Christ died on the Cross to pay for man's violation of the Law. Risen from the dead, He has the judicial right to bestow His righteousness and daily help upon those who receive Him.

Can salvation be obtained in any other way? No, the Bible says: "Neither is there salvation in any other: for there is none other name under heaven given among men, whereby we must be saved" (Acts 4:12).

With salvation comes a new mind and a new heart to use for God. At the resurrection, there will even be a new body! But the present miracle of the new birth is sufficient for present problems. God's Word states: "Therefore if any person is (ingrafted) in Christ, the Messiah, he is (a new creature altogether,) a new creation: the old (previous moral and spiritual condition) has passed away. Behold, the fresh and new has come!" (II Corinthians 5:17 ANT).

The Word of God Produces Faith

Psychologists and psychiatrists around the world are in general agreement that human beings need a faith. "Faith," they say, "is a necessary ingredient in the development of a well integrated personality." This is true. But where does faith come from? The Bible tells us: "So then faith cometh by hearing, and hearing by the Word of God" (Romans 10:17).

"Believing" was precisely the problem of a young man named Stanley. "I can't believe," he told Dr. Jackson, a beloved Christian physician.

"Why *can't* you believe?"

"I don't know; I just can't!"

"Do you really *want* to have faith in Christ?"

"Yes."

"Then," said the doctor, "you can. This is what you should do: Take a portion of God's Word — the book of John, for example. Then read it through again and again. Each time you read, ask God to reveal Himself to you and give you the little faith you need to believe. If you do this with an open heart, God will meet your need."

Stanley took Dr. Jackson's advice, and needless to say, he soon surrendered his life to the Lord. God *did* meet his unbelief by supplying him with faith.

Human beings are born to believe. This is the way God made them. This is instinctive. People are not satisfied unless they have something to believe in. But they are never completely happy until they have faith in God through His Son. In counseling you can help people meet this basic need of faith. Through the Word of God they can *place their trust in Christ.*

The Word of God Ushers in New Life — the New Birth

Someone has wisely said, "Man's greatest tragedy is to be born once without being born twice." When we look into the maze of life, we know this is true. As we study human beings we can see that man does not possess the seeds of perfection within his nature. He is out of fellowship with God, and his imperfect nature only begets further imperfection. Jesus clearly states, ". . . Verily, verily, I say unto thee, Except a man be born again, he cannot see the kingdom of God" (John 3:3). Thus being born again (accepting Christ as one's personal Saviour) is a *necessity.*

And how is the new birth accomplished? The answer, God points out, is extraneous to man's own efforts. It is the implanting of God Himself: "Being born again, not of corruptible seed, but of incorruptible, by the Word of God, which liveth and abideth for ever" (I Peter 1:23).

Doubtless, the crowning good of counseling with the Scriptures is that *a new life is communicated.* "And I give them eternal life, and they shall never lose it or perish throughout the ages — to all eternity they shall never by any means be destroyed. And no one is able to snatch them out of My hand. My Father, Who has given them to Me, is greater and mightier than all else; and no one is able to snatch (them) out of the Father's hand" (John 10: 28, 29 ANT).

Obviously a new life beginning with a personal faith in Christ miraculously changes the ability of a person to meet the vexing problems of life. Regeneration brings the blurred perception of man back into focus.

It is wonderful, but true, that through the use of God's Word the counselor may have a part in the bringing of eternal life.

The Word of God Offers Cleansing for the Believer

Daily cleansing is part of the believer's heritage. After salvation, he finds that although he is endued with a new nature imparted by God, he still must reckon with his *old* nature. As a result he may do things which are displeasing to God. But he need not continue in his sin or be tortured by the thoughts of his misdeeds.

It was after a Sunday evening church service that Mrs. "Smith," a well dressed lady came shyly to her pastor asking to speak to him about a personal problem.

In his office she began hesitantly, "As you know, I am an active member here, and it seems that everyone trusts me. But I feel I must explain some things to you." She paused, then continued: "I, I'm not really what folks think I am."

"Yes," the pastor said with continuing interest.

"Well, after your sermon tonight I just felt I must get this off my mind. I must, must tell you. Believe me, it takes all the strength I have to do this. I don't know if you can help me; I'm not sure *anyone* can help."

"You have something on your mind that is troubling you?"

"Yes. Oh, I only wish I could get this straightened out! I feel so mixed up. Sometimes I wonder if I am even saved. I can't see how a saved person would do such a thing . . . and yet I blame myself for doubting my experience."

"There is something you want to discuss and straighten out with God, isn't there?"

The lady said nothing, so he continued. "God knows all about it, doesn't He?"

"That's just it. I have prayed so much about it, but I just can't seem to get forgiveness. I feel like such a hypocrite!"

"Mrs. Smith," the pastor said, "why did Jesus die?"

"For our sins," she answered almost automatically.

"Then if He cannot forgive this sin of yours, He died in vain, didn't He?"

"Yes, that's right," she replied thoughtfully. After a moment she continued: "I don't know if you realize it or not, but I am divorced. My husband was untrue to me. That's why I divorced him."

At this point she was overcome with emotion. Words seemed to escape her. The pastor waited patiently. Finally she continued, "There was a man at my place of business — just the kind of man I'd like. We started dating. I did this secretly so no one in the church would know. The affair didn't last long. I broke it off. I had to!" At this she buried her head in her hands and wept. Finally she continued, "I'm just a no good sinner — I'm just as guilty as my husband. What I hated in him I have done myself."

"And this is so terrible," interjected the pastor, "that you think God could never forgive you?"

"That's it, Pastor. How could He ever forgive such a terrible sin!"

The pastor glanced at the Bible in her hand, then said, "May I see your Bible?"

She handed it to him and he turned to I John 1:9 and asked her to read.

"If we confess our sins, he is faithful and just to forgive us our sins, and to cleanse us from all unrighteousness."

"What does God say that you have to do in order to have this sin forgiven?" he asked.

"He says, 'confess.' But I have confessed my sins to Him many times. Why am I not forgiven?"

In reply to this, the pastor explained that the text said that He was faithful and just to forgive us our sins; that He could forgive because of Calvary; and that He would forgive because He promised to do so.

"Whose Word is this?" he asked.

"God's Word."

"Can God lie? Will He keep His Word?"

"No, He cannot lie," she said thoughtfully. "He will keep His Word."

"Then believe what He says," he urged.

"I know He does keep His Word. I do believe, but somehow I still feel guilty. Why is that?"

"Are you willing to forgive yourself, if God forgives you? Can you still hold the sin against yourself when God says that all is forgiven? In Romans 8:34 God says, 'Who is he that condemneth, it is Christ that died . . .'" They looked up the reference and read it together. Then the kind pastor continued. "You see, Mrs. Smith, when God has already forgiven us our sins, we fall into the devil's hands if we continue to condemn ourselves. It is Christ who died for those sins, and His atonement is the basis for all forgiveness. To hold our guilt after we have confessed our sin is to dishonor Christ. Take your forgiveness and *rejoice* in it. That is the only way you can show that you really believe His Word. Accept I John 1:9 and live in the truth of it."

They then prayed together. The wise pastor guided the woman as she prayed, suggesting that she ask God for faith to believe His promise and to never doubt His Word.

She arose with a smile of relief and peace on her face.

Shortly afterward Mrs. Smith had an opportunity to give a testimony at church. She beamed a smile toward the pastor, then turned to the people and began. "God has been so very real to me lately. It's almost like my Christian life was starting all over again. I have had such a wonderful answer to prayer. There is a verse that has come to mean everything to me, though I have read it many times before. It is I John 1:9." Then she quoted it with real feeling. In conclusion she added, "I just want to thank God for forgiveness. He is so real to me now!"

God's Word does offer the erring Christian renewed fellowship and fruitful relationship with God. He graciously says, "My little children, I write you these things so that you may not violate God's law and sin; but if anyone should sin, we have an Advocate (One Who will intercede for us) with the Father; (it is) Jesus Christ (the all) righteous — upright, just, Who conforms to the Father's will in every purpose, thought and action" (I John 2:1 ANT).

Daily forgiveness keeps a man mentally healthy. He no longer needs to think of the past and its sin. The Christian counselor, through the use of God's Word, can direct the counselee to forgiveness and fellowship with Christ. God assures us, "Now ye are clean through the word which I have spoken unto you" (John 15:3). And again, "Sanctify them through thy truth: thy word is truth" (John 17:17).

Indeed, no man need leave the office of a Christian counselor still bearing his own load of sin!

The Word of God Gives Unerring Guidance

It seems as though half the world is seeking advice — and the other half is giving it. Yet neither is satisfied.

True, men *do* need advice. God tells us that human beings are like sheep that have gone astray. Wandering through life without direction, they need help at every turn: friendships, marriage, children, education, vocation, religion, parents, sex, finances, death, and a host of other concerns. From the richest to the poorest, from one part of the world to another, from birth until death, all men need guidance. But man is not capable of self direction. His judgment is unreliable and influenced by Satan, the prince of the power of the air. Unerring guidance comes only from God, and it is vested in His flawless Word.

Divine guidance is freely assured those who accept God's counsel. Who can resist the wholesomeness of such a promise as this: "And the Lord shall guide thee continually, and satisfy thy soul in drought, and make fat (strong) thy bones: and thou shalt be like a watered garden, and like a spring of water, whose waters fail not" (Isaiah 58:11).

It is the counselor's unique privilege, through use of the Bible, to give unerring direction.

The Word of God Offers Discernment

Discernment between good and evil, between better or worse, is a faculty not readily available in man's twisted store of pragmatic philosophy. It is difficult to know what to do and what not to do. Confusion abounds on every hand. In fact, the Scriptures teach that in the last days confusion will be the norm: "For false Christs and false prophets will arise, and they will show great signs and wonders, so as to deceive and lead astray, if possible, even the elect (God's chosen ones)" (Matthew 24:24 ANT).

God's Word also warns that many false religions will rise up and prosper. "For the time is coming when (people) will not tolerate (endure) sound and wholesome instruction, but having ears itching (for something pleasing and gratifying), they will gather to themselves one teacher after another to a considerable number, chosen to satisfy their own liking and to foster the errors they hold, and will turn aside from hearing the truth and wander off into myths and man-made fictions" (II Timothy 4:3, 4 ANT).

But the Christian counselor knows that the Bible affords the metric system of all eternity for determining right from wrong. And this standard does not change with social cultures or world conditions. It is Divine. "Howbeit when He, the Spirit of truth, is come, he will guide you into all truth . . ." (John 16:13).

The Word of God Produces Knowledge

The twentieth century has catapulted man into a space age in which there is much to know and much being taught. Yet man's knowledge does not afford real satisfaction.

Where else than in the Holy Scriptures can man find such knowledge and wisdom? The Bible declares that all the treasures of wisdom and knowledge are vested in God and Christ: "That their hearts might be comforted, being knit together in love, and unto all riches of the full assurance of understanding, to the acknowledgement of the mystery of God, and of the Father, and of Christ: in whom are hid all the treasures of wisdom and knowledge" (Colossians 2:2, 3).

In some unregenerate circles the Bible is not recognized as the gateway to knowledge. Yet, it is general history that this Divine Book was the foundation and fountainhead of formal and informal knowledge in our colonial and early national history. And this has largely accounted for the progress and many blessings of America. The majority of our great educational institutions were founded on Christianity and the Bible. The vast and incalculable influence that was exercised upon our national origin by the Bible was largely because our forefathers well understood Proverbs 1:7, "The fear of the Lord is the beginning of knowledge."

And looking back through the annals of history far back to apostolic times, we see countless numbers of humble men and women who attained great stature and wisdom through God's

251

Word. Despite some erudite arguments to the contrary, the men who overturned the first century world were, for the most part, unschooled, plain folk whose glory was in the Scriptures. "Now when they saw the boldness and unfettered eloquence of Peter and John, and perceived that they were unlearned and untrained in the schools — common men with no advantages — they marvelled; and they recognized that they had been with Jesus" (Acts 4:13 ANT).

When the Christian counselor turns to the Bible, he offers unparalleled light to the counselee. "The entrance of Thy words giveth light; it giveth understanding to the simple" (Psalm 119: 130). This is not a flashlight beam into Monday morning blues or a ray through the black outlook of domestic and world affairs. It is the glorious sunburst of divine help from the One who said of Himself, "I am the light of the world" (Matthew 5:14).

Truly this is knowledge. But more than that, it is knowledge that satisfies — knowledge that is the foundation for a joyous, victorious life.*

The Word of God Offers Protection Against Sin

The most disturbing element in all the world is sin. It brings discouragement, failure, fear, perversion, frustration, confusion, jealousy, and every evil imagination. Sin not only exists, it *abounds*. And to walk in good mental health the unbeliever must seek protection against sin.

As a leader in high school, Jack was surrounded by unsaved friends. Although he tried to follow Christ, he found himself losing ground spiritually. Finally, he unburdened his heart to Mr. Stanton, a Christian teacher at the high school. Mr. Stanton turned to the Bible and explained that God had made provision for His children to have protection against sin. All Jack had to do was avail himself of it.

"The way to do this," said the teacher, "is to fortify yourself with God's Word. It isn't enough to read it each day; you must meditate and feed upon it, then hide it in your heart. If you do this daily, the Word will keep you from sin."

Jack took his teacher's advice and set up a schedule of read-

*For a detailed discussion of knowledge that satisfies, see an annotation of *This Way to Happiness,* Chapter 33.

ing and meditating on God's Word. Each day he selected a special verse to memorize. Writing the verse on a card, he carried it with him to school and looked at it between classes and during the lunch period. Jack soon learned that it *did* give him protection from sin.

Jesus, Himself, when tempted by Satan, rebuffed him and thrice won a victory by saying, "It is written." Satan was powerless against the bulwark of the Scripture.

Without apology, the counselor may urge the Word of God for protection against Satan's forces. Not as a fetish, of course. It's paper pages may not always stop bullets in battle. Yet, the contents of the pages are a complete and indestructible armor against all evil power and the very gates of hell.

In our modern system of economy, people tend to buy things in a package arrangement. For example, insurance companies are grouping many risks together under one policy and premium. However, these are effective only as far as human ability permits. They are a discreet gamble against studied safety norms. And they are certainly designed for profit making rather than for the sake of generosity alone. Many "fine lines" in the policy limit the liability of the company.

Not so, God's protection. It is unlimited. When God's Word is lodged in the heart, it affords *full* protection.

Too often the problems brought to the counselor by Christians are a result of sin in their lives. The way to combat these problems is to combat the sin. But even when Christians have been lifted out of a difficulty, they are apt to fall into Satan's snare again if precautions are not taken. The way to insure the counselee against problems arising because of sin in his life is to fortify him with the purity of God's Word.

"Thy Word have I hid in my heart that I might not sin against thee" (Psalm 119:11). God's Word is the force that overcomes sin.

The Counselor's Possession of God's Word

God's Word is not a good luck charm. It is not a stack of printed paper upon which to lay hands and swear pious oaths. Nor was it ever intended as an ornamental piece for the rituals of secret societies.

The Bible must be believed. "These are written (recorded) in order that you may believe that Jesus is the Christ, the Anointed

One, the Son of God, and that through believing and cleaving to and trusting in and relying upon Him you may have life through (in) His name (that is, through what He is)" (John 20:31 ANT).

The counselor must appropriate the Word of God, as well as believe it. That is, he must assimilate it. It is to be part of his innermost being — without reservations. How can we help others with something that has not helped us?

With believing comes obedience to the Word of God. The counselee stands in need of more than mere mental stimulation. He is not in need of dainty dishes of theological opinion. Whether he realizes it or not, he is in desperate need of God's direction in his life. God's wholesome statutes will give government to his being. He needs to obey the Word of God.

The Counselor will need to learn the Word of God. He must penetrate its message and apply it personally to his *own* life. Learning is a discipline of the mind. But learning Divine truth, also demands a discipline of the heart. The study of God's Word is more than a lazy amusement. We are instructed to "Study and be eager and do your utmost to present yourself to God approved (tested by trial), a workman who has no cause to be ashamed, correctly analyzing and accurately dividing — rightly handling and skillfully teaching—the Word of Truth" (II Timothy 2:15 ANT).

The best reference file for Bible passages is memory. Not every counselee will give his undivided attention while the counselor makes a desperate search for some important Scripture. Front line action demands a loaded gun instead of a requisition for ammunition from quartermaster stores. The enemy may overwhelm the position before the shells arrive and are unpacked.

Treasuring the Word of God in the heart has the double merit of keeping the Christian worker from sin and of making him a spiritual blessing to others. In our time, the Navigator movement has shown again the value of memorizing Scripture for use in vigorous Christian testimony. Thousands of young men and women in the armed forces memorized tens of thousands of Bible passages, enriching their own lives and communicating boundless wealth of hope, assurance and guidance to others. This is in keeping with Colossians 3:16, "Let the word (spoken by) the Christ, the Messiah, have its home (in your hearts and minds) and dwell in you in (all its) richness, as you teach and admonish and train one another in all insight and intelligence and wisdom (in spiritual things, and sing) psalms and hymns and spiritual songs, making melody to God with (His) grace in your hearts (ANT)."

Finally, let the Word of God mature you. Let it guide your daily living. Consider it in all your decisions, large and small. See it change your own life across the years. Only by such personal satisfaction in its wholesome help can you genuinely offer it to others. We are not "medicine men" who hawk healing panaceas from an irresponsible road show. We are ambassadors of the most high God!

The Effective Use of God's Word

Undoubtedly some Christian counselors are more successful than others because they are more skilled in the use of Scripture. The following suggestions will aid the counselor in presenting the precious Word of God.

During the interview *the counselor may want to read a certain portion of the Bible.* There is no substitute for the pure Bread of Life. A counselee may respond to it more quickly than to anything a counselor might say. God's Word has in it an eternal power not found in any classic, common literature or man made suggestion.

A more abiding impression of God's Word may be made when *the counselee is handed the Bible and asked to read an indicated portion.* In many instances holding a Bible and reading it aloud is a new and unique experience — one which God uses to press His claims on the reader. If in secular salesmanship, personal identification with a product awakens a desire to buy, then it is an even more important aim in awakening a soul to the claims of Christ.

When the counselor suggests that the counselee *memorize a Bible verse or a portion of Scripture,* the effect may be even greater. As a harpoon is thrown into the body of a whale, so has God's Word been fixed in many hearts that have had no previous thought of accepting the Saviour. Many miles may be traveled, and many further ideas entertained, but God may pull in the line of imbedded Scripture and bring the wandering one to Himself. A memorized verse is one which continues to witness throughout the day. Again, it may be as a delayed action bomb revealing its power at some later, unexpected time.

Often the counselor will want to read a passage and ask the

counselee to *repeat or reread the passage after him*. A double emphasis is afforded in this way and the words may have more opportunity for permanent lodgment. There is also a deliberateness of treatment evident beyond a casual or careless reading habit. God's Word merits this.

The Holy Spirit may have opportunity to fix and apply the passage to the heart of the counselee through still another method. It may be found richly profitable to *call attention to the person or the setting of the verse*. Offer such background as (a) where it took place, (b) to whom it refers, (c) the outcome, (d) the application for us. For example, Acts 16:31: "Believe on the Lord Jesus Christ, and thou shalt be saved, and thy house." It is of great interest that this Scripture, the door of salvation to millions, was uttered by the Apostle Paul when he was a prisoner in the Roman garrison town of Philippi. Paul had been cruelly beaten for preaching the Gospel. Then in the dead of night while Paul and Silas prayed and sang, God sent a great earthquake so that the foundations of the prison were shaken and the doors were opened and everyone's bands were loosed. Fearful that his prisoners might have escaped, thus bringing a serious penalty on himself, the jailer was ready to take his own life. But Paul urged him not to harm himself. Then to his question concerning how to be saved, the apostle gave the glorious and well known answer: "Believe on the Lord Jesus Christ, and thou shalt be saved, and thy house."

A favorite way of applying Scripture to the counselee is to *personalize it*. Indeed it is a marvelous discovery to see that not only did "God so love the world," in John 3:16, but that specifically "God so loved 'James Jones' that He gave His only begotten Son, that 'James Jones' (whosoever) who believeth in Him, should not perish but have everlasting life."

Counselors should select Scriptures carefully. While all the Bible is God's Word, it is not likely that some remote passage from Ezekiel will have the same value in pinpointing the need and provision of salvation that is seen in John 3:16, and other clear, key Scriptures that summarize the burden of the entire Bible.

Discretion in the amount of verses used is extremely important. The commercial salesman also knows that too extensive an array of goods displayed before the buyer may confuse his mind and numb his response. Better to remember that there is an absorption limit. Keep the presentation simple. Do not muddy the issue with a barrage of side items.

The counselor may wish to analyze a verse. This merely means opening it up, examining it carefully, so that it can be understood and applied. Take, for an example, the meaning of the Christian armor passages in Ephesians 6:13-17: God's Word asks us to "put on the whole armor of God." This must be personal. It is needed by *you.* You need it because you are in warfare. Armor protects and *shields* the soldier. It must be *complete* or whole. You may be badly injured if part of it is not worn. Leave no piece off. It is *not ordinary* armor. It is supernatural in its protection: *salvation* for the helmet, the shield of *faith* for the enemy's fiery darts, the preparation of the gospel of *peace* for the feet, *truth* for the loins, and *righteousness* for a breastplate. And of course, all of these through *Christ, alone.*

For those unfamiliar with Bible passages it is often a favor to suggest *marking a number of key verses in the Bible.* Marks and notations in a book are like furniture and other conveniences in a home. They become familiar and cherished. Several fine methods of Bible marking are available, and may be commended to one whose Bible will now become personally precious.

Finally, the counselee may find much blessing in *reviewing certain Scriptures.* This can be the follow-up of previous reading, memorization, or marking. It cannot fail to bring bearing upon previously discussed problems. Besides adding a measure of coherence to a counseling session, it affords opportunities to inquire into spiritual progress. It will draw Scriptural answers from the sincere, searching heart.

SELECTED SCRIPTURES FOR USE IN COUNSELING

The following portions of Scripture have been selected because of their unique suitability for counseling purposes. They may be used both in individual and group counseling.

Undoubtedly one major weakness in counseling is a lack of knowledge of *available* Scripture as it applies to human problems. The Christian counselor may wish to duplicate these portions, then add to them, thus developing his own growing source for counseling as well as writing or speaking responsibilities.

Selected Scriptures for Use in Counseling

ANXIETY AND WORRY

Psalm 43:5

Why art thou cast down, O my soul? and why art thou disquieted within me? hope in God: for I shall yet praise Him, who is the health of my countenance, and my God.

Matthew 6:31, 32

Therefore take no thought, saying, What shall we eat? or, What shall we drink? or, Wherewithal shall we be clothed?

(For after all these things do the Gentiles seek:) for your heavenly Father knoweth that ye have need of all these things.

Philippians 4:6, 7

Be careful for nothing; but in every thing by prayer and supplication with thanksgiving let your requests be made known unto God. And the peace of God, which passeth all understanding, shall keep your hearts and minds through Christ Jesus.

Philippians 4:19

But my God shall supply all your need according to His riches in glory by Christ Jesus.

I Peter 5:7

Casting all your care upon Him; for He careth for you.

BEREAVEMENT AND LOSS

Deuteronomy 31:8

And the Lord, He it is that doth go before thee; He will be with thee, He will not fail thee, neither forsake thee: fear not, neither be dismayed.

Psalm 27:10

When my father and my mother forsake me, then the Lord will take me up.

Psalm 119:50

This is my comfort in my affliction: for Thy Word hath quickened me.

Psalm 119:92

Unless Thy law had been my delights, I should then have perished in mine affliction.

II Corinthians 6:10

As sorrowful, yet always rejoicing; as poor, yet making many rich: as having nothing, yet possessing all things.

Philippians 3:8

Yea doubtless, and I count all things but loss for the excellency of the knowledge of Christ Jesus my Lord: for whom I have suffered the loss of all things, and do count them but dung, that I may win Christ.

COMFORT

Psalm 23:4

Yea, though I walk through the valley of the shadow of death, I will fear no evil: for Thou art with me; Thy rod and Thy staff they comfort me.

Lamentations 3:22, 23

It is of the Lord's mercies that we are not consumed, because his compassions fail not.

They are new every morning; great is thy faithfulness.

Matthew 5:4

Blessed are they that mourn: for they shall be comforted.

Matthew 11:28-30

Come unto me, all ye that labour and are heavy laden, and I will give you rest.

Take my yoke upon you, and learn of me; for I am meek and lowly in heart: and ye shall find rest unto your souls.

For my yoke is easy, and my burden is light.

John 14:16, 18

And I will pray the Father, and He

shall give you another Comforter, that He may abide with you for ever;

I will not leave you comfortless: I will come to you.

Romans 15:4
For whatsoever things were written aforetime were written for our learning, that we through patience and *comfort of the Scriptures* might have hope.

II Corinthians 1:3, 4
Blessed be God, even the Father of our Lord Jesus Christ, the Father of mercies, and the God of all comfort.

Who comforteth us in all our tribulations, that we may be able to comfort them which are in any trouble, by the comfort wherewith we ourselves are comforted of God.

II Thessalonians 2:16, 17
Now our Lord Jesus Christ himself, and God, even our Father, which hath loved us, and hath given us everlasting consolation and good hope through grace.

Comfort your hearts, and stablish you in every good word and work.

CONFIDENCE (Developing)

Psalm 27:3
Though an host should encamp against me, my heart shall not fear: though war should rise against me, in this will I be confident.

Proverbs 3:26
For the Lord shall be thy confidence, and shall keep thy foot from being taken.

Proverbs 14:26
In the fear of the Lord is strong confidence; and His children shall have a place of refuge.

Isaiah 30:15
For thus saith the Lord God the Holy One of Israel; In returning and rest shall ye be saved; in quietness and in confidence shall be your strength.

Galatians 6:9
And let us not be weary in well doing: for in due season we shall reap, if we faint not.

Ephesians 3:11, 12
According to the eternal purpose which

He purposed in Jesus Christ our Lord: In whom we have boldness and access with confidence by the faith of Him.

Philippians 4:13
I can do all things through Christ which strengtheneth me.

Philippians 1:6
Being confident of this very thing, that He which hath begun a good work in you will perform it until the day of Jesus Christ:

Hebrews 10:35
Cast not away therefore your confidence, which hath great recompence of reward.

I Peter 2:9
But ye are a chosen generation, a royal priesthood, an holy nation, a peculiar people; that ye should shew forth the praises of Him who hath called you out of darkness into His marvellous light.

DANGER (Protection from)

Psalm 23:4
Yea, though I walk through the valley of the shadow of death, I will fear no evil; for Thou art with me; Thy rod and Thy staff they comfort me.

Psalm 32:7
Thou art my hiding place, Thou shalt preserve me from trouble; Thou shalt compass me about with songs of deliverance.

Psalm 34:7
The angel of the Lord encampeth round about them that fear him, and delivereth them.

Psalm 34:17
The righteous cry, and the Lord heareth, and delivereth them out of all their troubles.

Psalm 34:19
Many are the afflictions of the righteous: but the Lord delivereth him out of them all.

Psalm 91:1
He that dwelleth in the secret place of the Most High shall abide under the shadow of the Almighty.

Psalm 91:11
For He shall give His angels charge over thee, to keep thee in all thy ways.
Psalm 121:8
The Lord shall preserve thy going out and thy coming in from this time forth, and even for evermore.
Isaiah 43:2
When thou passest through the waters, I will be with thee; and through the rivers, they shall not overflow thee; when thou walkest through the fire, thou shalt not be burned; neither shall the flame kindle upon thee.
Romans 14:8
For whether we live, we live unto the Lord; and whether we die, we die unto the Lord: whether we live therefore, or die, we are the Lord's.

DEATH
Psalm 23:4
Yea, though I walk through the valley of the shadow of death I will fear no evil: for thou art with me; thy rod and thy staff they comfort me.
Psalm 116:15
Precious in the sight of the Lord is the death of his saints.
Lamentations 3:32, 33
But though He cause grief, yet will He have compassion according to the multitude of His mercies.
    For He doth not afflict willingly nor grieve the children of men.
Romans 14:8
For whether we live, we live unto the Lord; and whether we die, we die unto the Lord: whether we live therefore, or die, we are the Lord's.
II Corinthians 5:1
For we know that if our earthly house of this tabernacle were dissolved, we have a building of God, an house not made with hands, eternal in the heavens.
Philippians 1:21
For me to live is Christ, and to die is gain.
I Thessalonians 5:9, 10
For God hath not appointed us to wrath, but to obtain salvation by our Lord Jesus Christ,
    Who died for us, that, whether we wake or sleep, we should live together with Him.
II Timothy 4:7, 8
I have fought a good fight, I have finished my course, I have kept the faith:
    Henceforth there is laid up for me a crown of righteousness which the Lord, the righteous judge, shall give me at that day: and not to me only, but unto all them also that love His appearing.
Hebrews 9:27
And as it is appointed unto men once to die, but after this the judgment:
Revelation 21:4
And God shall wipe away all tears from their eyes; and there shall be no more death, neither sorrow, nor crying, neither shall there be any more pain: for the former things are passed away.

DIFFICULTIES (Discipline through)
Romans 8:28
And we know that all things work together for good to them that love God, to them who are the called according to His purpose.
II Corinthians 4:17
For our light affliction, which is but for a moment, worketh for us a far more exceeding and eternal weight of glory.
Hebrews 5:8
Though he were a Son, yet learned He obedience by the things which He suffered;
Hebrews 12:7
If ye endure chastening, God dealeth with you as with sons; for what son is he whom the father chasteneth not?
Hebrews 12:11
Now no chastening for the present seemeth to be joyous, but grievous: nevertheless, afterward it yieldeth the peaceable fruit of righteousness unto them which are exercised thereby.

Revelation 3:19
And as many as I love, I rebuke and chasten: be zealous therefore and repent.

DISAPPOINTMENT

Psalm 43:5
Why art thou cast down, O my soul? and why art thou disquieted within me? hope in God: for I shall yet praise Him.

Psalm 55:22
Cast thy burden upon the Lord, and He shall sustain thee: He shall never suffer the righteous to be moved.

Psalm 126:6
He that goeth forth and weepeth, bearing precious seed, shall doubtless come again with rejoicing, bringing his sheaves with him.

John 14:27
Peace I leave with you, my peace I give unto you: not as the world giveth, give I unto you. Let not your heart be troubled, neither let it be afraid.

II Corinthians 4:8, 9
We are troubled on every side, yet not distressed; we are perplexed, but not in despair;
Persecuted, but not forsaken; cast down, but not destroyed;

DISCOURAGEMENT

Joshua 1:9
Have not I commanded thee? Be strong and of a good courage; be not afraid, neither be thou dismayed: for the Lord thy God is with thee whithersoever thou goest.

Psalm 27:14
Wait on the Lord: be of good courage, and He shall strengthen thine heart: wait, I say, on the Lord.

Psalm 43:5
Why art thou cast down, O my soul? and why art thou disquieted within me? hope in God: for I shall yet praise Him Who is the health of my countenance, and my God.

John 14:1
Let not your heart be troubled: ye believe in God, believe also in Me.

John 14:27
Peace I leave with you, my peace I give unto you: not as the world giveth, give I unto you. Let not your heart be troubled, neither let it be afraid.

John 16:33
These things I have spoken unto you, that in me ye might have peace. In the world ye shall have tribulation: but be of good cheer; I have overcome the world.

Hebrews 4:16
Let us therefore come boldly unto the throne of grace, that we may obtain mercy, and find grace to help in time of need.

I John 5:14
And this is the confidence that we have in Him, that if we ask anything according to His will, He heareth us.

FAITH

Romans 4:3
For what saith the scripture? Abraham believed God, and it was counted unto him for righteousness.

Romans 10:17
So then faith cometh by hearing, and hearing by the word of God.

Ephesians 2:8, 9
For by grace are ye saved through faith; and that not of yourselves; it is the gift of God:
Not of works, lest any man should boast.

Hebrews 11:1
Now faith is the substance of things hoped for, the evidence of things not seen.

Hebrews 11:6
But without faith it is impossible to please Him: for he that cometh to God must believe that He is, and that He is a rewarder of them that diligently seek Him.

Hebrews 12:2
Looking unto Jesus the author and finisher of our faith; Who for the joy that was set before Him endured the cross, despising the shame, and is set

down at the right hand of the throne of God.

James 1:3

Knowing this, that the trying of your faith worketh patience.

James 1:5, 6

If any of you lack wisdom, let him ask of God that giveth to all men liberally, and upbraideth not; and it shall be given him. But let him ask in faith, nothing wavering. For he that wavereth is like a wave of the sea driven with the wind and tossed.

I Peter 1:7

That the trial of your faith, being much more precious than of gold that perisheth, though it be tried with fire, might be found unto praise and honour and glory at the appearing of Jesus Christ.

FEAR

Psalm 27:1

The Lord is my light and my salvation; whom shall I fear? the Lord is the strength of my life; of whom shall I be afraid?

Psalm 56:11

In God have I put my trust: I will not be afraid what man can do unto me.

Proverbs 3:25

Be not afraid of sudden fear, neither of the desolation of the wicked, when it cometh.

Isaiah 51:12

I, even I, am He that comforteth you: who art thou, that thou shouldest be afraid of a man that shall die, and of the son of man which shall be made as grass.

John 14:27

Peace I leave with you, my peace I give unto you: not as the world giveth, give I unto you. Let not your heart be troubled, neither let it be afraid.

Romans 8:31

What shall we then say to these things? If God be for us, who can be against us?

II Timothy 1:7

For God hath not given us the spirit of fear; but of power, and of love, and of a sound mind.

I John 4:18

There is no fear in love; but perfect love casteth out fear: because fear hath torment. He that feareth is not made perfect in love.

FORGIVENESS OF SIN

Psalm 32:5

I acknowledged my sin unto Thee, and mine iniquity have I not hid. I said, I will confess my transgressions unto the Lord: and Thou forgavest the iniquity of my sin.

Psalm 51 (all)

Psalm 103:3

Who forgiveth all thine iniquities; Who healeth all thy diseases;

Proverbs 28:13

He that covereth his sins shall not prosper: but whoso confesseth and forsaketh them shall have mercy.

Isaiah 1:18

Come now, and let us reason together, saith the Lord: though your sins be as scarlet, they shall be as white as snow; though they be red like crimson, they shall be as wool.

Isaiah 55:7

Let the wicked forsake his way, and the unrighteous man his thoughts: and let him return unto the Lord, and He will have mercy upon him; and unto our God, for He will abundantly pardon.

I John 1:9

If we confess our sins, He is faithful and just to forgive us our sins, and to cleanse us from all unrighteousness.

James 5:15, 16

And the prayer of faith shall save the sick, and the Lord shall raise him up; and if he have committed sins, they shall be forgiven him.

Confess your faults one to another, and pray one for another, that ye may be healed. The effectual fervent prayer of a righteous man availeth much.

FORGIVING OTHERS

Matthew 5:44-47

But I say unto you, love your enemies, bless them that curse you, do good to them that hate you, and pray for them which despitefully use you, and persecute you.

That ye may be the children of your Father which is in heaven: for He maketh His sun to rise on the evil and on the good, and sendeth rain on the just and on the unjust.

For if ye love them which love you, what reward have ye? do not even the publicans the same?

And if ye salute your brethren only, what do ye more than others? do not even the publicans so?

Matthew 6:12
And forgive us our debts, as we forgive our debtors.

Matthew 6:14
For if ye forgive men their trespasses, your heavenly Father will also forgive you:

Mark 11:25
And when ye stand praying, forgive, if ye have ought against any: that your Father also which is in heaven may forgive you your trespasses.

Ephesians 4:32
And be ye kind one to another, tenderhearted, forgiving one another, even as God for Christ's sake hath forgiven you.

Colossians 3:13
Forbearing one another, and forgiving one another, if any man have a quarrel against any: even as Christ forgave you, so also do ye.

FRIENDS AND FRIENDLINESS

Proverbs 18:24
A man that hath friends must shew himself friendly: and there is a friend that sticketh closer than a brother.

Matthew 22:39
And the second is like unto it, Thou shalt love thy neighbor as thyself.

John 13:35
By this shall all men know that ye are my disciples, if ye have love one to another.

John 15:13
Greater love hath no man than this, that a man lay down his life for his friends.

John 15:14
Ye are my friends, if ye do whatsoever I command you.

Galatians 6:1
Brethren, if a man be overtaken in a fault, ye which are spiritual, restore such an one in the spirit of meekness; considering thyself, lest thou also be tempted.

Galatians 6:10
As we have therefore opportunity, let us do good unto all men, especially unto them who are of the household of faith.

GROWING SPIRITUALLY

Ephesians 3:17-19
That Christ may dwell in your hearts by faith; that ye, being rooted and grounded in love,

May be able to comprehend with all saints what is the breadth, and length, and depth, and height;

And to know the love of Christ, which passeth knowledge, that ye might be filled with all the fulness of God.

Colossians 1:9-11
For this cause we also, since the day we heard it, do not cease to pray for you, and to desire that ye might be filled with the knowledge of His will in all wisdom and spiritual understanding;

That ye might walk worthy of the Lord unto all pleasing, being fruitful in every good work, and increasing in the knowledge of God;

Strengthened with all might, according to His glorious power, unto all patience and longsuffering with joyfulness;

Colossians 3:16
Let the word of Christ dwell in you richly in all wisdom; teaching and admonishing one another in psalms and hymns and spiritual songs, singing with grace in your hearts to the Lord.

I Timothy 4:15
Meditate upon these things; give thyself wholly to them; that thy profiting may appear to all.

II Timothy 2:15
Study to shew thyself approved unto God, a workman that needeth not to be ashamed, rightly dividing the word of truth.

I Peter 2:2
As newborn babes, desire the sincere milk of the Word. that ye may grow thereby.

II Peter 1:5-8
And beside this, giving all diligence, add to your faith virtue; and to virtue knowledge;

And to knowledge temperance; and to temperance patience; and to patience godliness;

And to godliness brotherly kindness; and to brotherly kindness charity.

For if these things be in you, and abound, they make you that ye shall neither be barren nor unfruitful in the knowledge of our Lord Jesus Christ.

II Peter 3:18
But grow in grace, and in the knowledge of our Lord and Saviour Jesus Christ. To Him be glory both now and for ever. Amen.

GUIDANCE

Psalm 32:8
I will instruct thee and teach thee in the way which thou shalt go: I will guide thee with mine eye.

Isaiah 30:21
And thine ears shall hear a word behind thee, saying. This is the way, walk ye in it, when ye turn to the right hand, and when ye turn to the left.

Isaiah 58:11
And the Lord shall guide thee continually, and satisfy thy soul in drought, and make fat thy bones: and thou shalt be like a watered garden, and like a spring of water, whose waters fail not.

Luke 1:79
To give light to them that sit in darkness and in the shadow of death, to guide our feet in the way of peace.

John 16:13
Howbeit when He, the Spirit of truth, is come, He will guide you into all

truth: for He shall not speak of Himself: but whatsoever He shall hear, that shall He speak: and He will show you things to come.

HELP AND CARE

II Chronicles 16:9
For the eyes of the Lord run to and fro throughout the whole earth, to shew Himself strong in the behalf of them whose heart is perfect toward Him. Herein thou hast done foolishly: therefore from henceforth thou shalt have wars.

Psalm 34:7
The angel of the Lord encampeth round about them that fear him, and delivereth them.

Psalm 37:5
Commit thy way unto the Lord; trust also in Him; and He shall bring it to pass.

Psalm 37:24
Though he fall, he shall not be utterly cast down: for the Lord upholdeth him with His hand.

Psalm 55:22
Cast thy burden upon the Lord, and He shall sustain thee: He shall never suffer the righteous to be moved.

Psalm 91:4
He shall cover thee with his feathers, and under His wings shalt thou trust: His truth shall be thy shield and buckler.

Isaiah 50:9
Behold, the Lord God will help me; who is he that shall condemn me? Lo, they all shall wax old as a garment; the moth shall eat them up.

Isaiah 54:17
No weapon that is formed against thee shall prosper; and every tongue that shall rise against thee in judgment thou shalt condemn. This is the heritage of the servants of the Lord, and their righteousness is of me, saith the Lord.

Hebrews 4:16
Let us therefore come boldly unto the throne of grace, that we may obtain

mercy, and find grace to help in time of need.

Hebrews 13:5
Let your conversation be without covetousness; and be content with such things as you have: for He hath said, I will never leave thee, nor forsake thee.

Hebrews 13:6
So that we may boldly say, The Lord is my helper, and I will not fear what man shall do unto me.

I Peter 5:7
Casting all your care upon Him; for He careth for you.

LONELINESS

Psalm 23

Psalm 27:10
When my father and my mother forsake me, then the Lord will take me up.

Isaiah 41:10
Fear thou not; for I am with thee: be not dismayed; for I am thy God: I will strengthen thee; yea, I will help thee; yea, I will uphold thee with the right hand of My righteousness.

Matthew 28:20
Teaching them to observe all things whatsoever I have commanded you: and, lo, I am with you alway, even unto the end of the world. Amen.

Hebrews 13:5
Let your conversation be without covetousness; and be content with such things as ye have: for He hath said, I will never leave thee, nor forsake thee.

LOVE (God's)

John 3:16
For God so loved the world, that He gave His only begotten Son, that whosoever believeth in Him should not perish, but have everlasting life.

John 15:9
As the Father hath loved me, so have I loved you: continue ye in my love.

Romans 5:8
But God commendeth His love toward us, in that while we were yet sinners, Christ died for us.

Romans 8:38, 39
For I am persuaded that neither death, nor life, nor angels, nor principalities, nor powers, nor things present, nor things to come, nor height, nor depth, nor any other creature, shall be able to separate us from the love of God, which is in Christ Jesus our Lord.

I John 3:1
Behold, what manner of love the Father hath bestowed upon us, that we should be called the sons of God: therefore, the world knoweth us not, because it knew Him not.

OBEDIENCE

I Samuel 15:22
And Samuel said, Hath the Lord as great delight in burnt offerings and sacrifices, as in obeying the voice of the Lord? Behold, to obey is better than sacrifice, and to hearken than the fat of rams.

Psalm 111:10
The fear of the Lord is the beginning of wisdom: a good understanding have all they that do His commandments: His praise endureth for ever.

Psalm 119:2
Blessed are they that keep His testimonies, and that seek Him with the whole heart.

Matthew 6:24
No man can serve two masters; for either he will hate the one, and love the other; or else he will hold to the one, and despise the other. Ye cannot serve God and mammon.

John 14:15
If ye love me, keep my commandments.

John 14:21
He that hath my commandments, and keepeth them, he it is that loveth me: and he that loveth Me shall be loved of my Father, and I will love Him, and will manifest myself to him.

James 2:10
For whosoever shall keep the whole law, and yet offend in one point, he is guilty of all,

I John 3:22

And whatsoever we ask, we receive of Him, because we keep His commandments, and do those things that are pleasing in His sight.

PEACE OF MIND

Isaiah 26:3

Thou wilt keep him in perfect peace, whose mind is stayed on thee: because he trusteth in Thee.

John 14:27

Peace I leave with you, My peace I give unto you: not as the world giveth, give I unto you. Let not your heart be troubled, neither let it be afraid.

John 16:33

These things I have spoken unto you, that in Me ye might have peace. In the world ye shall have tribulation: but be of good cheer; I have overcome the world.

Romans 5:1

Therefore being justified by faith, we have peace with God through our Lord Jesus Christ.

Philippians 4:7

And the peace of God, which passeth all understanding, shall keep your hearts and minds through Christ Jesus.

Colossians 3:15

And let the peace of God rule in your hearts, to the which also ye are called in one body; and be ye thankful.

PERSECUTION

Matthew 5:10, 11

Blessed are they which are persecuted for righteousness' sake: for their's is the kingdom of heaven.

Blessed are ye, when men shall revile you, and persecute you, and shall say all manner of evil against you falsely, for my sake.

Matthew 10:22

And ye shall be hated of all men for My Name's sake; but he that endureth to the end shall be saved.

Acts 5:41

And they departed from the presence of the council, rejoicing that they were counted worthy to suffer shame for His name.

Acts 9:16

For I will shew him how great things he must suffer for my name's sake.

Romans 8:17

And if children, then heirs; heirs of God, and joint-heirs with Christ; if so be that we suffer with Him, that we may be also glorified together.

II Timothy 3:12

Yea, and all that will live godly in Christ Jesus shall suffer persecution.

Hebrews 11:25

Choosing rather to suffer affliction with the people of God, than to enjoy the pleasures of sin for a season;

1 Peter 2:20

For what glory is it, if, when ye be buffeted for your faults, ye shall take it patiently? but if, when ye do well, and suffer for it, ye take it patiently, this is acceptable with God.

PRAISE AND GRATITUDE

I Samuel 12:24

Only fear the Lord, and serve Him in truth with all your heart: for consider how great things He hath done for you.

Psalm 34:1

I will bless the Lord at all times: His praise shall continually be in my mouth.

Psalm 50:23

Whoso offereth praise glorifieth me: and to him that ordereth his conversation aright will I shew the salvation of God.

Psalm 51:15

O Lord, open thou my lips; and my mouth shall shew forth thy praise.

Psalm 69:30

I will praise the name of God with a song, and will magnify Him with thanksgiving.

Psalm 107:8

Oh that men would praise the Lord for His goodness, and for His wonderful works to the children of men!

Psalm 139:14

I will praise thee; for I am fearfully and wonderfully made: marvelous are Thy works; and that my soul knoweth right well.

Ephesians 5:20
Giving thanks always for all things unto God and the Father in the Name of our Lord Jesus Christ.

Hebrews 13:6
So that we may boldly say, The Lord is my helper, and I will not fear what man shall do unto me.

Hebrews 13:15
By him therefore let us offer the sacrifice of praise to God continually, that is, the fruit of our lips, giving thanks to His name.

PROVISION

Psalm 34:10
The young lions do lack, and suffer hunger: but they that seek the Lord shall not want any good thing.

Psalm 37:3, 4
Trust in the Lord, and do good; so shalt thou dwell in the land, and verily thou shalt be fed.

Delight thyself also in the Lord; and He shall give thee the desires of thine heart.

Psalm 84:11
For the Lord God is a sun and shield: the Lord will give grace and glory: no good thing will He withhold from them that walk uprightly.

Isaiah 58:11
And the Lord shall guide thee continually, and satisfy thy soul in drought, and make fat thy bones: and thou shalt be like a watered garden, and like a spring of water, whose waters fail not.

Matthew 6:33
But seek ye first the kingdom of God, and His righteousness; and all these things shall be added unto you.

II Corinthians 9:8
And God is able to make all grace abound toward you; that ye, always having all sufficiency in all things, may abound to every good work.

Philippians 4:19
But my God shall supply all your need

according to His riches in glory by Christ Jesus.

RETURN OF CHRIST

Luke 21:36
Watch ye therefore, and pray always, that ye may be accounted worthy to escape all these things that shall come to pass, and to stand before the Son of Man.

Acts 1:11
Which also said, Ye men of Galilee, why stand ye gazing up into heaven? this same Jesus, which is taken up from you into heaven, shall so come in like manner as ye have seen Him go into heaven.

I Thessalonians 4:16-18
For the Lord Himself shall descend from heaven with a shout, with the voice of the archangel, and with the trump of God: and the dead in Christ shall rise first:

Then we which are alive and remain shall be caught up together with them in the clouds, to meet the Lord in the air: and so shall we ever be with the Lord.

Wherefore comfort one another with these words.

Titus 2:13
Looking for that blessed hope, and the glorious appearing of the great God and our Saviour Jesus Christ;

I John 3:2, 3
Beloved, now are we the sons of God, and it doth not yet appear what we shall be: but we know that, when He shall appear, we shall be like Him; for we shall see Him as He is.

And every man that hath this hope in Him purifieth himself, even as he is pure.

SICKNESS

Psalm 41:3
The Lord will strengthen him upon the bed of languishing: thou wilt make all his bed in his sickness.

Psalm 103:3
Who forgiveth all thine iniquities; Who healeth all thy diseases;

Matthew 4:23
And Jesus went about all Galilee, teaching in their synagogues, and preaching the gospel of the kingdom, and healing all manner of sickness and all manner of disease among the people.

John 11:4
When Jesus heard that, He said, This sickness is not unto death, but for the glory of God, that the Son of God might be glorified thereby.

James 5:15, 16
And the prayer of faith shall save the sick, and the Lord shall raise him up: and if he have committed sins, they shall be forgiven him.

Confess your faults one to another, and pray one for another, that ye may be healed. The effectual fervent prayer of a righteous man availeth much.

SIN

Isaiah 53:5, 6
But he was wounded for our transgressions, He was bruised for our iniquities: the chastisement of our peace was upon Him; and with His stripes we are healed.

All we like sheep have gone astray; we have turned every one to his own way; and the Lord hath laid on Him the iniquity of us all.

Isaiah 59:1, 2
Behold, the Lord's hand is not shortened, that it cannot save; neither His ear heavy, that it cannot hear:

But your iniquities have separated between you and your God, and your sins have hid His face from you, that He will not hear.

John 8:34
Jesus answered them, Verily, verily, I say unto you, Whosoever committeth sin is the servant of sin.

Romans 3:23
For all have sinned, and come short of the glory of God.

Romans 6:23
For the wages of sin is death; but the gift of God is eternal life through Jesus Christ our Lord.

Galatians 6:7, 8
Be not deceived; God is not mocked: for whatsoever a man soweth, that shall he also reap.

For he that soweth to his flesh shall of the flesh reap corruption; but he that soweth to the Spirit shall of the Spirit reap life everlasting.

SORROW

Proverbs 10:22
The blessing of the Lord, it maketh rich, and He addeth no sorrow with it.

Isaiah 53:4
Surely He hath borne our griefs, and carried our sorrows: yet we did esteem Him stricken, smitten of God, and afflicted.

John 16:22
And ye now therefore have sorrow: but I will see you again, and your heart shall rejoice, and your joy no man taketh from you.

II Corinthians 6:10
As sorrowful, yet always rejoicing; as poor, yet making many rich; as having nothing, and yet possessing all things.

I Thessalonians 4:13
But I would not have you to be ignorant, brethren, concerning them which are asleep, that ye sorrow not, even as others which have no hope.

Revelation 21:4
And God shall wipe away all tears from their eyes; and there shall be no more death, neither sorrow, nor crying, neither shall there be any more pain: for the former things are passed away.

STRENGTH

Deuteronomy 33:25
As thy days, so shall thy strength be.

Psalm 27:14
Wait on the Lord: be of good courage, and He shall strengthen thine heart: wait, I say, on the Lord.

Psalm 28:7
The Lord is my strength and my shield: my heart trusted in Him, and I am

helped: therefore my heart greatly rejoiceth; and with my song will I praise Him.

Isaiah 40:29, 31

He giveth power to the faint; and to them that have no might He increaseth strength.

But they that wait upon the Lord shall renew their strength; they shall mount up with wings as eagles; they shall run, and not be weary; and they shall walk, and not faint.

Isaiah 41:10

Fear thou not; for I am with thee: be not dismayed; for I am thy God: I will strengthen thee; yea, I will help thee; yea, I will uphold thee with the right hand of my righteousness.

II Corinthians 12:9

And He said unto me, My grace is sufficient for thee: for My strength is made perfect in weakness. Most gladly therefore will I rather glory in my infirmities, that the power of Christ may rest upon me.

Philippians 4:13

I can do all things through Christ which strengtheneth me.

SUFFERING

Romans 8:18

For I reckon that the sufferings of this present time are not worthy to be compared with the glory which shall be revealed in us.

II Corinthians 1:5

For as the sufferings of Christ abound in us, so our consolation also aboundeth by Christ.

Philippians 1:29

For unto you it is given in the behalf of Christ, not only to believe on Him, but also to suffer for His sake.

Philippians 3:10

That I may know Him, and the power of His resurrection, and the fellowship of His sufferings, being made conformable unto His death;

II Timothy 2:12

If we suffer, we shall also reign with Him: if we deny Him, He also will deny us:

I Peter 2:19

For this is thankworthy, if a man for conscience toward God endure grief, suffering wrongfully.

I Peter 4:12, 13

Beloved, think it not strange concerning the fiery trial which is to try you, as though some strange thing happened unto you: But rejoice, inasmuch as ye are partakers of Christ's sufferings; that, when His glory shall be revealed, ye may be glad also, with exceeding joy.

I Peter 4:16

Yet if any man suffer as a Christian, let him not be ashamed; but let him glorify God on this behalf.

I Peter 5:10

But the God of all grace, who hath called us unto His eternal glory by Christ Jesus, after that ye have suffered a while, make you perfect, stablish, strengthen, settle you.

TEMPTATION

I Corinthians 10:12, 13

Wherefore let him that thinketh he standeth take heed lest he fall. There hath no temptation taken you but such as is common to man: but God is faithful, who will not suffer you to be tempted above that ye are able; but will with the temptation also make a way to escape, that ye may be able to bear it.

Hebrews 2:18

For in that He Himself hath suffered being tempted, He is able to succour them that are tempted.

James 1:2, 3

My brethren, count it all joy when ye fall into divers temptations, knowing this, that the trying of your faith worketh patience.

James 1:12

Blessed is the man that endureth temptation: for when he is tried, he shall receive the crown of life, which the Lord hath promised to them that love Him.

James 1:14
But every man is tempted, when he is drawn away of his own lust, and enticed.

I Peter 1:6
Wherein ye greatly rejoice, though now for a reason, if need be, ye are in heaviness through manifold temptations:

II Peter 2:9
The Lord knoweth how to deliver the godly out of temptations, and to reserve the unjust unto the day of judgment to be punished.

Jude 24
Now unto Him that is able to keep you from falling, and to present you faultless before the presence of His glory with exceeding joy.

TRUSTING

Psalm 5:11
But let all those that put their trust in thee rejoice; let them ever shout for joy, because thou defendest them: let them also that love thy name be joyful in Thee.

Psalm 18:2
The Lord is my rock, and my fortress, and my deliverer; my God, my strength, in Whom I will trust; my buckler, and the horn of my salvation, and my high tower.

Psalm 37:5
Commit thy way unto the Lord; trust also in Him; and He shall bring it to pass.

Proverbs 3:5, 6
Trust in the Lord with all thine heart; and lean not unto thine own understanding.

In all thy ways acknowledge Him, and He shall direct thy paths.

Isaiah 12:2
Behold, God is my salvation; I will trust, and not be afraid: for the Lord Jehovah is my strength and my song; He also is become my salvation.

VICTORY

II Chronicles 32:8
With him is an arm of flesh; but with us is the Lord our God to help us, and to fight our battles. And the people rested themselves upon the words of Hezekiah king of Judah.

Romans 8:37
Nay, in all these things we are more than conquerors through Him that loved us.

I Corinthians 15:57
But thanks be to God, which giveth us the victory through our Lord Jesus Christ.

II Corinthians 2:14
Now thanks be unto God, which always causeth us to triumph in Christ, and maketh manifest the savour of his knowledge by us in every place.

II Timothy 2:19
Nevertheless the foundation of God standeth sure, having this seal, The Lord knoweth them that are His. And, Let every one that nameth the name of Christ depart from iniquity.

I John 5:4
For whatsoever is born of God overcometh the world: and this is the victory that overcometh the world, even our faith.

Revelation 3:5
He that overcometh, the same shall be clothed in white raiment; and I will not blot out his name out of the book of life, but I will confess his name before my Father, and before His angels.

Revelation 21:7
He that overcometh shall inherit all things; and I will be his God and he shall be My son.

SELECTED SCRIPTURES FOR USE IN SOUL WINNING

As the believer studies God's Word and witnesses for Him, he is led to certain portions of Scripture which he uses effectively. These

Bible verses vary somewhat from person to person. Yet a study of Scriptures used in soul winning indicates that certain portions are used frequently by nearly all personal workers.

The following portions of Scripture have been selected for use by the soul winner because they represent many of the verses that God has honored in drawing men and women to Himself.

MAN'S NEED OF SALVATION

Isaiah 64:6
But we are all as an unclean thing, and all our righteousnesses are as filthy rags; and we all do fade as a leaf; and our iniquities, like the wind, have taken us away.

Romans 3:10
As it is written, There is none righteous, no not one.

Romans 3:23
For all have sinned, and come short of the glory of God.

Romans 5:12
Wherefore, as by one man sin entered into the world, and death by sin; and so death passed upon all men, for that all have sinned.

Romans 6:23
For the wages of sin is death; but the gift of God is eternal life through Jesus Christ our Lord.

Hebrews 9:27
And as it is appointed unto men once to die, and after this the judgment.

I John 1:10
If we say we have not sinned, we make Him a liar, and His word is not in us.

JESUS CHRIST IS THE SAVIOUR OF THE WORLD

Matthew 1:21
And she shall bring forth a son, and thou shalt call His name Jesus, for He shall save His people from their sins.

Luke 19:10
For the Son of man is come to seek and to save that which was lost.

John 3:16
For God so loved the world, that He gave His only begotten Son, that who-soever believeth in Him should not perish, but have everlasting life.

John 14:6
Jesus saith unto him, I am the way, the truth, and the life: no man cometh unto the Father, but by me.

Acts 4:12
Neither is there salvation in any other; for there is none other name under heaven given among men, whereby we must be saved.

Romans 5:8
But God commendeth His love toward us, in that, while we were yet sinners, Christ died for us.

Ephesians 1:7
In whom we have redemption through His blood, the forgiveness of sins, according to the riches of His grace.

I John 5:12
He that hath the Son hath life; and he that hath not the Son of God hath not life.

GOD'S WORD GIVES THE PLAN OF SALVATION

Isaiah 55:7
Let the wicked forsake his way and the unrighteous man his thoughts; and let him return unto the Lord and He will have mercy upon him; and to our God for He will abundantly pardon.

John 1:12
But as many as received Him, to them gave He power to become the sons of God, even to them that believe on His name.

John 3:3
Jesus answered and said unto him, Verily, verily, I say unto thee, except a man be born again he cannot see the Kingdom of God.

John 5:24

Verily, verily, I say unto you, he that heareth My word, and believeth on Him that sent Me, hath everlasting life, and shall not come into condemnation; but is passed from death unto life.

Romans 10:9

That if thou shalt confess with thy mouth the Lord Jesus, and shalt believe in thine heart that God hath raised Him from the dead, thou shalt be saved.

Ephesians 2:8, 9

For by grace are ye saved through faith; and that not of yourselves: it is the gift of God: not of works, lest any man should boast.

Titus 3:5

Not by works of righteousness which we have done, but according to His mercy He saved us, by the washing of regeneration, and renewing of the Holy Spirit.

I John 1:9

If we confess our sins, He is faithful and just to forgive us our sins, and to cleanse us from all unrighteousness.

Revelation 3:20

Behold, I stand at the door, and knock, if any man hear my voice, and open the door, I will come in to him, and will sup with him, and he with Me.

ASSURANCE OF SALVATION

Matthew 24:35

Heaven and earth shall pass away, but my words shall not pass away.

John 5:24

Verily, verily, I say unto you, he that heareth My word and believeth on Him that sent me, hath everlasting life, and shall not come into condemnation; but is passed from death unto life.

John 6:37

All that the Father giveth me shall come to me; and him that cometh to me I will in no wise cast out.

John 10:28

And I give unto them eternal life, and they shall never perish, neither shall any man pluck them out of my hand.

John 20:31

But these are written that ye might believe that Jesus is the Christ, the Son of God; and that believing ye might have life through His name.

Romans 8:16

The Spirit itself beareth witness with our spirit, that we are the children of God.

I John 5:13

These things have I written unto you that believe on the name of the Son of God, that ye may know that ye have eternal life.

OVERCOMING TEMPTATION

Isaiah 41:10

Fear thou not; for I am with thee: be not dismayed; for I am thy God: I will strengthen thee; yea, I will help thee; yea, I will uphold thee with the right hand of my righteousness.

Matthew 26:41

Watch and pray, that ye enter not into temptation: the spirit indeed is willing, but the flesh is weak.

I Corinthians 10:13

There hath no temptation taken you but such as is common to man: but God is faithful, who will not suffer you to be tempted above that ye are able; but will with the temptation also make a way to escape, that ye may be able to bear it.

Philippians 1:6

Being confident of this very thing, that He which hath begun a good work in you will perform it until the day of Jesus Christ.

II Thessalonians 3:3

But the Lord is faithful, who shall stablish you and keep you from evil.

II Peter 2:9

The Lord knoweth how to deliver the godly out of temptations, and to reserve the unjust unto the day of judgment to be punished.

LIVING THE CHRISTIAN LIFE

Psalm 119:11
Thy Word have I hid in mine heart, that I might not sin against Thee.

John 15:7
If ye abide in me, and my words abide in you, ye shall ask what ye will, and it shall be done unto you.

II Corinthians 5:17
Therefore if any man be in Christ, he is a new creature: old things are passed away; behold, all things are become new.

Colossians 2:6
As ye have therefore received Christ Jesus the Lord, so walk ye in Him.

I Peter 2:2
As newborn babes, desire the sincere milk of the Word, that ye may grow thereby.

I John 1:7
But if we walk in the light, as He is in the light, we have fellowship one with another, and the blood of Jesus Christ His Son cleanseth us from all sin.

CHRISTIAN FELLOWSHIP

Matthew 18:20
For where two or three are gathered together in My name, there am I in the midst of them.

John 13:34
A new commandment I give unto you, That ye love one another; as I have loved you, that ye also love one another.

Acts 2:42
And they continued stedfastly in the apostles' doctrine and fellowship, and in breaking of bread, and in prayers.

Hebrews 10:25
Not forsaking the assembling of yourselves together, as the manner of some is; but exhorting one another: and so much the more, as ye see the day approaching.

I John 1:3
That which we have seen and heard declare we unto you, that ye also may have fellowship with us: and truly our fellowship is with the Father, and with His Son Jesus Christ.

WITNESSING FOR JESUS CHRIST

Psalm 66:16
Come and hear, all ye that fear God, and I will declare what he hath done for my soul.

Mark 5:19
Go home to thy friends, and tell them how great things the Lord hath done for thee, and hath had compassion on thee.

Luke 24:48
And ye are witnesses of these things.

Acts 1:8
But ye shall receive power, after that the Holy Ghost is come upon you: and ye shall be witnesses unto me both in Jerusalem, and in all Judaea, and in Samaria, and unto the uttermost part of the earth.

32 | TERMS

ADJUSTMENT MECHANISMS: Indirect and typically unconscious ways of gratifying or compensating for a repressed desire. Attempts to deal with CONFLICT. Such MECHANISMS are used to some extent by everyone. They are attempts to protect and enhance the person's SELF CONCEPT.* (See MENTAL MECHANISMS).

ADOLESCENCE: The period when a child is *becoming an adult*. It begins at PUBERTY (approximately 10-14) and ends when the person comes of age (approximately 17-19).

AGGRESSION: Attack upon an object, person or idea that stands in a person's way. This attack may be (1) an actual *physical* one or (2) a *verbal* one. It may take place (1) in REALITY or (2) in FANTASY. A common example of verbal AGGRESSION in REALITY is when a person openly attacks the validity of the Bible because its precepts stand in the way of his committing some favorite sin.

ALCOHOLISM: Addiction to alcohol. A diseased condition caused by habitually drinking too much alcoholic liquor. (Removal of inhibition at the expense of lowering of efficiency, neglect of responsibility.) It threatens mental and physical health. In severe cases it may lead to an alcoholic PSYCHOSIS. Usually associated with one or more of the following PERSONALITY characteristics: (1) *anxious* — worried, insecure (2) *moody* — easily depressed (3) *sensitive* — touchy (4) *withdrawn* — alone, unwanted (5) *resentful* — chip on shoulder (6) *un-*

* Capitalized words are defined in this glossary.

reliable — quitter, failure (7) *dependent* — needs to lean on people, finds companionship with other alcoholics at bar.

AMBIVALENCE: A conflicting attitude toward an object — more than one feeling at the same time. More or less balanced *love* and *hate* toward a person, idea or thing. Positive and negative feelings are approximately equal. Lasting decisions are made virtually impossible: The person vacillates constantly between alternatives. (See James 1:8.) Decisive actions can be taken only after the successful SUPPRESSION of either the positive or the negative aspect. Ambivalent people often act on impulse to keep from being deadlocked by their conflicts, thus making them unable to act at all.

AMNESIA: Pathological, partial or total loss of memory. In extreme cases a person may forget his own name or identity. As to cause, there are two main types: (1) organic: due to brain damage or disease. For example, a man's skull was fractured in an auto accident. He developed complete and permanent AMNESIA for the day preceding the accident. (2) PSYCHO-LOGICAL (emotional): due to severe emotional shock. For example, a woman saw her husband shot to death by a robber. She developed total AMNESIA She could not even remember her name. After a period of time her memory returned. (See DISSOCIATION.)

ANXIETY: A state of being uneasy, apprehensive, or worried about what may happen. FEAR many times without a real cause or far out of proportion to the real cause. Produces the same basic bodily changes as actual FEAR. However, because ANXIETY has its main source inside the mind, it is often harder to expel than FEAR. ANXIETY typically leads a person to use DEFENSE MECHANISMS. When these are used excessively, mental illness may result. The Bible gives an excellent anti-dote for ANXIETY (Philippians 4:6, 7).

APTITUDE: An inborn, potential ability to learn a specific kind of activity. Some types of aptitudes are: mechanical, clerical, numerical (arithmetical), abstract reasoning, verbal (word usage) and space perception. APTITUDE should not be con-fused with ACHIEVEMENT. ACHIEVEMENT means amount already learned in a particular field. APTITUDE is potential.

Probably no one ever achieves the level of his APTITUDE. God holds us responsible for using the APTITUDES He has given us (Matthew 25:14-30).

BED WETTING (ENURESIS): Involuntary urination while asleep continued past the usual age (4-5). Sometimes associated with EMOTIONAL IMMATURITY. See SLEEPWALKING.

CATHARSIS: The healthful (THERAPEUTIC) "talking out" of painful ideas to an understanding listener. It is like an emotional excretion of material that had been poisoning the mind. Hence, the word, CATHARSIS. As such, it may be disagreeable for an inexperienced counselor to accept. However, accepting the material without getting upset and encouraging a complete elimination is *most important* if a counselor is to help the counselee face his problem. Confession of sin can be a form of CATHARSIS and thus can have psychological as well as spiritual benefits. (Compare I John 1:9 — *catharize* — to cleanse.)

COMPENSATION: A MENTAL MECHANISM, often operating on an UNCONSCIOUS level. A person attempts to make up in some other way for a real or imagined deficiency. An individual often covers up or disguises an undesirable trait by calling into play a desirable one and exaggerating its manifestations. This may be healthy. Some people, for example, compensate for childhood weakness and develop a robust physique and personality as well. Excessive COMPENSATION, however, can lead to severe personality problems.

COMPULSION: An apparently meaningless impulse to do a certain thing. A person may compulsively count the steps in a·flight of stairs. He may count the cracks in the pavement or feel he must step on each one. Mild COMPULSIONS of this sort are common in everyday life. COMPULSIONS are sometimes an attempt to *substitute* a harmless act for an *unconscious* unacceptable impulse. Failure to carry out a compulsive act "to the letter" often results in ANXIETY. People who have *excessively* rigid standards are called *compulsive personalities* (see PERFECTIONISM). More serious COMPULSIONS are associated with mental illness. COMPULSIONS to do illegal acts are called *impulsions.* Examples are *Kleptomania* (COMPULSIVE stealing) and *Pyromania* (COMPULSIVE setting of fires).

CONFLICT: Stress characterized by incompatible desires, needs or environmental demands. The competition of two or more contradictory impulses. This is usually accompanied by emotional tension.

CONVERSION: An UNCONSCIOUS process. By it, inner CONFLICTS, *instead* of leading to ANXIETY, are *converted* into physical, physiological and psychological symptoms. This psychological term should not be confused with spiritual conversion — the process of salvation.

COUNSELING: The use of various techniques to help a person solve a CONFLICT or better his life adjustment. Used where the problems are basically SITUATIONAL. Problems involving mental illness require PSYCHOTHERAPY — treatment by a trained therapist.

DAYDREAMING: Wishful or purposeless thinking during waking hours. A form of FANTASY. Everyone does some DAYDREAMING. This is normal. But when DAYDREAMING becomes a constant *substitute for action,* mental health may be in danger. An increase in DAYDREAMING can be expected during ADOLESCENCE when desires are strong but there are many barriers to fulfillment and self-confidence is shaky. However, *excessive* DAYDREAMING may be a symptom of a deeper problem.

DEFENSE MECHANISMS: See MENTAL MECHANISMS.

DEFENSIVENESS: Being "on guard." A natural tendency to show only one's "good side." DEFENSIVENESS may stand in the way of gaining INSIGHT. We may be DEFENSIVE when meeting a stranger or when forced to talk about intimate matters. When DEFENSIVENESS has been reduced to a minimum, there is RAPPORT. (See INSIGHT.)

DELUSION: A belief which is out of keeping with REALITY and the level of maturity of the person who holds it. May be a sign of PSYCHOSIS. There are several kinds of DELUSIONS. The most common are: (1) DELUSIONS of *grandeur:* exaggerated ideas of one's importance. (2) DELUSIONS of *persecution:* ideas that one has been *singled out* for persecution. (3) DELUSIONS of *reference*: assuming wrongly that other people are "talking about me." (See PARANOIA.)

DENIAL: A MENTAL MECHANISM. A person disowns an intolerable thought, wish or need. He actually believes he does not have it. An effort to allay ANXIETY and resolve CONFLICT. Everyone uses this MECHANISM from time to time. However, it is usually ineffective in the long run. It can lead to serious mental illness when overused. DENIAL is often supported by PROJECTION and FANTASY. The only real cure for DENIAL is *confession* (owning up to one's faults). (See I John 1:8-10.)

DEPRESSION: Undue sadness, dejection or melancholy. Feeling of worthlessness and guilt and often, apprehension. Stems primarily from inner emotional causes. There is usually no (or an inappropriate) *outer* cause. DEPRESSION is unrealistic grief as ANXIETY is unrealistic fear. Some PERSONALITIES are characteristically mildly DEPRESSED and pessimistic. These are called *depressive personalities*. More serious DEPRESSION is a symptom of a NEUROSIS or PSYCHOSIS. It sometimes leads to suicide. (See INVOLUTIONAL PSYCHOSIS and MANIC-DEPRESSIVE PSYCHOSIS.)

DISILLUSIONMENT: To free from illusion. When a child is young he has little *past experience* in terms of which to judge what he learns. Thus he accepts fact and fiction alike. Later, when his reasoning powers have come of age, he re-examines many of the things he had taken for granted. The fairy castles crumble. With them, SPIRITUAL values that have not been thought through and firmly established may topple as well. The pendulum swings — from the child's dependence on external authorities (parents, teachers) to the ADOLESCENT's often premature dependence on *self* (and PEERS). Some DISILLUSIONMENT is normal. The child's dream-world is usually prettier than the real. But severe DISILLUSIONMENT may lead to bitterness, pessimism and HOSTILITY toward authority. Worse still, it may cause REGRESSION, flight into FANTASY and possibly SCHIZOPHRENIA. Parents can minimize DISILLUSIONMENT in their children by being straightforward and honest with them (on the level of their understanding) from the start.

Terms

DISORIENTATION: Mental confusion with respect to time, place or person. When a person is DISORIENTED, he has lost awareness of his own position with respect to one or more of these three spheres:
(1) Time: date and approximate time of day
(2) Place: *where* he is
(3) Person: *who* he is, his family and friends
DISORIENTATION is often a sign of acute emotional shock or PSYCHOSIS.

DISPLACEMENT: A MENTAL MECHANISM. Transfer of an emotional attitude or symbolic meaning from one object or concept to another. For example: Hostility aroused by one's boss may be taken out on one's wife. DISPLACEMENT occurs in the formation of a PHOBIA.

DISSOCIATION: Separation of mental processes in such a way that they become split off from the main personality or they lose their normal thought effect relationships. May result in AMNESIA, fainting, FUGUE state or the rare "alternating (or multiple) PERSONALITY" (Jekyl-Hyde). Associated with NEUROSES (severe mental illnesses).

DRIVES: (See PHYSIOLOGICAL DRIVES.)

EMOTION: An experience or mental state characterized by a strong degree of feeling and usually accompanied by motor expression often quite intense. Any of various complex reactions with both psychical and physical manifestations as fear, anger, love and hate. In mental illness, the cause of the EMOTION may not be known to the person himself. Continual unpleasant EMOTIONAL stimulation may do permanent harm to the body because the body is kept at "battle stations," ready for a *non-existent* emergency situation at all times. As the emotional cause is *inside,* these outside defenses are useless and place a great drain on the body's vitality.

EMOTIONAL CONFLICTS: See CONFLICT.

EMOTIONAL IMMATURITY: Incomplete development of EMOTIONAL control. Failure to develop normal adult degrees of independence and self-reliance, and inability to maintain equilibrium under stresses which most people can meet satisfactorily. Childish tantrums, sulking, crying, attention-getting and similar childish behavior. Many who are adults in a physical sense are more or less EMOTIONALLY IMMATURE. This may not be apparent to a person's casual acquaintances but will be obvious to family and close friends. Serious EMOTIONAL IMMATURITY may border on mental illness but usually it merely makes the person concerned (and his friends) unhappy.

EMOTIONAL TENSION: An aroused EMOTIONAL state (anger, fear, etc.) in which the body's *preparation for action* has not been *consummated* in action. INHIBITION of the basic EMOTIONAL response (Anger — to strike out; Fear — to run away) tends to keep the body in an *emergency* state instead of letting it return to normal. Continued too long or repeated often, EMOTIONAL TENSION can cause psychological and physiological harm.

EMOTIONALIZED ATTITUDES: Attitudes which have *emotional* rather than *rational* causes. Although often very strong, such attitudes cannot be logically defended even though an attempt to RATIONALIZE (make them logical) will usually be made. For example, George dislikes a certain race. He can give no reason for this attitude. He believes that all men are equal in God's sight. Yet he cannot get rid of this EMOTIONALIZED ATTITUDE. Its roots are in early childhood. He accepted it from his parents while too young to see its unreasonableness.

EMPATHY: *Intellectual* (objective) awareness and understanding of the feelings, emotions and behavior of another person. Differs from SYMPATHY which is the emotional (subjective) IDENTIFICATION with the feelings and behavior of another. For example, a minister could *empathize* with a man who had committed adultery. He could understand and accept the needs, conflicts and emotions which led to the act. However, his convictions would prevent him from sympathizing (emotionally agreeing) with this sin. Christ empathized with *sinners* whose *sin* He condemned (John 8:3-11).

ENDOCRINE GLANDS: Important group of glands which secrete hormones. These hormones regulate body functions and growth. When the balance of hormones in the body is seriously disturbed, personality changes as well as physical disturbances can result. This condition can often be treated successfully by an ENDOCRINOLOGIST.

ENDOCRINOLOGIST: A medical doctor who specializes in the treatment of the ENDOCRINE GLANDS and the internal secretions of the body. The glandular functioning of the body is closely related to emotional, mental and physical well-being.

ENVIRONMENT: The world a person lives in. Such as home, school, office, family, church and other social contacts. The ENVIRONMENT exerts a profound influence on the personality. Habits, attitudes and values are shaped by parents, teachers, friends and things which help to make up a person's ENVIRONMENT. The Christian believer has a new (Spiritual) ENVIRONMENT which is superimposed on the old (II Corinthians 5:7).

EPILEPSY: A chronic disease of the nervous system, characterized by convulsions and often unconsciousness. There are two main types (1) GRAND MAL (major): symptoms — gross convulsive seizures with loss of consciousness (often tongue is chewed). (2) PETIT MAL (minor): symptoms — lesser convulsive seizures or momentary loss of consciousness. The lapse of consciousness may be so slight that the person seems only to be in thought for a few seconds (but will not remember events during those seconds). EPILEPSY is basically *organic* in cause. It may often be controlled by certain drugs.

ESCAPE FROM REALITY: An attitude looking toward flight or avoidance which an individual may assume with respect to certain situations. When the real world becomes *too* unpleasant most people will seek some means of escape. Sometimes it is healthy to step back for a moment to take a good look at one's situation. However, when a person DENIES the REALITY of a situation and substitutes his own FANTASY in its place, he needs professional help. Healthy solutions to conflict must be sought in terms of REALITY, not in spite of it. God is ultimate REALITY. It is useless to try to escape from Him.

EXHIBITIONISM: This has several forms: (1) Childhood "showing-off" behavior. (2) In SUBLIMATED form, the exhibition of talent, clothes, physical attributes, intellect. (3) *Sexual* exhibitionism — normal in small children (love of nudity). A perversion in adults (exhibiting the sex organs to the opposite sex). It is often a form of AGGRESSION against members of the opposite sex — an attempt to (symbolically) violate them sexually. MASTURBATION or actual sexual attack often accompanies EXHIBITIONISM.

EXTROVERSION: Turning one's interests *outward*. Interest in environment and in other people more than in one's self. Interest in external and social activities. EXTROVERTS are people who display EXTROVERSION to an extreme degree. They tend to be sociable, happy-go-lucky, stable, optimistic and practical. They are the *opposite* of INTROVERTS. Most people are a balance of the two.

FAMILY BACKGROUND: A person's family provides his HEREDITY and much of his childhood ENVIRONMENT. Thus FAMILY BACKGROUND has a profound effect on PERSONALITY. It helps answer the question, "How did he get this way?" This is the reason a PSYCHIATRIST normally gets a complete family "history" from his patient before administering treatment. For the born-again Christian, his *new* FAMILY BACKGROUND also helps explain the amazing changes of PERSONALITY that often follow genuine conversion (John 1:12, 13, 42).

FANTASY: A MENTAL MECHANISM. Faced by CONFLICT, a person may resort to *imagining* solutions instead of actively working them out. As long as imagination is a *preparation for action*, it is good. But when it becomes an *end in itself* it can be a threat to mental health. A common form of FANTASY is DAYDREAMING. When a person can no longer distinguish his FANTASY from REALITY, he is PSYCHOTIC.

FEAR: A basic emotion characterized by a feeling-tone of unpleasantness and accompanied by activity of the sympathetic nervous system. Physiological changes associated with FEAR throw our bodies into "high gear." This helps us protect ourselves against dangers. Like a car, our bodies cannot remain at "full throttle" too long without damage. When we suffer from prolonged ANXIETY (excessive, uncalled-for FEAR), physiological damage or malfunction can result. The Bible says the best remedy for FEAR is LOVE (I John 4:18).

TERMS

FRUSTRATION: Thwarting of a need or desire. The blocking of a person's efforts to satisfy basic needs and drives. May lead to the use of MENTAL MECHANISMS.

FUGUE: A form of DISSOCIATION. A term applied to episodes of non-remembered activity of considerable duration, usually involving disappearance. One forgets (AMNESIA) and leaves his usual ENVIRONMENT. He may wander about in a confused fashion — perhaps in some strange city. He has forgotten who he is. This may go on for days or months. He may assume some new role and carry on unsuspected. After his recovery, he usually cannot remember the events of the episode. A person in a FUGUE state needs professional help.

HABIT: A pattern of activity which, through repetition, has been learned to the point that it has become automatic. It can be carried on with a minimum of conscious attention. The HABIT pattern of driving a car is very strong in most of us. Under normal driving conditions we give little thought to shifting gears or stepping on the brake pedal. These have become HABITS. They are automatic. We can talk to a friend or listen to the radio and still drive. HABITS may be difficult to break. Especially harmful ones that are often reinforced by powerful MOTIVES. Then we need to turn to Him who can give us SELF CONTROL (Galatians 5:22, 23).

HALLUCINATIONS: A sensation which seems real to a person but which has no outside cause (stimulus). "Seeing (or hearing) things" that are not there. More rarely, there are HALLUCINATIONS of smell, taste or touch. HALLUCINATIONS may be brought about by certain drugs, including ALCOHOL. They also occur in certain types of PSYCHOSES.

HEREDITY: The pattern of characteristics and potentials which a person receives from his parents. Physical characteristics such as hair and eye color are determined chiefly by HEREDITY. So are potentials such as INTELLIGENCE and APTITUDE. PERSONALITY is influenced partly by HEREDITY and partly by ENVIRONMENT. One of the reasons our PERSONALITY changes when we are saved is that God gives us a new HEREDITY, a spiritual nature. We are born anew (John 3:5) and become children of God (John 1:12, 13).

HETEROSEXUALITY: The *normal* sexual attraction, interests and physical relationships between male and female. This is opposed to HOMOSEXUALITY.

HOMOSEXUALITY: Inverted sexual orientation, sexual attraction or relationship between members of the *same* sex. Three levels may be distinguished: (1) *Latent* (hidden): many persons who appear normal sexually (i.e. who are normal physically, date, marry and have children) may have homosexual tendencies of which even they themselves are unaware. This sometimes shows itself as weakened or absent HETEROSEXUAL interests or (through COMPENSATION) as abnormally increased HETEROSEXUALITY. (2) Passive: Persons at this level usually engage in homosexual acts only when invited by an active homosexual and may play a passive (feminine) role. They may also be capable of normal HETEROSEXUAL relations. (3) Active: Those at this level actively solicit others to engage in homosexual acts and may commit homosexual rape. Often active homosexuals are revulsed by the thought of relations with the opposite sex. They may wear the clothes of the opposite sex and even change their names. The Bible mentions HOMOSEXUALITY in Romans 1:24-32.

HOSTILITY: A feeling of enmity, ill will, unfriendliness or antagonism. It often operates on an UNCONSCIOUS level and may be directed toward certain persons.

HYPERACTIVITY: Being *too* active. In some cases this is caused by a "flight into activity" (a form of escape). There is an attempt to avoid facing some CONFLICT by plunging into activity to "keep the mind busy." (See COMPULSION and PERFECTIONISM). HYPERACTIVITY may also be caused by improper balance of the ENDOCRINE GLANDS.

IDENTIFICATION: A MENTAL MECHANISM. A person attempts (UNCONSCIOUSLY) to make himself like another person. He may *automatically* take over another's characteristics. IDENTIFICATION plays a major role in the development of a child's personality. The child unconsciously copies the characteristics of his parents and other persons important to him. An emotional tie unconsciously causing a person to act as he imagines the person with whom he has the tie, does.

284

Idiot: A mentally defective person. Lowest grade of mentality. The I.Q. is below 20. (See intelligence, mental age.)

Imbecile: A mentally defective person. In the second lowest classification of intelligence. The I.Q. is approximately 20 to 49. (See mental age.)

Inferiority Complex: Strong feelings of inadequacy and insecurity which color an individual's entire adjustive efforts. A tendency to dwell on and overemphasize the normal feelings of self-doubt which all of us have from time to time. Often associated with feelings of unworthiness and guilt. (See self control). It may result in compensation. That is, a person may develop unrealistic ambition or a "superiority complex" to cover up his feelings of inferiority. For example, Joe was very unsure of himself. Often he would dread having to go to a party or other social gathering. But when he was with people he was just the opposite. Joe "knew it all," had "been everywhere," had "done everything" there was to do — just a little bit better than the next person. This usually "went over like a lead balloon" with his friends — who became fewer and fewer. And Joe? He dreaded going to those parties more each time.

Inhibit: To retard, restrain, hold back or prevent a response. Where inhibitions are excessive there will often be a damming up of emotional tension. This can result in considerable mental and physical discomfort. In serious cases it can lead to mental illness.

Insecurity: Lack of confidence because of unsureness of the love and support of others. Many Christians are insecure because they forget that they have the love and support of God (Psalm 37:1; I Peter 5:7). For example, ever since Mary could remember, she had been insecure. She tried to take her problems to her parents, but they were rarely home. If they were, they brushed her off and told her to "go out and play." Gradually it dawned on Mary that she was *unwanted*. Psychologically *alone*, Mary lost her self-confidence. Her personality began to wither. But then Mary found Christ. She now knew that God loved her — even if her parents did not.

She was confident of His support. With this new found security, Mary's PERSONALITY broadened and matured.

INSIGHT: Self-understanding. The ability to see and understand clearly the inner nature of things. The extent to which a person understands his *real* motives, conflicts and defense mechanisms. INSIGHT is hampered by DEFENSIVENESS. For example, Henry had been extremely "nervous" for some time. Finally he agreed to see a PSYCHOLOGIST. He was encouraged to talk out his problems. Henry didn't see the value of it but he did as he was asked. As he unburdened his heart, his DEFENSIVENESS melted away. He began to see himself realistically. The fog began to lift and solutions to his problems appeared. As he achieved INSIGHT his "nervousness" began to disappear.

INTEGRATION: Oneness, the organization of various traits or tendencies into one harmonious personality. The absence of CONFLICT. Three levels may be defined:

(1) *Personal* INTEGRATION: harmony within the personality.

(2) *Social* INTEGRATION: a generally harmonious relationship with other people.

(3) *Spiritual* INTEGRATION: peace with God. Often one kind of INTEGRATION is sacrificed to obtain another. Lack of INTEGRATION results in MALADJUSTMENT. Jesus, as Perfect Man, was integrated on all levels (Luke 2:52).

INTELLECTUALIZATION: An ego defense mechanism. A person avoids the emotionally disturbing aspects of something by attempting to treat it in a detached, "objective" way. The person is often unaware that he is doing this. This is a favorite defense among *educated people* or those who wish to consider themselves educated. Through INTELLECTUALIZATION a deeply disturbed person may sometimes deceive even a trained counselor (as well as himself) into believing that he "has no problems."

INTELLIGENCE: A person's potential ability to adjust to life. Three aspects of general INTELLIGENCE are often defined:

(1) *Abstract* (symbolic): ability to deal with words, symbols and concepts.

(2) *Mechanical* (motor): ability to deal with physical objects, develop physical skills.

(3) *Social* (interpersonal): ability to deal with people, to influence and understand them.

The accepted measure of INTELLIGENCE is the I.Q. (INTELLIGENCE quotient). An I.Q. between 90 and 110 may be considered "average" (See MENTAL AGE).

INTERPERSONAL RELATIONSHIPS: Relationships between people. (See INTEGRATION and MALADJUSTMENT.)

INTROVERSION: Turning one's interests *inward*. Preoccupation with self. Lessening of interest in the outer world. INTROVERTS are people who display INTROVERSION to an *extreme* degree. They tend to be shy, rigid, flighty, pessimistic and introspective. They are the opposite of EXTROVERTS. Most people are at neither extreme.

INVOLUTIONAL PSYCHOSIS: A serious mental illness which occurs during the climacteric (menopause) period of life (40-55 years), usually due to overconcern about declining sexual and physical vigor. It may take the form of DEPRESSION. It tends to last a long time. Symptoms include guilt, ANXIETY, DELUSIONS, insomnia and excessive concern over bodily condition.

MALADJUSTMENT: The inability of an individual to adapt himself to the conditions of his environment. Disharmony or lack of INTEGRATION. Three levels may be defined: (1) personal (psychological), (2) social (inter-personal) and (3) spiritual (between the person and God). MALADJUSTMENT at one level is usually reflected at the other levels. See INTEGRATION.

MANIC-DEPRESSIVE PSYCHOSIS: A type of mental disorder characterized by alternating periods of exaltation and depression. Tends to recur again and again. There are two types: (1) *depressed*: symptoms — DEPRESSION of mood, slowed down thinking and physical activity. (2) MANIC: symptoms — elation, over-talkativeness, extremely rapid ideas, increased physical activity. (A person may swing back and forth from one to the other.)

MASOCHISM: Sexual deviation in which an individual obtains sexual gratification from having pain inflicted upon him. Pleasure in *suffering* pain, physical or psychological. Often an attempt to atone for guilt. Many heathen religions have MASOCHISTIC practices for this purpose. It is the opposite of SADISM.

MASTURBATION: Self-stimulation of the sex organs (autoerotism). Often a HABIT in young children and common in adults. Contrary to popular belief, it does not normally cause mental or physical illness. However, *guilt* and ANXIETY over MASTUR-BATION can threaten one's feelings considerably.

MENTAL AGE: Age level of a child's mental ability. It is determined by a standard INTELLIGENCE test appropriate for the child's age. MENTAL AGE (M.A.) may be greater or less than chronological (actual) age (C. A.) The well known I. Q. (intelligence quotient) for children is calculated as follows: $\frac{M.A.}{C.A.} \times 100 = $ I.Q. For instance, Terry is 10 with a MENTAL AGE of 12. He has an I.Q. of 120 (Superior).

MENTAL MECHANISMS: Indirect and typically unconscious manners of gratifying a repressed desire. Ways of dealing with CONFLICT. They are attempts to *protect* and *enhance* the person's SELF CONCEPT. Each MECHANISM is used to some extent by everyone. Some persons, however, use certain MECHANISMS *too much*. This can damage their mental health. The MECHANISMS described in this glossary are:

COMPENSATION	PROJECTION
DENIAL	RATIONALIZATION
DISPLACEMENT	REACTION FORMATION
FANTASY	REPRESSION
IDENTIFICATION	SUBLIMATION
INTELLECTUALIZATION	WITHDRAWAL

MENTALLY DEFECTIVE: When a person's INTELLIGENCE is below an I.Q. level of approximately 70 he is said to be MENTALLY DEFECTIVE. This condition may be caused by HEREDITY, injury or disease. Three levels of the MENTALLY DEFECTIVE are generally accepted:

(1) MORON: I.Q. 50 - 69
(2) IMBECILE: I.Q. 20-49
(3) IDIOT: I.Q. below 20

These conditions are generally permanent. Special training may help the higher INTELLIGENCE defectives. The lower must usually be placed in an institution.

MORON: A MENTALLY DEFECTIVE person. I.Q. is between 50 and 69. (See INTELLIGENCE and MENTAL AGE.)

MOTIVE (motivation): A conscious experience or sub-conscious condition which serves as a factor in determining an individual's behavior. The psychological force which disposes a person to act in a certain way. Often the true MOTIVE for an act may be unknown to the person (UNCONSCIOUS MOTIVATION). When the MOTIVE is unacceptable, a *more acceptable* MOTIVE will often be offered as the true one. (See RATIONALIZATION.)

NEGATIVISM: Doing the opposite of (or resisting) the suggestions and commands of others. "Contrariness" in children. It reaches a peak between 2 and 3 years of age, declines and usually shows itself in a different form in ADOLESCENCE. A defense among people who feel "pushed around." A way of asserting independence (especially important to ADOLESCENTS.) Occasionally results in severe conflict with authority. May be a factor in criminality. Children go through a negative stage. For example, Sandra is 2½ years old. Every time her mother asks her to do something there is one standard answer. "No!" Sandra will outgrow this.

NEUROLOGIST: A medical doctor who specializes in diseases of the nervous system. Nervous diseases with a *psychological* cause are usually treated by a PSYCHIATRIST or PSYCHOLOGIST.

NEUROSIS (PSYCHONEUROSIS): A functional personality disorder without severe loss of contact with reality. It often causes much psychological discomfort to the patient and his family. However, few NEUROTICS must be hospitalized. (See PSYCHOSIS.)

OBESITY: Excessive fatness. A result of overeating. (1) May be due to psychological causes: Dependent, insecure people — especially ADOLESCENTS — often turn to overeating as a DEFENSE against ANXIETY. (2) May also be due to improper balance of the ENDOCRINE GLANDS which can occur especially during the fast-growth period of ADOLESCENCE.

OBSESSION: A persistent idea or thought which the individual recognizes as irrational but cannot seem to eliminate. An unwanted thought which repeatedly and insistently intrudes into consciousness. It is highly charged with UNCONSCIOUS emotional significance. Its function is to *substitute* a comparatively acceptable thought for an unacceptable UNCONSCIOUS one. A COMPULSION does the same thing by substituting an action. Both are efforts to prevent an overflow of UNCONSCIOUS CONFLICTS and the resultant ANXIETY.

PARANOIA: A PSYCHOSIS (Quite rare). It is characterized by gradually developing logical, well systematized DELUSIONS — of persecution or grandeur. The person may seem quite normal in every respect, outside of his DELUSIONAL area. PARANOIA must be distinguished from its more common "cousin," Paranoid SCHIZOPHRENIA.

PEERS: Equals in age group and status. A child's playmates are called his PEERS.

PERFECTIONISM: Excessive attention to detail. Often with COMPULSIVE inability to be satisfied with the work of self or others. It may be a DEFENSE against guilt or ANXIETY.

PERSONALITY: The sum total of a person. His attributes, DRIVES, aspirations, INHIBITIONS, strengths, weaknesses, INTERESTS, APTITUDES, INTELLIGENCE. The psychological term PERSONALITY differs from the popular word, "personality," which often refers only to the attractive qualities of a person. Everyone has the same "amount" of PERSONALITY in the psychological sense. But the make-up of PERSONALITY differs from person to person.

PHOBIA: An irrational fear. The individual may realize its irrationality but be unable to dispel it. A familiar example is *claustrophobia* — fear of closed spaces. PHOBIAS are usually created by the DISPLACEMENT of an ANXIETY from its real (UNCONSCIOUS) object to a substitute. When a person *avoids* the PHOBIC object he is also (symbolically) avoiding the real UNCONSCIOUS object of his ANXIETY.

PHYSIOLOGICAL DRIVES: The basic biological needs of a person. These include: hunger, thirst, sleep, sex, elimination and others. They can be strong MOTIVES of behavior.

PRODIGIOUS APPETITES: See OBESITY.

PROJECTION: An ego defense MECHANISM in which the individual places the blame for his difficulties upon others or attributes to them his own unethical desires and impulses. Unwilling to criticize himself, he can now criticize others for the characteristics which he had imputed (projected) to them. For example, Larry complained bitterly to his teacher that Jim and Harry were cheating. Investigation showed that only one child was cheating. It was Larry, himself. Both Christ and Paul spoke of PROJECTION (Matthew 7:1-5; Romans 2:1-3, 21-23).

PSYCHIATRIST: A medical doctor (M.D.) who specializes in the treatment of emotional illness (mental disorders). He practices *psychiatry*.

PSYCHOANALYST: A PSYCHIATRIST (or, rarely, a PSYCHOLOGIST) with special additional training in *psychoanalysis* — Freud's method of treating mental illness.

PSYCHOLOGIST: A person usually holding an M.A. or Ph.D. degree in psychology. In many states he is also required to pass special examinations and be certified. He may work in one of several fields: (1) *Clinical* — with mental patients (usually collaborating with a *Psychiatrist*). (2) *Experimental* — in laboratory research with animals and people. (3) *Industrial* — with personnel problems in industry. (4) *School* — with students, teachers, administrators and parents.

PSYCHONEUROSIS: See NEUROSIS.

PSYCHOPATHIC PERSONALITY: A person characterized by emotional instability and lack of sound judgment. He does not "learn" by experience and is not restrained by the threat of punishment. He is often impulsive, perverse and irresponsible and cares little about the consequences of his behavior. He has no conscious sense of guilt for his wrongdoing. He gratifies selfish desires (at the expense of others), when and how he wishes. Many (but *not* all) criminals, sex offenders and delinquents are PSYCHOPATHIC PERSONALITIES.

PSYCHOSIS: A severe mental disorder. Usually requires hospitalization. Often characterized by DELUSIONS and/or HALLUCINATIONS and a loss of contact with REALITY. There are several kinds of PSYCHOSES. The most frequent is SCHIZOPHRENIA. (See NEUROSIS.)

PSYCHO-THERAPY: Treatment of emotional illness by various psychological techniques. Used when the source of the problem is chiefly *personal* (not *situational*) as in COUNSELING.

PUBERTY: The beginning of ADOLESCENCE (between 10 and 14 years of age). The time when the sex organs begin to mature. Menstruation commences in the girl. Her breasts begin to develop. The boy's voice grows deeper. Beard begins to appear on his face. Gradually body hair appears. Figures in both sexes mature toward the characteristic adult physique. This may be a time of increased psychological stress for the boy or girl, a time when they need the guidance of adults in understanding what is happening to them. Adequate prior and current information about sex will help boys and girls pass through pubescent years with wholesome, desirable attitudes.

RAPPORT: An interpersonal relationship characterized by a spirit of cooperation, confidence and harmony; usually between therapist and patient. A minimum of DEFENSIVENESS. Usually essential for the patient to make progress in PSYCHOTHERAPY or COUNSELING.

RATIONALIZATION: An ego defense MECHANISM. A person imagines a *more acceptable* reason for why he does something than the *real* reason (MOTIVE). Daily life abounds with examples of RATIONALIZATION. A familiar form is "sour grapes." According to the fable, the fox saved face by claiming the *grapes* were sour instead of admitting that *he* could not reach them. An opposite form is "sweet lemon." A person who was swindled often convinces himself that he got a good deal.

REACTION FORMATION: A MENTAL MECHANISM in which a person exhibits (and consciously believes he possesses) the *opposite* feelings from those he has on the UNCONSCIOUS level. For example, a father may UNCONSCIOUSLY REJECT his son. Through a REACTION FORMATION he "bends over backwards" to show love and concern for his son. He buys him toys and overprotects him. But his UNCONSCIOUS REJECTION is sensed by his son·and results in HOSTILITY toward his father — which the father cannot understand.

Terms

REALITY: The real world in which a person lives — as it actually is — physical, social and spiritual. Ability to perceive reality is often severely impaired in serious mental illness. (See ESCAPE FROM REALITY and FANTASY.)

REGRESSION: Reversion to earlier behavior patterns, as to escape from an unpleasant situation. Physical illness, excitement, fatigue and intoxication may cause varying degrees of *temporary* REGRESSION. More serious and lasting REGRESSION is often found in severe mental illness. Dick, for example, an ADOLESCENT boy, became frightened by the challenge of young manhood — dating, competition with other boys, decisions, responsibilities. Unable to go on toward maturity, he turned back on the road of life to more childish ways of behaving. These were familiar to him; he had used them before. He felt more secure with them. His REGRESSION continued until Dick succumbed to a PSYCHOSIS: SCHIZOPHRENIA.

REJECTION: The (*often* UNCONSCIOUS) denial of genuine affection — usually to a child. Often, an "unwanted child" that was *not planned* or a child *conceived out of wedlock* is the victim of REJECTION. The parents may make an honest effort to accept the child, yet they may harbor UNCONSCIOUS resentment against the small intruder. They may try to make up for their lack of love with toys and gifts. They may "overprotect" the child. But their REJECTION will be sensed by the child. (See INSECURITY and REACTION FORMATION.)

REPRESSION: A defense MECHANISM in which the individual forces ideas and impulses, painful to the conscious mind, into the unconscious where they still modify his behavior or remain dynamic. Under certain conditions, REPRESSED conflicts may disguise themselves as symptoms of mental illness. Normally however, REPRESSION acts to protect mental health. By removing contradictory elements it permits a person to make decisions and to resolve CONFLICT. For example, Frieda loved her mother. But she also had *hate* feelings toward her mother for favoring (she thought) her sister. Frieda successfully REPRESSED the hatred. She then could IDENTIFY with her mother — copy her as a model of womanhood. Barbara had a similar problem. But she failed to completely REPRESS her hatred. She became AMBIVALENT and later developed a NEUROSIS.

SADISM: Pleasure in inflicting pain — physical or psychological — on another person. A sexual deviation in which sexual gratification is obtained by the infliction of pain upon others. It is the reverse of MASOCHISM. SADISM plays an important role in "sex psychopaths." (See PSYCHOPATHIC PERSONALITY.)

SCHIZOPHRENIA: A major psychotic disorder characterized by distortions and disturbances in thought processes and a withdrawal from reality. Approximately one half of all PSYCHOTICS are SCHIZOPHRENICS. Chief types of SCHIZOPHRENIA are (a) *simple*: symptoms — WITHDRAWAL (apathy) lack of feeling — progressively gets worse. (b) *Hebephrenic:* symptoms — silly behavior, unpredictable giggling, mannerisms, bizarre behavior — social and personal habits deteriorate. (c) *Catatonic:* symptoms — *either* stupor, rigidity, refusal to talk or (the opposite) violent excessive activity. (d) *Paranoid:* symptoms — unrealistic thinking, DELUSIONS of *persecution* (and possibly grandeur), very HOSTILE, possibly obscene.

SECLUSIVENESS: See WITHDRAWAL.

SELF-ACCEPTANCE: Realization and acceptance of the *objective* abilities, interests, strengths, weaknesses and other aspects of one's PERSONALITY. This provides a basis for good mental health and for PERSONALITY growth. It should not be confused with *self-satisfaction* — its imposter. This leads only to stagnation and blindness to one's responsibilities.

SELF CONCEPT: A person's evaluation or picture of himself. It is largely determined by the way he has been treated by his parents and other significant persons — especially in early childhood. For example, Sally was constantly belittled by her parents. Her school work, appearance, speech were always being criticized and compared to her more accomplished sister. Sally developed a shriveled SELF CONCEPT — a deep INFERIORITY COMPLEX. She would never try anything new and was afraid to meet people. She felt deeply unworthy and unwanted. She was actually attractive and many times young men asked her for a date. But she always refused — afraid she would do something wrong. After a while they didn't ask her any more.

SELF-CONSCIOUSNESS: Excessive concern with self — especially with the impression one is making on others. Often accentuated in ADOLESCENCE. May result in shyness or (as a COMPENSATION) show-off behavior (EXHIBITIONISM). The self-conscious person may not realize that other people have problems too. He may feel that everyone is busy looking at him. Taking an interest in other people — their problems and fears — often is the best cure for SELF-CONSCIOUSNESS.

SELF-CONTROL: Self-Discipline. Control of one's own emotions, desires and actions. SELF CONTROL (temperance) is named as one of the fruits of the Spirit (Galatians 5:22, 23). As such, it is possible in a true sense for the believer only. The believer's new HEREDITY (John 3:3-6) provides him with God's set of spiritual DRIVES to pit against the old ones. When the unregenerate person attempts SELF CONTROL, he must pit one natural drive against another. That this is not always effective will be obvious to those with spiritual insight.

SELF-UNDERSTANDING: (See INSIGHT.)

SLEEPWALKING: (Somnambulism). Involuntary walking and other coordinated physical activity while asleep. May be related to BED WETTING and EMOTIONAL IMMATURITY. SLEEPWALKING tends to occur more often when the person is under psychological stress. It is sometimes an aspect of DISSOCIATION.

SOCIAL ADJUSTMENT: INTEGRATION at the social level. Generally harmonious relations with other people.

SOCIAL APPROVAL: A strong human MOTIVE. The desire to have people like us makes us fall in line with the customs of society. It may cause us to strive for goals valued by society. This is natural and good. Sometimes, however, CONFLICT arises when the values of society clash with our own desires, or with spiritual laws. SOCIAL APPROVAL should, in the latter case, be forgone in favor of the higher good (Acts 5:29).

SPECIAL APTITUDE: Exceptional talents. (See APTITUDES.)

SUBLIMATION: The unconscious process of diverting unacceptable DRIVES into personally and socially acceptable channels. An indirect gratification of the original DRIVES is sometimes obtained in this way.

SUPPRESSION: The conscious effort to push unacceptable thoughts "out of the mind." Directing attention away from undesirable thoughts, objects or feelings. SUPPRESSION differs from REPRESSION, which is UNCONSCIOUS. The best method of SUPPRESSION is displacing unwanted ideas with positive ones (see Philippians 4:8, 9).

THREAT: A situation that is perceived (often UNCONSCIOUSLY) as dangerous to the PERSONALITY. It will normally increase DEFENSIVENESS or call for certain MENTAL MECHANISMS.

TRANSFERENCE: Reaction toward people in present situations as one felt and acted toward important people in early life. Otherwise puzzling behavior and feelings toward certain people can often be explained in terms of TRANSFERENCE. For example, Ray was surprised and chagrined over his almost uncontrollable resentment toward his new boss. His boss had never done anything to hurt Ray — nothing Ray could put his finger on. But still, Ray couldn't stand him. One day he had to turn and walk away to keep from saying something unpleasant to his boss. It was some months later that Ray was reading his psychology assignment and came across the word TRANSFERENCE. That was it! It suddenly dawned on Ray how much his boss reminded him of his oldest brother — with whom he certainly did *not* get along! Ray had reacted to his boss the way he was accustomed to act toward his brother. This was why the intensity of his feeling was so *out of proportion* to the situation.

UNCONSCIOUS: The sum of all thoughts, impulses, desires and feelings of which the individual is not conscious but which influence his behavior. That part (or aspect) of the mind which acts as a "safe deposit vault" for past experiences that have been "forgotten." (See REPRESSION.) Probably no "forgotten" conflicts, feelings, experiences, are ever really lost. They continue to exist in the UNCONSCIOUS. They exert a subtle influence on *conscious* thinking and behavior. UNCONSCIOUS (childhood) ways of meeting CONFLICT are often dusted off and put to work on CONFLICTS in adult life. Acts which seem "out of character" for the person concerned may be due to UNCONSCIOUS MOTIVATION.

VOCATIONAL INTERESTS: A special interest in a given occupation, profession or career. Research has shown that most successful people in a given occupation have a similar pattern of interests. This pattern will differ more or less from that of other occupational groups. Thus, it has been possible to construct tests which will compare a person's interests with those of many occupational groups. The result is a prediction to what extent he will enjoy certain kinds of work: a measure of his VOCATIONAL INTERESTS. This, together with the results of APTITUDE tests, can be very helpful in VOCATIONAL counseling.

VOYEURISM: "Peeping Tom" activity. A perversion in which sexual gratification is obtained through "peeping," particularly at the nude body of others. Often accompanied by MASTURBATION. May be followed by actual sexual attack. A form of psychological AGGRESSION against the opposite sex. See EXHIBITIONISM and COMPULSION.

WITHDRAWAL: A MENTAL MECHANISM. *Retreat* from a CONFLICT situation. One may do this (1) by physically removing himself from the situation or (2) by psychologically "turning a deaf ear to it" so that he is not emotionally moved. The second alternative usually takes the form of *apathy* toward a situation that others would consider disturbing. For example, Miriam is entering ADOLESCENCE. She is ANXIOUS. She wants to remain in the security of girlhood. But she knows she is expected to grow into womanhood. She is awkward and unsure of herself. She feels SELF-CONSCIOUS — that people are laughing at her. So Miriam WITHDRAWS from contact with other people. She becomes SECLUSIVE and INTROVERTED. She remains a little girl at heart while physically growing up.

33 | BOOKS AND RECORDINGS

BOOKS

Bakwin, Harry, and Ruth M.: *Clinical Management of Behavior Disorders in Children,* W. B. Saunders Co., 1953.

This volume is designed as a practical guide not only for the physician but for professional workers in the field of child psychology. It brings together from many sources and from the clinical experience of the authors (both medical doctors and pediatricians) helpful information on the psychologic aspects of child care. Although the principal purpose is presentation of the clinical management of behavior disorders, consideration is also given to psychologic development and normal variability and to psychologic care.

Common problems such as eating habits, enuresis, thumb-sucking, and difficulties of adolescence are included as well as many disturbances less often encountered. Etiology, diagnosis, and treatment of these disorders are described and are related to the total care of children.

This book contains excellent headings for quick reference. It is replete with research summaries. Secular.

Coleman, James C.: *Abnormal Psychology and Modern Life,* Scott Foresman and Company, New York, 1950. 657 pp.

Part I (two chapters) traces the historical changes in theories and treatment of mental illness since the time of the ancients.

Part II (two chapters) lays the theoretical groundwork for an understanding of the dynamics of personality development and adjustment and of the types of factors that contribute to the development of abnormal behavior.

Part III (seven chapters) is concerned with symptoms, dynamics, therapy, and prognosis of the various abnormal reaction patterns.

Part IV (four chapters) deals with modern theories and methods of diagnosis, therapy, and prevention.

This book is widely used in colleges throughout America. Secular.

English, Horace B. (Editor): *Comprehensive Dictionary of Psychological and Psychoanalytical Terms,* Longmans, Green and Company, New York, 1958.

This is a large, comprehensive dictionary of psychological and psychoanalytical terms that counselors find helpful.

Harriman, Philip L. (Editor): *Dictionary of Psychological Terms,* Littlefield, Adams and Company, 1959.

This dictionary of psychological terms is suitable for the counselor. It is not as large nor as comprehensive as the dictionary edited by Horace B. English.

Jacobsen, Margaret B.: *The Child in the Christian Home,* Scripture Press, Wheaton, 1959.

This 200 page book is thoroughly Christian. It contains many photographs and deals primarily with children between the ages of one and ten.

It discusses many practical problems of younger children in the Christian home. It is useful as a guide in counseling parents. It also lends itself to parent and teacher study groups.

Jenkins, Gladys Gardner, and others: *These Are Your Children: A Text and Guide on Child Development,* Scott-Foresman, rev. ed., 1954.

This is a widely used book on child growth and development. It contains many excellent photographs and is well organized with splendid headings for quick reference.

It discusses the growth and development of children through each stage of childhood. It is suitable as a guide for counseling parents and it lends itself to parent and teacher study groups. Secular.

Lewin, S. A. and Gilmore, John: *Sex Without Fear,* The Medical Research Press, New York, 1950.

This is a marriage manual for counselors and married couples. It is clearly and frankly written, discussing most areas dealing with the sexual aspects of marriage. It is used widely. Secular.

Lewis, Richard S.: *Other Child: The Brain-Injured Child,* Grune and Stratton, Inc., 1951.

This specialized book deals with one problem: brain injury in children. Both counselors and parents have found this volume particularly helpful in understanding the child who is neurologically impaired. It contains suggestions for handling and educating brain-injured children.

Los Angeles County Superintendent of Schools Office: *Guiding Today's Children,* California Test Bureau, May, 1959.

This comprehensive book is intended for classroom teachers, administrators and guidance specialists. It concerns children in the elementary school.

Part I discusses methods of studying all boys and girls. Part II concerns children who have special needs. Part III is devoted to the school personnel functioning as a team, and Part IV presents an outline for evaluating guidance services.

The appendix contains many helpful forms, including some for use in making special studies of children. It also contains a list of test publishers and tests.

It is helpful as background information for the counselor. It is also suitable for teacher and parent study groups. Secular.

Narramore, Clyde M.: *How to Tell Your Children About Sex,* Zondervan Publishing House, Grand Rapids, 1958.

This book is a Christian book for parents whose children range in age from infants to adolescents. It deals with more than twenty basic considerations of sex education.

The information presented in this book is essential to counselors and parents. It is suitable for teacher and parent study groups.

Narramore, Clyde M.: *How to Understand and Influence Children,* Zondervan Publishing House, Grand Rapids, 1957.

This Christian book for parents and teachers of primary age children, contains three major sections. Part I discusses techniques of teaching children. Part II discusses growth and developmental factors of children. Part III suggests a number of ways to influence children for Christ. It is suitable for those who counsel with parents. It also lends itself to parent and teacher study groups.

Narramore, Clyde M.: *Life and Love,* Zondervan Publishing House, Grand Rapids, 1956.

This Christian book is intended as a Christ-centered introduction to the subject of sex education. Beside chapters on *Dating, Looking Toward Marriage* and *What the Bible Says About Sex,* it contains three chapters on the sexual functioning of the human body. One chapter is devoted to definitions.

This book, containing a number of schematic drawings, has three major uses: (1) to be given to young people, (2) to use in counseling young people and (3) to use as a guide in a series of meetings with young people on the subject of personal living. It is also available in Swedish.

Narramore, Clyde M.: *This Way to Happiness,* Zondervan Publishing House, Grand Rapids, 1958.

This Christian book deals with the basic psychological needs of man, showing how each is met most fundamentally through knowing Christ and living the dynamic Christian life.

Pastors and other Christian counselors report its effectiveness as (1) outline material for messages, (2) reading material for the unsaved, and (3) reading material for the believer. It is especially suitable for adults.

Narramore, Clyde M.: *Young Only Once,* Zondervan Publishing House, Grand Rapids, 1957.

This Christian book is comprehensive in nature, dealing with the major concerns of young people: Fun, Dating, Personality, Parents, Manners, Looks, Education, Life's Work, Conversation, Military Service, Wedding Bells and God's Will.

In addition to its use with young people, it furnishes the youth counselor much information on all of the above topics. It also lends itself to youth study and discussion groups.

Stone, Hannah M., and Abraham: *A Marriage Manual,* Simon & Schuster, rev. ed., 1952.

This volume, both in its original and revised editions, has proven helpful to many marriage counselors and married couples.

It is clearly and frankly written in question and discussion style. It covers most areas dealing with the sexual aspects of marriage. Secular.

RECORDINGS

Only recently Christian recording companies have begun to produce records which are particularly helpful to counselors. These recordings are valuable (1) as information for counselors and (2) as suitable material for group counseling and study seminars.

Christian counselors will want to keep abreast of currently produced recordings that may assist them in their work. Among the recordings helpful to counselors are two albums by the author.*

Psychology for Living

This album contains 24 sides, each of which plays approximately 22 minutes. These recordings are designed especially for information and for use with discussion and study groups. Several titles are intended for leaders and counselors, others for parents and teachers, and some for adolescents.

In conducting study and discussion groups it is suggested that the leader describe the recording to be heard, requesting the group to take notes during the playing. Afterward the leader will want to raise such questions as "What, do you feel, are the most significant points discussed?" "Have you thought of other points that were not discussed?" "What questions did this discussion raise in your mind?" "Were

---

*Audio-Bible Society of America, 1061 Memorial Avenue, Williamsport, Pennsylvania.

there points with which you did not entirely agree?" In this manner the group members will share their learnings with each other.

Contents of this album include such topics as — The Psychology of Conversion, Guides for Understanding People, Gaining Self-Confidence, Improving Your Personality, Influencing and Winning Children to Christ, Discipline in the Christian Home, The Kind of Parents Young People and Children Want, Sex Education in the Christian Home, Children Who Are Adopted, Children With Emotional and Behavior Problems, Delinquency: — Its Early Signs and Solutions, Helping Teen-agers to Become Mature, What Makes a Good Marriage?, Knowing God's Will, and How to Improve Your Leadership Skills.

Golden Meditations

This album contains 30 sides, each playing nearly 10 minutes. Titles include 30 of the major themes of the Bible. Appropriate scriptures and organ background are included in each.

These recordings are designed to bring spiritual teaching and inspiration. They are suitable not only for devotionals, but for use in counseling with groups and shut-ins.